# The Dark Ground of Spirit

Friedrich Wilhelm Joseph Schelling is widely regarded as one of the most difficult and influential of German philosophers. In this book, S.J. McGrath not only makes Schelling's ideas accessible to a general audience, he uncovers the romantic philosopher's seminal role as the creator of a concept which shaped and defined late nineteenth- and early twentieth-century psychology: the concept of the unconscious.

McGrath shows how the unconscious originally functioned in Schelling's philosophy as a bridge between nature and spirit. Before Freud revised the concept to fit his psychopathology, the unconscious was understood largely along Schellingian lines as primarily a source of creative power. Schelling's lifelong effort to understand intuitive and non-reflective forms of intelligence in nature, humankind, and the divine has been revitalised by Jungians, as well as by archetypal and trans-personal psychologists. With the new interest in the unconscious today, Schelling's ideas have never been more relevant.

*The Dark Ground of Spirit* will therefore be essential reading for those involved in psychoanalysis, analytical psychology and philosophy, as well as anyone with an interest in the history of ideas.

**S.J. McGrath** is an associate professor of philosophy at Memorial University of Newfoundland, Canada. His areas of specialisation include phenomenology, German philosophy, and the philosophy of religion.

# The Dark Ground of Spirit

## Schelling and the Unconscious

## S.J. McGrath

Routledge
Taylor & Francis Group

LONDON AND NEW YORK

First published 2012
by Routledge
27 Church Road, Hove, East Sussex BN3 2FA

Simultaneously published in the USA and Canada
by Routledge
711 Third Avenue, New York NY 10017

*Routledge is an imprint of the Taylor & Francis Group, an Informa business*

*British Library Cataloguing in Publication Data*
A catalogue record for this book is available from the British Library

*Library of Congress Cataloging-in-Publication Data*
McGrath, S. J., 1966-
   The dark ground of spirit : Schelling and the unconscious / S.J. McGrath.
      p. cm.
   Includes bibliographical references and index.
   ISBN 978-0-415-49209-6 (hbk.) – ISBN 978-0-415-49212-6 (pbk.)
1. Schelling, Friedrich Wilhelm Joseph von, 1775-1854. 2. Subconsciousness.
3. Psychology and philosophy. I. Title.
   BF315.M39 2012
   154.2–dc23

                                                                    2011030911

ISBN: 978-0-415-49209-6 (hbk)
ISBN: 978-0-415-49212-6 (pbk)
ISBN: 978-0-203-13439-9 (ebk)

Typeset in Times by Garfield Morgan, Swansea, West Glamorgan
Paperback cover design by Andrew Ward

MIX
Paper from
responsible sources
FSC® C004839
www.fsc.org

Printed and bound in Great Britain by
TJ International Ltd, Padstow, Cornwall

Only in personality is there life, and all personality rests on a dark ground.

(Schelling, 1809: 75)

# Contents

# Acknowledgements

The generous support of the Humboldt Stiftung enabled me to spend sixteen months over the course of four years researching this book in Freiburg, Germany, with many trips to nearby Zurich and a memorable visit to the *Bibliotheca Philosophica Hermetica* in Amsterdam. Prof. Dr Michael Schulz, Faculty of Theology, University of Bonn, was a key early supporter of this project. Prof. Dr Markus Enders, Chair of the *Arbeitsbereich Christliche Religionsphilosophie* at the University of Freiburg, supported the book at every step. Prof. Dr James Bradley at the Department of Philosophy of Memorial University of Newfoundland provided valuable comments on the work in progress. Christina Galego lent her talented editing skills to the penultimate draft. Last but not least, the graduate students at Memorial suffered me to carry out my education in public over the course of four seminars, respectively on psychoanalysis (2007), Schelling (2008), the history of the unconscious (2009), and German Idealism (2010).

Part of Chapter 3 appeared as Is Schelling's nature-philosophy Freudian?, *Analecta Hermeneutica*, *3*. Parts of Chapter 4 appeared as Schelling and the unconscious, *Research in Phenomenology*, *40*, 72–91 and Boehme, Hegel, Schelling and the Hermetic Theology of Evil, *Philosophy and Theology*, *18*, *257–285*.

I dedicate this book to my son, Ethan Simon Patrick Squires McGrath, who knows all about tending the dark fire, at the age of five.

# Abbreviations

BSS Jacob Boehme. 1960. *Sämtliche Schriften*. Faksimile-Neudruck der Ausgabe von 1730 in elf Bänden. Ed. Will-Erich Peuckert. Stuttgart: Frommann-Holzboog.

BSW Franz Xaver von Baader. 1963. *Sämtliche Werke*. 16 vols. Neudruck der Ausgabe Leipzig 1851–1860. Ed. Franz Hoffmann and Julius Hamberger. Darmstadt: Scientia Verlag Aalen.

CW C.G. Jung. 1953–1977. *The Collected Works of C.G. Jung*. 20 vols. Ed. H. Read, Michael Fordham and Gerhard Adler. Trans. R.F.C. Hull. London: Routledge.

SSW F.W.J. Schelling. 1856–1861. *Sämtliche Werke*. 14 vols. Ed. K.F.A. Schelling. Stuttgart and Augsburg: J.G. Cotta.

# Chapter 1

# Introduction

"Someday we shall be able to see by what torturous paths modern psychology has made its way from the dingy laboratories of the alchemists, via mesmerism and magnetism . . . to the philosophical anticipations of Schopenhauer, Carus and von Hartmann" (Jung, CW 4: 748). This remark by Carl Jung reveals both the breadth of his understanding of the lineage of the unconscious and an important oversight. Missing from the genealogy is German Idealism, most notably, F.W.J. Schelling (1775–1854), who is, we will argue, the philosopher with the greatest claim to being the original theoretician of the unconscious. And behind him stands the massively underrated figure of Jacob Boehme (1575–1624), whom Hegel called "the first German philosopher" (Hegel, 1896: 188), but whom we could just as accurately describe as the first depth psychologist. Prototypes for three of the major models of the unconscious in the twentieth century, the Freudian bio-personal unconscious, the Jungian collective unconscious, and the Lacanian semiotic unconscious, can be traced back to Schelling. Unlike Jacques Lacan, neither Sigmund Freud nor Jung read the German Idealists carefully, but they did not need to: by the end of the nineteenth century, German Idealism had infiltrated most fields of German academic life, either negatively, inspiring materialist reactions in logic, metaphysics, and natural science, or positively, influencing historiography, hermeneutics, and the burgeoning science of dynamic psychiatry. Late nineteenth-century psychologists no longer speculated about demons, spirits of the dead or mysterious invisible fluids to explain non-rational psychological phenomena; they had their theoretical model, the unconscious psyche, handed to them on a platter so to speak, not only theoretically well developed, but to some degree over-developed in hugely popular studies such as Eduard von Hartmann's 1869 *Philosophy of the Unconscious* (a bricolage of Schelling, Hegel and Schopenhauer, which everybody seems to have read). Jung singles out Schopenhauer's "anticipations" of psychoanalysis without reflecting on the relative lateness of Schopenhauer's contribution or showing any sense that Schelling might be the missing link he seeks. The historical claim of this book is that Jacob Boehme's alchemico-theosophical psychology, modified and given metaphysical grounding by Schelling, is the origin of the psychodynamic notion of the unconscious.

## The unity of Schelling's thought

The interpreter of Schelling faces a particularly difficult hermeneutical challenge: as soon as Schelling had developed a workable theoretical frame (say nature-philosophy or identity-philosophy), he seems to have abandoned it. Schelling appears to have been repulsed by the prospect of settling down into a system, as though the real always beckoned to him from the far side of whatever set of categories were recommending themselves, compelling him to leave for others the frame he had constructed while he continued his restless search for the logical and historical relation between the infinite and the finite. For Heidegger, Schelling's flagrant neglect of the canons of consistency and coherence is not a sign of the weakness of his thought, but exactly the opposite: thinking, according to Heidegger, never enjoys arrival, certainty, or stability (Heidegger, 1971). Schelling, whose philosophy was always underway, is the quintessential Heideggerian thinker.[1]

Schelling's inconsistencies notwithstanding, we can discern a set of recurring concerns in Schelling's collected works, leitmotifs, which do not a system make, but constitute a style of philosophizing which we can call Schellingian. First in appearance is a theme most characteristic of Schelling's nature-philosophy, but which also plays a central role in the philosophy of freedom and returns in the Trinitarian metaphysics of the late lectures: the notion of polarity. Schelling remains convinced, from his earliest treatises to his last lectures, that all intelligible structure, mental or material, physical or metaphysical, finite or divine, is characterized by polarity, opposition, and the creative and dynamic tension between incommensurables, a tension which must not be abrogated in a spurious logic that presumes to deny the principle of contradiction (Hegel's). The production of being in Schellingian ontology is not by means of Hegel's *qualitative* differentiation, the collapse of the identical into the play of contradictories and the subsequent negation of and re-inscription of difference into a higher standpoint, but by means of *quantitative* intensification of power, generation of difference within an essential identical being through progressive potentization, which renders the latent power of anything available. For Schelling, contradictories are never fused, and the opposition between them highlights the primacy of will over thought, for in the face of incommensurable options, thinking can go no further until the will *decides*. However, Schelling is not Kierkegaard: all polarities are undergirded by a concealed commonality, a deep ground of unity that makes the opposites possible, for only that which is in secret alliance, according to Schelling, can be truly opposed. Thus the other-side of Schellingian polarity is the crucial notion of teleology: polarity is never something that just happens to be; it is always something that has come to be for the sake of a higher development, be it life, consciousness, the personalization of God, or the production of love. The one divides into two so that it might give birth to a one that knows itself as such and can be lovingly related to others.

The second recurring theme in Schellingian thought is the finitude of human experience, which is, for Schelling, neither a dogmatic assertion nor romantic *Schwärmerei*, but an experience of the crucifixion of thought against the real. The sense for finitude draws the middle Schelling to theosophy, but the late Schelling will re-consider this move, distancing himself from theosophy because the theosophist's enthusiasm for the non-rational is too cheaply purchased. For Schelling, the understanding must go the distance with thought, concept, and logic, a distance which cannot be measured a priori but must be traversed to be known. The late Schelling stages a critique of "negative philosophy," rationalist idealism, which he more or less invented and Hegel perfected, but he nonetheless insists that the passage to "positive philosophy," the philosophy of existence, is only by means of negative philosophy. We cannot deduce existence from concepts but neither can we understand existence without concepts.[2] Carried as far as it goes, the understanding discovers unsurpassable limits, whether this be the subject–object identity of the early Schelling, the contingencies of history of the middle period, or, in the later Schelling, the existence of reason itself, but these are not concepts (Hegel is thus far correct, concepts represent no real limit to thought); they are, rather, existential realities. For the early Schelling, an anticipation of the real shows itself in the symbolic and aesthetic patterns of experience, which always disclose more than reflective reason can ever comprehend; in the late Schelling, the real is not only an aesthetic experience, it is a religious experience, a revelation. The resistance of the real to idealization is at the heart of Schelling's dispute with Hegel. To make the rational coextensive with the world, that is, to correlate logic or the symbolic with the whole of nature and culture, may in fact be an inevitable move for philosophy, which finds intelligibility everywhere it looks, structure that appears to be little more than an expression or exteriorization of the implicit logic of reason itself. But Hegel's absolute idealism explains nothing, for the whole of the rational is not intelligible in terms of itself, it does not explain itself; as the brute fact of intelligibility, it is as absurd as it is meaningful.[3] In the light of this fundamental antinomy of the existence of reason, the late Schelling regards logic as "negative," a non-knowledge, a play of concepts, the significance of which remains opaque to philosophy.

The third Schellingian theme is contingency: the teleology of spirit is undergirded, qualified, and to some degree undercut by the formlessness of matter: older than order is accident, more basic than necessity is freedom. About this proto-existentialist/proto-materialist/proto-Marxist Schelling, much has been said.[4] Schelling's "irrationalism" can be overstated: without order and necessity, thought cannot exist, for the ordered, the ruled, and the necessary constitute the proper medium of thought, the warp and woof of the ideal. From his earliest rebellion against subjectivistic interpretations of transcendental philosophy, to his re-evaluation of negative philosophy at the end of his career, Schelling rejects any suggestion that ideality, however insufficiently explanatory, is illusion, virtual, a merely subjective synthesis. Ideality is one face of the absolute; it is not the whole, but neither is it merely reflective of "the hard-wiring" of the mind. The absolute manifests itself in the ideal to some degree and therefore order and necessity are undeniable on a certain level of experience. In the maximum reach of the understanding, every order is revealed to be *in fact* contingent, grounded in something "ruleless," something out of which order has been brought but which is not itself ordered.

We see these three motifs, polarity, finitude, and contingency, in the early Schelling, especially in the nature-philosophy; we also see them at play in the middle Schelling, in the dialectic of ground and existence and the combustive interaction of the three potencies; and in the late Schelling, the motifs come to mature expression in the last version of the doctrine of the potencies and the distinction between negative and positive philosophy. That said, Schelling's work can hardly be described as a continuous evolution of thought: a sea-change separates the later from the early Schelling. Schelling's thought was transformed when he moved to Munich in 1806, whether this be because he came to a new appreciation for the Catholic Middle Ages (Laughland, 2007), or discovered the significance of Jacob Boehme for the question concerning nature (Fuhrmans, 1954; Brown, 1977), or had a religious experience (Horn, 1954/1997), or perhaps all three. But what does remain consistent between the later and the early Schelling is the refusal to follow the trajectory of early modernity and split spirit from nature. It is in this historical context that we must read the *Freedom* essay: Schelling attempts to resolve the modern philosophical problem of freedom by moving the discussion to a deeper level of analysis in which both freedom and determinism can be understood as essential moments in freedom's experience of itself.

The early notion of nature as "visible spirit" (Schelling, 1797: 202) becomes, in the middle Schelling, "ground," God's dark other, which leaves its trace in the impenetrable and inexplicable reality of things, "the irreducible remainder" (*der nie aufgehende Rest*), never to be subsumed into a concept and frustrating reason's every attempt at system (Schelling, 1809: 29). The *Freedom* essay is a continuation of nature-philosophy by other means: Schelling's impulse – to bring freedom and nature within one comprehensive view – remains the same as in his first explorations of post-Fichtian metaphysics. For the middle Schelling, the opposition between freedom and nature is overcome when nature is no longer understood positivistically as a substance or a network of substances, but rather onto-dynamically as difference, non-being, potency, desire: "Nature in general is everything that lies beyond the absolute being of absolute identity" (Schelling, 1809: 28). Essential to this naturalization of freedom is the middle Schelling's replacement of the Kantian notion of existence (position in space and time) with the neo-Oetingerian notion of life as spontaneous self-revelation.[5] Freedom is the potentization of organic life, just as organism is the potentization of non-organic life, a perfection of the power of internal causality that is latent in the non-organic and first manifest in the lowest living organism. The archetype of both human freedom and organic life is the self-actualizing freedom of God.[6] As image of God, nature is no mechanism but an evolving, self-moving life, the pinnacle of which is reached in man, who not only moves according to internal principles, but brings the dynamic of self-movement to its highest expression by authoring himself.

Although the absolute in itself, the unground, lacks nothing, the middle Schelling sometimes speaks of it as though it did, for what is brought about by the unground's decision – creation, difference, consciousness – is understood after the 1809 personalist turn as a real increase in being. By the late philosophy of mythology and revelation, Schelling will change his view yet again and insist that God as a free and personal creator lacks nothing and does not depend upon creation to become personal. This is where we would do well to emphasize the tension (not the split) between Schelling's identity-philosophy, which explores the impersonal and eternal self-sufficiency of the absolute, and the 1809 philosophy of freedom, with its breakthrough to the concept of personality. Identity-philosophy argues that, from the vantage point of the absolute, multiplicity, consciousness, and history are appearances produced by deficiencies in knowledge, degrees of separation from intellectual intuition: "All that is is, to the extent that it is, One: namely, it is the eternally self-same identity, the One that alone exists, and that therefore is all that can be known" (Schelling, 1804a: 153). In his middle period, Schelling argues, to the contrary, that difference is not an imperfection: the absolute is in process, giving birth to itself as a divine personality by means of duality, multiplicity, and history. The late Schelling returns to the assumption of the divine aseity characteristic of the identity-philosophy and corrects his theological "error" of ascribing historical development to God; in the same moment Schelling's theology becomes less psychologically relevant. If we suspend the theological problems resulting from a God who begins imperfect and creates the world to perfect himself and, for a moment, follow Žižek in interpreting the theogony of the middle Schelling as a metapsychology, or better, a speculative psychology, a metaphysical analysis of the structure of personality by means of a projection of these structures onto a model of the absolute personality – for whatever else the middle Schelling is doing he is clearly also writing a psychology of the unconscious – we discover a narrative that anticipates not only Lacan and the resolution of the Oedipal complex in psychoanalysis but also the birth of the hero in analytical psychology: a being that begins in unconscious unity with the system that produces and initially sustains it, achieves personal consciousness, individuality, and freedom by dissociating from that system and establishing a conscious relationship to it.

## Historical immanentism

German Idealism is often identified with the thesis of historical immanentism, the metanarrative that describes the history of being as a dialectical process through which God achieves consciousness of himself. The thesis is essential to the genesis of the notion of the unconscious, for it offered thinkers like Schelling, Hegel, Schopenhauer, and von Hartmann (among others less known) a speculative tableau upon which they could sketch a history of mind, which psychoanalysis and analytical psychology later "discover" coincides to a significant degree with the development of the human personality. We call the thesis "historical" because it breaks with modern (pre-Kantian) a-historical metaphysics and insists on the inclusion in philosophy of the material and cultural reality of world-history: not all times and places are metaphysically equivalent, for being itself has a history, which coincides with man's changing understanding of it. We call the thesis "immanentist" because it subsumes God into history: God does not begin conscious, he becomes conscious of himself through the developing consciousness of man, which presupposes the entire trajectory of natural and cultural evolution. Historical immanentism identifies the divine and the human mind through the medium of history, which could either mean that philosophy now finds a metaphysical way of expressing the Christian dogma, that God becomes man, or, that God as the transcendent origin and destiny of being does not in fact exist – what Christianity means by God is nothing other than man, as Feuerbach puts it.

Historical immanentism is arguably the young Schelling's invention (even though Hegel deserves full credit for developing the thesis into a working system), an invention which came to haunt Schelling, for as Hegel makes clear, it implies that there are no real contingencies in the world just as there are no real limits to reason.[7] The late Schelling breaks with the thesis: the freedom of the individual, the real contingency of material and cultural history, and the finitude of reason, not only in the face of matter, but in the light of revealed religion, strike him as too high a price to pay for a system of nature and history. And yet historical immanentism (re-conceived as "negative philosophy") remains for Schelling to the end of his career the only adequate system of philosophy – its inadequacy to reality grants him the decisive impetus he needs to transcend the boundary between philosophy and religion in the *Philosophy of Revelation*.

The thesis of historical immanentism is founded upon the presumption that a system must comprehend all things as a unity, not simply a collection;

rather, everything in the system must be demonstrated to be necessary to the dramatic unfolding of the logical pattern. The unity of being cannot be static – this was the mistake of Spinozism – it must have the character of an event: all things, material, cultural, spiritual, must be conceived as moments in a developmental process. History cannot be merely a theatre of accidents and arbitrary acts of will; it can only be a logical development, a movement from a lower or primitive ontological position to a higher standpoint, which includes the lower within itself even as it overpasses it. The significance of the existence of the individual being as such disappears behind its mediating role in bringing the whole of being into actuality: the idea, as Hegel puts it, is the truth of the individual, the truth that the individual as such has no truth. Historical immanentism can hardly be described as indifferent to theology: the whole of material and cultural history is grounded in the being of God. However, the historical immanentist's God is no longer conceived as *ens perfectissimum* or *actus purus*, whole, complete or perfectly actual being; following Fichte's notion of the self, and receiving decisive impulses from Eckhart (God needs me to be God), the Kabbalah (the doctrine of divine contraction or *zimzum*), and Boehme (God gives birth to himself), historical immanentism conceives of a God who becomes God by positing his other and becoming self-conscious by means of his opposition to it.

Historical immanentism is the entry point for the first philosophical figure of the unconscious in the Western tradition: the unconscious as the divine abyss out of which God emerges as an infinite drive for self-knowledge. Henceforth dissociation from a primitive fullness of being, the introduction of lack and absence into the infinite, is understood to be essential to the growth of personal identity: God only acquires self-knowledge by dissociating from his eternity, his infinite and undifferentiated unity with being, and inaugurating the drama of creation, posting another to himself, contracting himself from unrelated infinity into one who has another and finding himself in it. In human self-consciousness, God achieves his goal, consciousness of himself; therefore God's consciousness is not other than man's consciousness. God's desire for consciousness drives world-history, his dissatisfaction with his own unconsciousness is the driving force of being, for consciousness requires duality, the opposition of self and other. God cannot remain in his primordial state of undifferentiated self-identity for without the infinite–finite duality, God is less than fully actual; he is driven by the inadequacy of his initial state of being into dialectical development. The paradox at the heart of the thesis is the notion of the imperfection of infinity: God without world is less perfect than God with world. The world adds something essential to the infinite: relationship. The creation of the world, therefore, is not a free and arbitrary act that adds nothing to God, but neither is it a spontaneous emanation: these two alternatives, respectively classical theism and classical pantheism, are fused in historical immanentism. Creation for the historical immanentist is like an emanation insofar as it is an emergence of being *ex Deo* (not a creation *ex nihilo*), but it is not simply an involuntary process such as the emergence of light from the sun; creation is born of a crisis, a decision or break guided by a final cause: creation is for the sake of God's becoming free, self-conscious, and personal. God's becoming conscious, then, is identified with material and cultural history, with the historical dialectic of events and concepts, all of which only appear contingent but are in fact necessary. With this thesis, a priori metaphysics, seemingly abolished by Kant, returns with a vengeance in German Idealism and absorbs history into itself.

The working out of the thesis of historical immanentism is the central trajectory of German Idealism, from its inception in Fichte's *Science of Knowledge*, through the treatises of the early Schelling, to the final form of Hegel's system in the *Encyclopedia of the Philosophical Sciences*. The history books have allotted Schelling the minor role of passing the historical immanentist torch from Fichte to Hegel and adding the reminder that nature, the "not I" in Fichte's system, is as essential to the development of consciousness as the transcendental ego.[8] In fact, Schelling seems to have become bored with historical immanentism after working out its rough outlines in the 1800 *System of Transcendental Idealism*, dropping it for a more classical Neoplatonic emanationism in the identity-philosophy, only to re-awaken his interest in the idea in his middle period under the influence of Boehme and new psychological questions concerning the history of the personality. Identity-philosophy does not deny the articulation of the self-sufficient absolute in hierarchically ordered levels of being; it denies the autonomous ontological reality of the hierarchy and thus does not seriously consider history as an event in the life of God. In its most mature expression, the 1804 Würzburg lectures (Schelling, SSW 6: 71–576), identity-philosophy insists on an abiding identity of reason with the absolute, the non-duality of being, which is essentially non-conscious. But this absolute unconsciousness is not a deficiency; rather, consciousness, characterized by the subject–object distinction and the experience of quantitative (comparative) differences among individuals, is a decline from the absolute, a descent into non-being, the "infinite fracture of the crystalline monolith of reason into the endless repetition of finite subject–objects" (Vater, 2000: 220). Schelling wavers back and forth in the 1801–1804 heyday of identity-philosophy on the question of whether philosophy possesses an intellectual intuition of the non-dual absolute or merely negatively, therapeutically, facilitates the recovery of such an intuition by removing obstacles to it (the last of which is philosophy itself). In the 1804 *Philosophy and Religion* essay, which inclines towards the latter, therapeutic, view of philosophy, Schelling describes intellectual intuition as the substantial being of the soul.[9] Schellingian philosophy is always de-centred, thought thinking itself in the finite thinking subject, and, to this degree, the absolute indifference of the identity-philosophy is immanent in history. But the history in which the absolute is immanent in identity philosophy is not yet a real history and a history of the real. On the contrary, for identity-philosophy God does not need history or human consciousness which is its fruit; in the strongest sense of the notion of being, neither truly exists. For historical immanentism *sensus strictus* it is not enough to say that my knowing is God's knowing of himself, one must also add that God needs my knowing in order to know himself.

In 1809 Schelling returns to historical immanentism in a more robust sense than the 1800 *System of Transcendental Idealism* had articulated, driven by new questions about the anarchic nature of "freedom," the contradiction between good and evil, and the irreducible remainder left out of every movement of idealization. These questions precipitate Schelling's personalist turn and culminate in the final disentangling of Christianity from idealism in *The Philosophy of Revelation*. In his late philosophy, Schelling denies historical immanentism altogether: the ontological difference between God and creation, between the absolute and the finite, between eternity and time, the late Schelling argues, underwrites all of the discontinuities in being which historical immanentism always glosses over. God is not an idea but being itself. Being is freedom; therefore that which God creates is contingently real. The history of consciousness remains a central theme of the late philosophy, only now it is the history of human consciousness, teleologically evolving out of matter toward personhood and friendship with the always already individuated God.

Given that he cut his teeth in the opposite camp, in transcendental idealism, how does Schelling arrive at the extreme form of transcendental realism characteristic of his late period, alternatively described as the overcoming of idealism (Fuhrmans, 1940) or its completion (Schulz, 1955)? The answer to this question would involve us in a systematic overview of Schelling's long career, only the main moves of which can be outlined here.[10] Identity-philosophy is the first step towards positive philosophy since it problematizes the main assumption of historical immanentism, that the absolute could be contained within a historical world-process. Identity-philosophy produced a conundrum for Schelling for it presumed to deploy absolute knowledge, intellectual intuition, but only by denying the reality of freedom, contingency and the finite. Schelling's disciple C.H. Eschenmayer suggested a solution: we must distinguish the appearance of being, with its dualities of subject–object, substance–attributes, infinite–finite, from being itself, which is one, undivided and timeless; philosophy concerns itself with the former, finite being sundered into inevitable dichotomies, religion with the latter, the absolute in itself.[11] Schelling's answer to this suggestion was the 1804 *Philosophy and Religion* treatise (Schelling, 1804b), the text often referred to as the turning point in Schelling's career. Schelling argues against Eschenmayer that finitude is more than mere appearance; it is, rather, an indication of a historical break in the absolute. The question then becomes: why did this break with the absolute occur? The answer Schelling provides in 1809 is the great thought of his later period, perhaps his one great thought, which had to be wrested from his own pantheistic inclinations: being is free and freedom is anarchic, the capacity for good and evil (*ein Vermögen des Guten und des Bösen* (Schelling, 1809: 23)). The unity of the absolute is not necessary to spirit and the break with unrelated infinity ushers in not only human self-consciousness and responsibility but all of the evils of finite existence: sin, disease, madness and death. The 1809 turn in Schelling's thought is not merely a qualification of the identity-philosophy's impersonal notion of the absolute (the timelessly undifferentiated), it is also the dawning of a new concern in Schelling's work: the real problem for philosophy is not the absolute as such but the freedom which has deprived us of it.

Why does such freedom exist? What purpose does it serve? It is clear enough to Schelling in 1809 that freedom must be able to disrupt the absolute, otherwise nothing would exist. But since such disruption must be possible, the monism of identity-philosophy is thrown into question: only a real power can disrupt reality. The existence of such freedom, Schelling concludes, cannot be known a priori; hence the identity-philosophy, which aimed at the construction of an a priori system, was not wrong in denying the existence of negative freedom; it was only wrong in assuming that idealist philosophy could be adequate to reality. The existence of negative freedom can only be discovered a posteriori, in real history, especially the religious history recounted in the Old and New Testaments. In the Bible, philosophy discovers a religious solution to its problem, albeit one that still needs to be thought through philosophically: the break with the absolute can only be the result of a rebellion of freedom. Evil now becomes a real issue for Schelling, and he sympathizes greatly with Jacob Boehme, for whom it is *the* only issue, one that drove Boehme to overhaul conventional understandings not only of God, but of the nature of the human being. Evil is not simply a power of self-destruction original to man, as Kant would have it, it is the primal otherness in being for which God himself must be ultimately responsible, else he is not God.

Schelling's 1809 turn pivots on a new assessment of personality, relationality, and self-differentiation: no longer conceived as departures from reality, degenerations of the absolute, or surface distinctions that do not apply to the depths of being, they are now regarded as conditions of the possibility of love. It is in this personalist context that Schelling sets to work on what Fuhrmans has aptly named "a teleology of evil" in the 1810 *Stuttgart Seminars* (Fuhrmans, 1940: 43). Schelling asks: how could evil make the revelation of the divine possible? How could evil be in itself contingent but historically necessary to the revelation of God? If it is not to lead to a gnostic dualism of equal and opposing forces, the reality of evil must be a later development in being, which once again must be understood to have a history. Evil cannot be something which develops necessarily out of being, the way the essential properties of a thing develop necessarily out of the concept of the thing, it can only be an event, a disruption in excess of its occasioning causes. The immanentist's dream of an a priori history is dashed against the surd of sin: the reality of evil means that history cannot be understood as a continuous development but only as a series of ruptures, and, to that degree, as irrational, but nevertheless culminating in something glorious, the incarnation of God. The concept of the individual also changes under the force of Schelling's new questions: no longer a mere medium of spirit, the person becomes a God-like being with anarchic power to disrupt the ideal, a self-determining and absolutely responsible being. By means of these ideas, which Schelling explores in a patchwork of small publications between 1809 and 1815, Schelling arrives at his psychodynamic concept of personality. The self, of course, was a constant theme of German Idealism, but under the scrutiny of the later Schelling, the elaboration of the theme changes; it is no longer a question of the relation of the I to the not-I, but a question concerning the developmental structure of the whole personality, of which the I could only be a part.[12]

## The Schellingian unconscious

The three leitmotifs of Schellingian thought, polarity, finitude, and contingency, underscore the centrality of the concept of the unconscious for all phases of his thinking: the unconscious is the other pole of consciousness, the limit to the ego, and the abyss of unfathomable freedom at the ground of culture and nature. At its base, the Schellingian unconscious is non-dual, but since consciousness presupposes duality, first a developmental logic and then a voluntarist teleology are introduced to explain the transition from the monism of absolute being to the dualism of personal being. For the unconscious to give rise to consciousness, unity must divide itself, and the one give rise to two, so that the one might know itself and become capable of relationship. Uncovering the secret of this happening, above all explaining why it should have happened, the ultimate purpose served by the absolute's break with itself, is the fundamental impulse of the second half of Schelling's career. Although Kant and Fichte provide arguments for the notion of an essential duality in consciousness, Schelling's real guide here is Boehme: without duality, Boehme argues, there can be no self-revelation (Boehme, BSS 7: 3.22), and what else is consciousness, Schelling adds, but the self's revelation of itself to itself? The one divides so that it might be revealed to itself, and thereby love itself, that is, so that love might be.

"My ego contains a being that precedes all thinking and representing," Schelling declares in his first major philosophical work, *On the I* (SSW 1: 167). The young Schelling's idea of a non-representable and pre-cognitive other of the self is little more than a development of Fichte's assumption of a primordial act at the foundation of transcendental subjectivity, which is in turn an elaboration of Kant's conclusion that the activity of the noumenal ego, which can never be fully recovered by reflection, grounds all subjective synthetic acts. The inception of the Schellingian unconscious is therefore a Kantian figure, but Schelling develops it in ways unanticipated by Kant or Fichte. The unconscious act of self-constituting subjectivity is connected to the Fichtian "not-I," empirical nature in Schelling's nature-philosophy of 1797–1799. This first original form of the Schellingian unconscious (visible spirit/invisible nature) is succeeded by the absolute identity of subject and object in the 1800 *System of Transcendental Idealism* – in effect two variations on a theme. For the early Schelling the unconscious is emphatically impersonal. What Schelling discovers in Boehme in 1806 is the volitional unconscious, the unconscious of drives (as distinct from the epistemological unconscious, the Kantian unconscious of "dark representations"[13]). After the personalist turn, the other of subjectivity is no longer merely "the real," the "not-I," but "drive," "desire," and "will" (Furhmans, 1954: 230). That the acknowledged sources of Schelling's early philosophies of the unconscious are Spinoza, Kant, and Fichte does not diminish the significance of Schelling's 1809 return to Boehme. Schelling enters into the Boehmian labyrinth armed with the questions and concepts of modern philosophy, which had already led him in his early work to conclusions similar to the main tenets of Boehme's theosophy: the non-duality of the deep unconscious; the emergence of consciousness through self-division and self-return; the fallenness of time and materiality, et cetera. What is new for Schelling in 1809 – the biggest lesson he learns from Boehme – concerns the dynamic structure of the personality.

The subjective generation of a world in which consciousness can carry out its activities of knowing and willing is "noumenal" in Kant: it is to be affirmed without being understood. Just so, the Fichtian act of self-positing by which consciousness constitutes itself cannot itself be conscious. The I that posits itself first becomes conscious of itself through the positing of another, a not-I, in which it then recognizes the effects of its recurring synthetic acts. The self-positing that produces consciousness cannot itself be conscious. Fichte understands the significance of this point to be primarily moral and practical: because the I can never recover the primordial act of its being posited, it is called to infinitely strive against that which resists reason, order, and the good. Schelling understands the point in a predominantly metaphysical way: lacking a full and transparent possession of the act that brings it into being, reason can never arrogate to itself mastery of the conditions of its own possibility. Schelling reconceives Fichte's self-positing I along the lines of Spinoza's substance, as a non-dual absolute, the original indifference of subject and object. Only the I that stands limited by an object, by nature, is conscious of itself. Hence in order to become a self-conscious I, the absolute I had to generate an opposite to itself and then forget that it had done so, for the I's positing of the not-I cannot be conscious if the latter is to truly function for it as a not-I. Conversely, the absolute I can never become an object for a knowing subject: when the absolute I becomes conscious of itself, it is no longer absolute.

Schelling's *Ideas on a Philosophy of Nature* (1797) and *On the World Soul* (1798) mark the beginning of his turn from Fichtian idealism to an increasingly de-subjectified nature-philosophy. Fired up by his Swabian sense for nature and a strong affinity for Spinoza, Schelling undertakes to show that nature is just as much "spirit" as subjectivity, only in a different sense: nature is spirit prior to self-consciousness, an unconscious subject out of which self-consciousness emerges. Kant had shown that nature must be thought of as an organism, a self-organizing teleological whole; such an organism requires a principle of organization, that is, a "world soul." Inorganic and organic forms develop through a natural process that mimics the dynamic Fichte describes as the law of subjectivity: mediated self-return through the overcoming of antitheses. Governing and motivating all dynamic exchanges between opposites is the spiritual principle in nature, the world soul, which is more than human if less than divine. It has not been sufficiently acknowledged that, by retrieving the notion of world soul, Schelling betrays his early theosophical proclivities. For Giordano Bruno, after whom Schelling titled one of his works (Schelling, 1802), the world soul holds together the infinity of the material universe, animating it with a single life and setting in motion the productive exchange of energies and forms. The Brunoian world soul is the vitalizing power that holds sway in the whole as much as in every part, a daemon that influences everything through love and hate, the motivator of all sympathy and antipathy in nature, all attraction and repulsion, and the condition of the possibility of "natural magic."[14] Similarly for the early Schelling, nature is an organic whole. The teleology that animates nature is not the result of a Kantian transcendental synthesis, an imposition of form upon matter that encases subjectivity in its representations; rather, it is an indication that what modernity holds to be exclusive to subjectivity – purposiveness, design, spontaneity, and freedom – is also found to a lesser degree in matter, which can and must be considered in some sense a subject in its own right.

The Fichtian works and the nature-philosophy had led Schelling on the hunt for a conception of unconscious knowledge – that is, knowledge without reflection and its inevitable dualisms (subject–object, mind–body, spirit–nature). In the 1800 *System of Transcendental Idealism*, unconscious productivity, intelligence free of reflection, emerges as the master concept. What nature produces with such purposiveness and design, she produces unconsciously. Art occupies a place of privilege in Schelling's *System* because artistic creation, like natural production, emerges spontaneously from the unconscious. By allowing herself to be a medium of spirit (rather than trying to control the means of production), the artist becomes the shaman of the absolute. Like a somnambulist, she knows what she is doing without knowing what she is doing and her activity is unhampered by the reflection that splits the absolute self into subject and object.

It is often noted that a "turn" in Schelling's thought already occurs in the 1804 *Philosophy and Religion* treatise (Schelling, 1804b). The real existence of the world, with its subject–object duality and its temporalized particulars, can only be a fall from the absolute: the finite is still denied full reality, but the emergence of the finite from the infinite is now thought of as catastrophe, collapse, and decline. The path to the positive philosophy begins here. The next move is to trace individuality, personal existence, and time itself to a dark volition in the divine, which Schelling, with Boehme's help, does in the *Freedom* essay and the three drafts of the unfinished *Ages of the World*. The philosophy of freedom (1809–1815) represents Schelling's most sustained effort to think the unconscious. On the grounds of a metaphysically reconstructed Boehmian theogony, Schelling constructs, in his own view, "the first clear concept of personality" (Schelling, 1809: 73). In the *Freedom* essay Schelling struggles to draw analogies between the God who births himself from darkness and the human personality which is beholden to an unconscious decision for good or evil. The fall of the absolute into finitude is now conceived as God's decision to allow for something rather than nothing, which God accomplishes by contracting his being and distinguishing within himself an unconscious ground and a conscious personality; this decision is then repeated in the prehistory of the individual, who contracts a character in an unconscious decision that marks the subject's descent from possibility into actuality.

In the *Ages* drafts, the three potencies are distinguished from "the will to revelation," which is latent in the unground and becomes manifest in third potency. God's decision to personalize himself is an actualization of the will to revelation, a decision that requires the splitting of the absolute into opposed desires, first and second potency, which creates the tension that calls for the resolution of third potency. The ultimate purpose of this resolution is not merely to heal the split but to reveal the Godhead to itself, that is, to personalize God. First potency is the new figure for the dark ground, distinct from the absolute and from the existence of that which it makes possible. It is negative, contractive, but also productive, a lack that generates determinate being. Where the absolute is wholly unconscious, first potency is relatively unconscious, a will moving with a dark presentiment of what is needed if it is to achieve its desire for existence, namely humility, subordination, what Boehme, following Eckhart, calls *Gelassenheit* (letting be). The dark ground, the negative desire for self without other, is now called "being" (*das Seyn*). Second potency, the positive, expansive desire for other without self, is still associated with existence (*das Seyende*) and consciousness, which Schelling seems to have always understood in a proto-

Heideggerian way, as ecstatic, a being outside of itself. Third potency is the unity of the first two, thus the unity of *Sein* and *das Seyende*, the real and the ideal, and the concrete realization of personality through the successful coordination of opposed desires. Third potency brings about a return to the unity of the unground, but unity in a new sense: the impersonal unground – non-dual, unrelated, and therefore unconscious – has become a personal God, self-mediated, self-related, and self-conscious. Understood psycho-dynamically, first potency is aggressively self-assertive, schizophrenically introverted, lost in an interiority without boundaries because it refuses to recognize the other. Second potency is ecstatically self-abnegating, a hysteric, whose whole identity is transferred to the other, to whom it defers in everything. First and second potency both lack boundary and psychic definition, but for different reasons: first potency does not recognize the other while second potency does not recognize itself. Third potency achieves a functional relation of self to other by integrating these opposite tendencies: it alone is capable of love in the genuine sense of the term.

The middle Schelling's model of divine personality, which the human personality mirrors, repeats in all essentials Boehme's triadic pattern of the self-revelation of God (see Figure 1.1). What is not explicitly found in Boehme is Schelling's notion of "the intelligible deed," the founding act of freedom, arguably the most profound development in Schelling's lifelong effort to think the unconscious.[15] The concept is a curious fusion of Kant's notion of a transcendental determination of character, Spinoza's idea of freedom, and the Lurianic Kabbalistic *zimzum* – set in the context of Schelling's repetition of Boehme's theogony. The greatness of the concept – often missed by commentators who see in it nothing more than an eccentric position on the relation of freedom to determinism – consists in its capacity to condense these diverse historical influences into a new paradigm for thinking the self. Schelling finally separates two ideas that had become fused in the modern philosophical tradition – spirit and consciousness – something he had been endeavouring to do, with varying degrees of success, since the nature-philosophy. Surely spirit is only free to the degree that it is conscious of what it does? But Schellingian spirit is not conscious of what it does when it makes the choice that determines its character (and thereby all subsequent choices): the unalterable decision for good or evil. Just as "self-revelation" comes out of the unground's separation into two wills, consciousness emerges out of but (does not precede) its fundamental choice. To be conscious is to be aware of who you have become, and by means of consciousness of having become someone, to have a past for the first time.[16] The decision by which an individual becomes the person he or she is destined to be separates time into a finite period prior to the decision (the eternal past) and a present that begins with the decision. Such an act must remain unconscious; to make it conscious would be to undo consciousness itself.

**Boehme's theogony**

Dark principle ↔ Light principle

↓

Self-revelation


**Schelling's psychology**

Ground ↔ Existence

↓

Personality

*Figure 1.1*

The intelligible deed is a finite repetition of the self-constituting act by which God becomes God, the decision by which the unground chooses to be revealed, a decision that entails allowing for the differentiations within it necessary for self-revelation and creation – in short, allowing for the basic duality of self and other. God "comes to be" a creator and self-conscious being in the same moment that the pre-personal divine retreats into the unknowable abyss. In *The Ages of the World*, God's "un-prethinkable decision" is described as the abrupt and arbitrary break with the rotation of opposed drives in the absolute, which, left to themselves, would endlessly repeat the succession of mutually exclusive emerging-into-prominence and withdrawing-into-latency. No beginning would be possible without this violent break with eternity, this "fall" from the absolute, for in the eternal tri-potentized divinity no potency is strong enough to hold its ground against the other two. But creation comes at a price. God can only create free persons if he allows them the possibility of evil, which is the possibility of self-willed psychosis. On the level of the finite, personality has the option of refusing the transition into light, of deliberately staying in the chaos of mutually antagonizing drives. Following Boehme closely, Schelling describes evil as the will of the ground dissociated from the will of love, thus a willing of self in denial of otherness, a refusal to acknowledge otherness, an incoherent and unsustainable will to be oneself the all and everything.

The late Schelling leaves the terrain of philosophical psychology for cultural and religious philosophy, and lectures for two decades on mythology and revelation, but even here, the unconscious (no longer named as such) plays a decisive role. Mythology, the late Schelling argues, is the progressive birth of the consciousness of God in man: from an original relative mono-theism, in which the human community is united as one people, speaking one language, and not yet reflectively aware of their differences or, indeed, of time itself (man not yet emerged from the unconscious), culture fragments into successive polytheism, which brings about the birth of nations, the diversity of languages and consciousness of history, only to be united in a fully spiritual sense under the revelation of the one God of the Jewish and Christian Bibles. The transitional period is the epoch of mythology, an era characterized by a proliferation of stories of the gods, which appear everywhere at the same time and repeat transcultural patterns. The birth of consciousness from the unconscious in the late Schelling is not an event in the life of God but the history of humanity, the drama by which God drives man out of a primordial unconscious unity with the divine (primitive or relative monotheism), into religious diversity (polytheism), and then into a personal relationship with himself (Christianity). In order to support this narrative, Schelling must assert a common foundation to human consciousness, a stratum of natural mental life structured a priori by the divine potencies.

On the Schellingian assumption that consciousness is a teleological development out of the unconscious – nature climbing toward absolute consciousness – the Schelling school of romantic psychiatry (Gotthilf Heinrich von Schubert, Karl Friedrich Burdach, Ignaz Troxler, and C.G. Carus) elaborated the unconscious in non-pathological terms.[17] Schubert's expression "the night-side of nature" (*die Nachtseit der Natur*) sums up the Schelling school's fascination with intuition, dreams, clairvoyance, hypnosis, and somnambulism – phenomena that not only give the lie to the self-mastery and self-possession of the Cartesian ego, but also indicate higher states of awareness in the unconscious. In *Die Symbolik des Traumes*, Schubert claims that in dreams the soul expresses itself more fully than in waking life, speaking a language of universal symbols. The poet "hidden in us" re-activates the original language of consciousness, for Schubert shares Schelling's contention that poetry precedes prose in the history of language (Shamdasani, 2003: 109). In several entirely forgotten works, Burdach develops the speculative psychology implicit in Schelling's nature-philosophy on the assumption that "the soul is not outside of nature, not supernatural, counternatural or unnatural," but the *inside* of nature (Burdach, cited in Orth, 1914: 23). Carus's *Psyche: Zur Entwicklungsgeschichte der Seele* outlines the various stages soul passes through in its evolution from primitive life forms to the human being.[18]

The elevation of certain unconscious states (inspiration, aesthetic experience, mystical experience, intellectual intuition) above reflective consciousness by Schelling and his followers inaugurates the era of romantic psychiatry. Bookended between the pathologizations of early mesmerism, with its diagnostics of "magnetic diseases," and early psychoanalysis, with its institutionalized hysterics and schizophrenics, romantic psychiatry lasted seventy-five years, from Anton Mesmer's 1776 defaming of the exorcist Josef Gassner, whose spectacular exorcisms Mesmer reproduced and explained in "scientific terms," to James Braid's 1851 coining of the term "hypnosis." Just as Mesmer took the steam from the baroque industry of exorcism, so did Baird take the steam from animal magnetism, with its occult notions of invisible fluids and spiritual energies. In between these events, Schellingian researchers run with Schelling's philosophy of the unconscious and construct medical anthropologies in which man is conceived as "a double star," consciousness concealing a creative unconscious centre of the personality that only gradually emerges into being through a series of transformations in the life of the individual. Their efforts are linked to allied movements in France, especially the transformation of mesmerism into animal magnetism by Armand Marie Jacques de Chastenet de Puységur (1751– 1825), who claims that the unconscious states enacted by the somnambulist are not lower but higher than ordinary consciousness. It is Hegel who first endeavours to call a halt to this subordination of reason to the non-rational in his 1830 lectures on madness where he characterizes the unconscious as a primitive stage of spirit (the moment of immediacy) that can only exist for rational mind as negated (Hegel, 1845 [1830]: 124–139). Moments of return to unconscious states are regressions, if not signs of perversity and delusion (genius, inspiration, and artistic creativity not excepted): at best these are merely natural moments in the development of spirit that must be raised to consciousness; if fetishized they become obstructions to the progress of spirit.[19]

Matthias Ffytche has broken the silence about the Schelling school's role in the history of psychiatry, in an article (Ffytche, 2008) and a book still forthcoming as this one goes to press (Ffytche, 2012). I have not had an opportunity to review the latter. In the 2008 article Ffytche takes the safe approach to the unconscious as a socially constructed phenomenon, adding a narrative elaboration as to when the construction began and what purposes it served. Ffytche locates the construction in German romanticism, which is not controversial (see Ellenberger, 1970; Shamdasani, 2003). What is new is Ffytche's socio-political argument for why the construct was undertaken. In Ffytche's reading of Schelling, Schubert, Carus and Freud, the unconscious served to protect the autonomy of the liberal subject against the encroaching determinism of nineteenth-century natural scientific and social political trends. The unconscious secured for the self an inscrutable and unrepresentable ground outside the material and historical nexus of causes. Of course, Kant did as much with his notion of transcendental freedom; the romantics added that freedom was not merely an ideal of reason, a practical belief necessary to the rational synthesis of moral life, it was also a trans-rational experience. In those areas where consciousness finds itself productively outflanked by motives and aims which it does not understand (somnambulism, trance, art, history, religious experience), the romantic subject experiences the agency of a self that is deeper and more essential than the conscious ego. Ffytche writes:

> The turn to the psyche involves not simply the attempt to produce an adequate language for the phenomena of inner life, but is at the same

time concerned to establish the metaphorical representation of autonomous individuality. The metaphors of obscurity serve, then, not only
as placeholders for kinds of process – moral, psychological, biological,
experiential – which are thought to be too complex to be represented
by simple "chains" of determination; they serve also to introduce the
notion that the self is radically self-caused by a logic which belongs
wholly to itself and thus is in some way inscrutable. In this resistance to
rational conceptions of causal process, the self has acquired a certain
inalienable freedom. It is here that psychology tips over into ontology
with moral and political implications for a theory of man. The
philosophers and anthropologists looked to psychiatry both because
they were interested in describing the basis of the individual mind and
because in doing so they were able to draw on a whole range of
metaphors – trance, seizure, unconsciousness, inner vision – with
which to supplant the language of determinism in their depictions of
the human world.

(Ffytche, 2008: 27)

The ensuing psychology of the unconscious fails for Ffytche because it
confuses two discourses that operate and, it seems, must operate according
to different methods, norms and sources: the medical science of the psyche
and the ontology of the self.

The problem is that such moral and existential discourses about
identity and the medical descriptions of psychic states belong within
different paradigms; there is no simple way to suture them together.
. . . These different languages of self-presence cannot simply be joined
together by hypothesizing some *innermost link* or yet-to-be discovered
substance. This is one reason why the language of the psyche remains
bound to a kind of obscurity and liminality – it remains inconsistent, in
its very essence, and this inconsistency can't be easily dispensed with.

(Ffytche, 2008: 25)

In a refreshing change from standard English-speaking practice of
treating only primary sources (as though no one before had written
anything worth consulting), Ffytche brings heavyweight scholarship to his
argument. The Freudo-centric reading of the history of the unconscious
must be put to rest once and for all, and in this regard Ffytche's project is
allied with our own. However, Ffytche's socio-political argument leaves
something to be desired. Does Ffytche not more or less concede that
psychology must be quantitative and reductively empirical, an assumption
that can only result in the abolition of precisely that which depth psychology ventures, an account of psyche *from within*? Isn't Ffytche in effect
capitulating to clinical psychology and psycho-pharmacology and denying

the possibility of psyche or soul altogether? Schelling is presented by Ffytche as attempting artificially to fold medicine into metaphysics when in fact what Schelling attempted was to build up a new medicine upon metaphysical grounds. Depth psychology is crypto-metaphysics, to be sure. One solution to this is to free it from metaphysics, overhaul the whole enterprise in the direction of clinical and statistical work (by and large the general trend in post-Freudian and post-Jungian psychology), thereby attempting to rescue Freud's and Jung's common dream of psychoanalysis as an empirical science. But another option is to follow the immanent logic of depth psychology and make its crypto-metaphysics explicit, perhaps even to improve it, not by more precise accommodation to clinical results, but by creating more adequate speculative concepts. This is what the Schelling school ventured with respect to the medical psychology of their day, mirroring in medicine the method of Schelling's nature-philosophy or "speculative physics" – not to deduce metaphysical principles from empirical results or hypothesize metaphysical structure only insofar as the empirical results warrant the hypothesis, but rather to fuse the a priori and the a posteriori element in psychology and *approach the empirical through the metaphysical*. This approach is still valid, however unpopular it might be in psychology departments. A speculative psychology would not grant empirical psychology its presumed metaphysical neutrality; on the contrary. The implicit metaphysics of empirical psychology (by and large Cartesianism) would be exposed and deconstructed, a critique that would happen on not only historical, but also explicitly metaphysical terrain.

We do not deny constructivism, for clearly the unconscious is a constructed concept, bearing the imprint – and the limitations – of modern presuppositions and values. But we are not so sure that its constructed nature means that it does not in fact reference a real phenomenon, which was experienced and named otherwise in different cultural epochs (the Dionysian in Greek religion, the *mundus imaginalis* in medieval Arabic thought, the *desiderium naturale* in Aristotelian Scholasticism, the will in medieval voluntarism, the *anima mundi* in Renaissance Hermeticism). The problem with constructivism is that it generally presupposes nominalism and rules out phenomenological and experiential sources of concepts, instead finding only political motives behind the construction of the stories we tell about ourselves. Thus we read in Ffytche that the agenda of the liberal self, to shield individual autonomy from representation, is the hidden and somewhat desultory motive of romantic psychiatry. When one notices the strong strain of pantheism in German romantic thought one wonders if this could indeed be true. For the romantics seem equally motivated by a desire to restore nature to the divine status which it lost with the ascendancy of the liberal self. Even the early Freud enthuses about nature as a transpersonal nexus of forces, to which the psyche belongs and by which it is to some degree ruled (Bishop, 2009: 14–17). Schelling's strategy is neither to opt for the subject nor for nature but for an absolute which grounds both. Ffytche does not seem to consider seriously the possibility that the romantics had an experiential basis for their reflections, that something which Enlightenment science and philosophy ignored was pressing on the romantic psyche and demanding to be expressed.

We will argue in tension with Ffytche's thesis that Schelling's notion of the unconscious originates in Western esoteric discourses, that is in premodern or alter-modern traditions. After decades of abuse in theology and pop psychology, the term "esotericism" is gaining respect in non-foundationalist academic circles. Emboldened by the work of scholars such as Gershom Scholem, Frances Yates, Gerhard Wehr and, more recently, Antoine Faivre and Wouter Hanegraaff, and in the postmodern absence of authoritative arguments for continuing to exclude whole genres of Western literature from more canonically respectable studies in religion and philosophy, Western esotericism has established itself as an inter-disciplinary domain in its own right.[20] The admittedly vague term "Western esotericism" refers to a stream of alternative Western religious and philosophical discourses which have been influential in the development of European thought, but which until now have found no venue for academic study.[21] These include gnosticism, Neoplatonism, Hermeticism, Kabbalah, alchemy, theosophy, especially as these discourses merge at various nodal points in European history, for example in the Renaissance (Paracelsus, Ficino, Pico, Boehme), in seventeenth- and eighteenth-century secret societies (Freemasonry, Rosicrucianism), nineteenth-century romanticism, early twentieth-century occultism, and, more recently, in New Age religions and self-help therapies. What is increasingly recognized is that, while Western esotericism is not reducible to any single doctrine or system, the major texts display certain easily recognizable common features. Faivre has summed these up under four headings: correspondences, living nature, imagination, transmutation (Faivre, 1994: 10–14). "Correspondences" refers to the macro-micro homology typical of Hermeticism and alchemy, the revived ancient metaphysics in which the universe is assumed to be a complex, hierarchically structured material-spiritual whole within which lower levels image higher levels and seemingly unrelated things resemble or correspond to each other (the medicinal qualities of certain plants, for instance, correspond to the qualities of certain metals and their allied planets, and more generally, everything corresponds in one way or another to qualities of the human being, the microcosm). "Living nature" refers to the notion of nature as an organic whole animated by a world soul. "Imagination" refers to the role of fantasy and symbol in the discernment of the encrypted relations of all things to each other and to the whole, and the general subordination of conceptualization and objectification to imaginal, intuitive and sensual modes of cognition, particularly, though not exclusively, in magical practices. Finally transmutation refers to the assumption that since everything is related, any entity on one level of being can be transformed into an entity on another level through an alchemical process of *solve et coagula*, the reduction of the thing to its component elements and the recombination of those elements on a higher level. If the term is properly understood, Faivre's four themes can be reduced to one: living nature. The notion of nature as animated organic whole touches the core thought in modern esotericism (from the Renaissance to the present day): the rejection of mechanism and quantitative, value-free science in favour of organicism, qualitative amplification and holistic approaches.[22]

I do not need to prove Schelling's interest in matters esoteric; it is soundly demonstrated in several classic studies of Schelling, alongside other lesser known but equally reliable accounts of Schelling's development from speculative Pietism, through pantheism, and back to Christianity via theosophy.[23] Yet to be done is a narration of the essential role of the esoteric in the development of the non-Freudian unconscious, a task I will undertake in a forthcoming book.[24] Contemporary forms of the non-Freudian unconscious (classical Jungian, archetypal, transpersonal, Deleuzian, etc.) are expressions of a counter-movement in Western intellectual history which is at least as old as Renaissance Hermeticism and as contemporary as Tolkien. The movement has no real homogeneity, varying from high-brow metaphysics and ultra-cool cultural studies to pulp fiction and Oprah Winfrey banalities, but the eclectic authors of this diverse literature are united by a common enemy: the desacralization of nature (material nature, human nature, cosmological nature) by techno-science and capitalist consumerism. Notwithstanding the massive commodification the esoteric has suffered in recent years, from the long-sighted perspective of the humanities its significance and influence are not easily dismissed. Its critics regard it as regressive or anti-modern, but this is a misreading; Western esotericism, at least in the forms it has assumed in the last 500 years, is an expression of the same wave of humanism that generated modernity, sharing the impulse toward human amelioration through science, although it articulates an alternative way of working with nature. Western esoteric nature-philosophy refuses to follow mainstream natural science and split mind from matter, spirit from animal, finite from infinite. Esoteric modernity is a road not *taken* in the history of science – here we depart from the Yates thesis that Hermeticism is the ancestor of modern science (Yates, 1964) – a modern approach to nature which was openly rejected in the seventeenth century because it did not grant us the calculative control which techno-science demanded of the Western mind (Foucault, 1966). Above all, esoteric philosophies of nature reject nominalism, with its subject–object dichotomy, its desacralized matter as value-free order of molecules-in-motion, its reduction of the many-sided qualities of things to homogeneous, manipulable quantities, and its apotheosis of instrumental or calculative thinking at the expense of the contemplative or what Heidegger calls meditative thinking (*besinnliches Denken*). A thorough reading of Schelling's life and works shows that Schelling's place in the history of Western esotericism is indisputable. The notion of "living nature" is the central assumption of his early work; he wrote and practised methods of what we would call holistic or alternative medicine, and was formally recognized for his contribution by the medical community, which granted him an honorary medical degree; clairvoyance, theosophy and alchemy are recurring themes of his middle period; even his more conservative later work shows the influence of esoteric notions: the collective and symbolic unconscious, for example, which is the presupposition of his approach to mythology, or the notion of corre- spondence in his doctrine of creation, in which ontological categories are held to correspond to natural forces because both have as their archetype spiritual potencies or divine attributes. With respect to the history of the unconscious, Schelling is the key node through which Western esoteric notions of will and the spirit–matter relation are transmitted to nineteenth- century medicine and psychology.

We will not be able to unpack all of the esoteric themes in Schelling for the esoteric unconscious is not our topic. But we will argue that Schelling cannot be understood without the most important figure in the history of German esotericism, Jacob Boehme. Through Boehme the Schellingian unconscious is animated by currents of thought older than romanticism – Kabbalah, Hermeticism, alchemy, and theosophy – which are passed on in more robust metaphysical form to his followers, including several influential figures in the history of psychology: C.G. Carus, Justinus Kerner, Ignaz Troxler, Gustav Fechner, Victor Cousin and Félix Ravaisson, among others.

## Schelling's Neoplatonic logic

In the chapters that follow, we will have occasion to examine in detail two famous diagrams for the absolute from different stages of Schelling's career: the equation from the 1801 *Presentation of my System of Philosophy* (SSW4: 137), and the 1815 "Formula of the World" (*Weltformel*) from *The Ages of the World* (Schelling, 1815: 89). I use the word "diagram" deliberately, for the formulas are meant to visually as well as algebraically represent the functions of their terms. While the diagrams represent quite different versions of the ideal–real relation (the 1801 diagram condenses Schelling's early monistic understanding of the relation; the 1815 *Weltformel*, by contrast, is an expression of the later Schelling's historical realism), they are nevertheless structured by a common logic, which is Neoplatonic in origin. This logical presupposition is key to understanding Schelling's difference from Hegel and the difference between the Schelling unconscious and the Lacanian unconscious. Let us put the two diagrams together and tease out the common logic.

$$\frac{\overset{+}{A = B} \qquad \overset{+}{A = B}}{A = A}$$

The 1801 formula of the absolute

$$\left(\frac{A^3}{A^2 = (A = B)}\right) B$$

The 1815 formula of the world

The principle structuring both diagrams is the Platonic argument that any two opposites must be grounded in a third term which is their relation and which makes possible their opposition by transcending it. Two can only be essentially opposed if they share some common ground which cannot be reduced to either one of them. The idea here is that opposition is not only disidentification, it is also a mode of relation: the one is related to its other as to that which it is not, and all such relations are only possible on the supposition of commonality. Thus the large can be opposed to the small because both are possible qualities of a body, which is in itself neither large nor small. Or in a more Schellingian key, mind can be opposed to matter because both are possible forms of some unknown order of being which is in itself neither mental nor material. The Neoplatonists used such arguments to make a case for spaceless and timeless forms as the ground of the variety of opposite determinations of beings we experience. Schelling uses the argument to overturn Cartesian dualism and to disidentify the absolute from concrete determinations that are proper to subjectivity (self-reflection, consciousness, immateriality, etc.). The latter point is crucial to Schelling's rehabilitation of nature as spirit in another modality, for so long as spirit is confused with subjectivity, nature remains without dignity, autonomy, and spiritual standing, save as the negative of the subject, the object which the subject needs in order to be a subject. Modern philosophy cleaves being into two opposed structures, subject and object, without indicating why the distinction is necessary or showing what makes it possible. The Cartesian systems of philosophy, Descartes', Kant's, and Fichte's, remain stuck in this unexplained duality, where all that is said is that subject is not object, even if it is never without it, a point we will formalize thus: $S \neq O$. Schelling's argument is that the subject–object distinction presupposes a common ground of the subject and the object which is neither subject nor object:

$$\frac{S \neq O}{X}$$

X is indifferent to but not identical with S and O, therefore X can ground both S and O. Thus is the oppositional relation of S and O explained even if X remains inscrutably mysterious – in fact its inscrutability is essential to its explanatory power, a point which becomes clearer in the 1815 *Weltformel*. To see how this Neoplatonic logic is also at work in the 1815 diagram, more exegesis is required (see page 141 following). Suffice it to say here that A2 and A3 must appear sequentially after A=B is posited because the duality latent in the first potency, A=B, requires us to posit a third term which is neither A nor B but which could ground both. A2 is the ground, the condition of the possibility of A=B, but since this reinstates another level of duality (that of A2 and A=B), A3 must be posited as the ground of the possibility of that opposition, and in order to avoid an infinite regress of grounding, B must be posited (or rather not-posited although always already assumed) as the unground, the ground which is never made explicit, the ground which presupposes no ground, which has no opposite, and which is necessarily presupposed in any systematic relation or system of relations, but which can never be brought before consciousness, can never be objectified as a term in the system.

To explain A=A, if it is not a tautology, means A≠A or A=B. But A=B introduces manifest opposition, for on some level A≠B. Hence out of the monad (A) emerges the dyad (A2), where A2=(A=B). The same argument which requires us to see A=A as an implicit dyad, as A=B, compels us to recognize A2=(A=B) as dyadic, that is, as the positing of two opposed terms, A2 and A=B. A3 then is the synthesis of the explicit antithesis between A2 and A=B. Out of the dyad comes the tetrad. But why not look for a further level, for is the tetrad not opposed to the dyad just as much as the dyad is opposed to the monad? Why not continue potentizing to infinity? Because an infinite regress explains nothing. If the potencies are to be sufficiently explanatory, there must be one excluded term, a nonpotency, a ground which is never foregrounded, objectified and made conscious in any equation. Just as the transcendental subject never becomes an object to itself, or as Wittgenstein puts it, the eye can never be given within its own visual field, just as the axiom upon which a Gödelian system rests cannot be explained but must be presupposed by that system, so does the Schellingian unground, the ground which is not itself grounded, withdraw from all positing and presentation. The fourth term, B, is not, then, the next level of potentization after the A3, but rather the always unmanifest ground of every potency; for this reason, it is outside the brackets in the *Weltformel*, i.e., outside the system of potencies.

Hegel, Lacan, and Žižek break with this Neoplatonic Schellingian metaphysics by following nominalism and refusing the move from opposition to common grounding in a third term. Opposites are merely the same thing in a process of necessary self-differentiation. Hegel's alternative logic is: S≠O means S=O. The second formula, S=O, is not a mystical *conjunctio oppositorum*; rather, it is a reinstatement of Cartesian dualism, but with a twist. The subject must alienate itself in a posited object because the subject is nothing other than that which intends an object, that which objectifies itself by disidentifying with its immediate experience. The subject by definition has no substantiality, but directs itself towards substance, either epistemically as knower or psychologically as desirer, and in both cases in an impossible intention toward a union which can never be fulfilled, for fulfilment would mean the extinction of the one who intends the union. The truth of Cartesian dualism, according to Hegel, is the claim that *res cogitans* and *res extensa* are dialectically related, one and the same being in a process of self-alienation and disidentification. S≠O means S=O, where O is S at a later moment of development (Hegel) or subjectivity in disavowal of itself, a constitutive repression, which cannot be undone without undoing subjectivity (Lacan/Žižek). For Hegel there is no logical necessity to posit a hidden ground of duality. The ineffability of the Schellingian X undermines the rationality of the real; only if reason's other is reason in a constitutive (dialectical) act of self-differentiation, the negative *of* reason (subjective genitive), only then can we say that the real *is* rational, that there is nothing outside the system of reason, which could render the system fragile, epistemically suspect or merely relative to our finite cognitive capacities. For Žižek (and by implication, Lacan), the Schellingian X is the fundamental fantasy, as such psychologically inevitable – but seeing through its merely apparent logical necessity is the crucial breakthrough in the Lacanian cure, the move from subjectivization to destitution. To take X for something real outside of the subject–object dyad is ideologically to hypostasize the Big Other. Hence Žižek's reading of the *Weltformel* as the very image of constitutive repression: B is not the unground in the Boehmian-Schellingian sense but the excremental remainder giving the lie to the symbolic, the Lacanian real, that which must always be excluded if the symbolic is to function as a substitute for natural life.[25] Schelling, according to Žižek, has correctly hit upon the formula of fundamental fantasy, but he does not see it as fantasy. Hegel does, hence his superiority.

## Reading Schelling against Schelling?

In spite of his impact on nineteenth-century psychology, Schelling is scarcely mentioned by historians of medicine.[26] In one of the few studies that exist on the Schelling school of psychology, Schelling's eclipse is attributed to the non-teleological character of "the exact sciences," which, following Herbart, was taken as a methodological ideal for psychology at the turn of the century (Orth, 1914: 3). In philosophy, Schelling has enjoyed a modest revival of late, but hardly enough to redress the century of neglect he suffered at the hands of Hegelian historians of philosophy. For the first time since 1800, when he shot to fame at the age of 25 with several widely influential books to his name, Schelling is almost relevant. Philosophers of mind find in the psycho-physical parallelism of the Schelling school a peculiarly contemporary alternative to property dualism (Heidelberger, 2004); speculative realists discover in Schelling resources for supporting their ongoing war on "correlationism" (Grant, 2006); Lacanians find in Schelling the father of the disjointed subject whose recoil from reality founds its own existence (Žižek, 1996; Johnston, 2008). That these retrievals are sometimes in direct contradiction to each other is testimony to the fertility and breadth of Schelling's oeuvre.

Yet another arena of relevance for Schelling has opened up with the advent of Web 2.0: personal identity theory. We appear to be moving beyond the era of self-psychology into an era of personality psychology. Identity is no longer primarily understood in terms of a substantial unity – the monolithic self with its hidden essence – but in terms of historico-geographical dissociation and social connectedness. No longer defined by place and time, personality is as multiple as its social contexts and "exists" to the extent that it is linked.[27] With the exponential increase in information access (everything available all the time) and, especially, the new forms of exchange and social role playing made possible by participation in virtual communities, personal identity is now conceived wholly in terms of relationality. Schelling's relevance to this discussion lies in his insistence, against pantheist, subjectivist, and mechanist impersonalism, on a positive sense of dissociation. Every act of becoming conscious is, for Schelling, a dissociation from that of which we are conscious. Dissociation in this sense is not an obstruction to personal identity but the condition of its possibility: only he who dissociates from who he once was emerges from the past and is able to establish a living relation to the present and the future (Schelling, 1813: 120). Positive dissociation must be distinguished from negative dissociation: where the former enlivens the relation to time, the latter encloses the personality in the past by dissociating from the dissociation life is demanding of the personality. Negative dissociation is wilful unconsciousness or what is commonly known as repression. The divide in the personality demarcated by consciousness–unconsciousness is, for Schelling, not so much a rigid binary as the axis around which revolve the multiple centres of the dissociative self. To be a personality in a Schellingian register is to be inextricably involved in such processes of dissociation and re-identification, of dialoguing with difference, and of consolidating an identity only to have time itself splinter the personality into an ever-greater number of constituent members. Like the divine persons of the Holy Trinity, each of the members of the dissociative self is defined by its relations to others. A certain face of the person emerges into the light of consciousness only at the expense of another receding into darkness. The Schellingian personality thrives in self-diversification much as living organisms grow by division and self-pluralization.[28]

We have Žižek to thank for reminding us of Schelling's continued psychological relevance (Žižek, 1996, 1997a). Although Žižek's interpretation of

Schelling as a misshapen Hegelian is slanted at almost every turn by his allegiance to Lacan's peculiar brand of transcendental-semiotic materialism, Žižek's Schelling studies nevertheless support the thesis of this book, that Schelling is the master architect of the notion of the unconscious, for not only can classical Freudian and Jungian thinking be traced back to Schelling, but to some degree so can Lacan's structuralist overhaul of Freud. Žižek shows how Schelling's neo-Kabbalistic notion of the contraction of being, which makes the finite order possible (God's decision to become a creator and thus bring an end to eternity), mytho-metaphysically dramatizes Lacan's developmental psychology: after the cut of the logos, the interdiction of the Father (*le nom/non du Père*), the pre-Oedipal unity of the child with the mother contracts into the ineffable and inassimilable "real" so that symbolically mediated ego-life can begin. To be sure, Žižek does not claim that Lacan's psychoanalysis is based on Schelling; rather, he claims that Schelling can be fruitfully read through Lacan. There is however more to the story. Žižek never mentions Lacan's collaboration with Alexander Koyré, the foremost interpreter of Boehme in the twentieth century, and he repeatedly underplays the significance of Boehme for Schelling. Lacan had read Koyré's *Böhme* as early as 1929 and participated in Koyré's seminar in 1934. The two became close collaborators in the 1950s (Burgoyne, 2003: 77). These historical facts are essential to understanding why Žižek's cross-reading of Schelling and Lacan works so well: Boehme's theosophy or Christian Kabbalism is a common denominator between Schelling and Lacan.[29]

Essential to Žižek's Lacanian reading of Schelling against Schelling is the discontinuity Žižek sees between the middle Schelling's Lacan-friendly notion of ground and the early Schelling's proto-Jungian notion of nature as unconscious spirit. Ground is interpreted as the fictionalized origin of God, "the Signifier," which stabilizes the symbolic by excluding itself from it. By means of this phantasmic theogony, the middle Schelling illustrates the positing of nature by subjectivity as the negative which positivizes its own vacuous pseudo-life, repeating in the dramatic fantasy of the birth of God the primal act of subjectivity constituting the symbolic by repression of the real and projection of the Big Other. The early Schelling's concept of nature as unconscious spirit out of which consciousness teleologically evolves is the very fantasy of pre-subjective cosmological order that the later theogony unmasks.

What fascinates Žižek most in the middle Schelling is how ground, a self-conflicting nest of cycles of expansion and contraction, the "rotary motion" of conflicting drives, must be "repressed" if consciousness is to exist. The decision that resolves the conflict is forever lost to the self, a "vanishing mediator" that must sink into unconsciousness the moment the decision is made. Lacanian consciousness is not a *synthesis* of conflicting *desires* but a *displacement* of *drives* – not a resolution of unconscious conflict, but a symptom of subjectivity forever out of sync with itself. For Žižek, the unconscious in the middle Schelling can no longer be thought of as the visible spirit of the nature-philosophy; it is instead the decision that is simultaneously the birth of consciousness and the ejection of ground. On this view, nature does not precede subjectivity; rather, it comes to be at the precise moment that subjectivity separates itself from its pre-symbolic life; the illusion of a natural order begins with the decision of the subject to be *for itself*, a decision that can only be made by setting up the *in itself* as that which the subject is not. Adrian Johnston calls this "a transcendental materialist theory of subjectivity" (Johnston, 2008: 69–122): transcendental because it begins with subjectivity and asks after the condition of its possibility; materialist because it discovers that the condition of the possibility of subjectivity is a denial of materiality. The denial is never entirely successful for the repressed always returns as irreducible remainder, reminding us that the ideal is a lie we tell ourselves in order to secure a place for subjectivity in a universe of unintelligible matter.[30]

In Žižek's reading, the eternal cycle of potencies in Schelling's God – the rotation of three mutually exclusive possibilities for will – becomes the infinite reflection of a primordial psychotic subject who cannot decide who or what it is, divided as it is by conflicting drives and incapable of authentic action because it lacks the requisite self-identity to act. Schelling's manifest argument, for Žižek, is that God can only be self-conscious if he allows for difference in being – that is, if he allows for the division of himself from his ground; of himself from creation; of every creature from every other. Psychoanalysed, the latent meaning of Schelling's argument is that subjectivity must repress its Oedipal psychosis if it is to exist at all. The life of the subject can therefore only be a divided life in which subjectivity stands over and against itself on some level – threatened, haunted, and erotically drawn to that which it is not, the pre-verbal mother–infant dyad (hypostasized as "nature"), that with which it could be united only at the expense of itself.

Žižek's psychoanalytical reading of Schelling (more accurately, a psychoanalysis of Schelling) highlights the radicality of the middle Schelling's ontology, which breaks with traditional metaphysics by grounding being in drive. Žižek helps us to see how and why ground is not an ontological foundation in a traditional sense, not a substance or a natural network of causes. Ground is less real than what it grounds: beneath that which exists lies that which does not exist but "longs" to. To say ground exists "prior" to being is to make a category mistake, applying a category, "existence," which is an ideal determination, to the real. The ground longs for existence, which means that it lacks existence. Where for Boehme and Schelling this indicates a mysterious purpose hidden in the deep unconscious of God, requiring limitation, negation, and finitude for the sake of love and community, for Žižek it indicates something far less sublime: at the origin of subjectivity lies a repression of the primordial absence of being necessary to consciousness. Žižek is the first, says Johnston, to overturn the common interpretation of psychoanalysis as a variety of determinism (Johnston, 2008: 115). Freedom is primordially pathological, formless and abyssal, that is why we habitually repress it. Žižek is particularly adept at demonstrating how Schellingian freedom does not choose between good and evil; as the capacity for both, freedom is beyond good and evil. The problem of the formal identity of good and evil is another puzzle that Schelling inherits from Kant.[31] Schellingian freedom does not respond to a pre-existing order of values; inasmuch as it makes possible the distinction between good and evil, freedom is itself neither good nor evil but equally open to both. What this means for Žižek is that evil must reside at the core of every good act as its repressed other: the good act is not one that has expelled the possibility for evil from freedom but has rather put it to use in another way. The subject's inexhaustible capacity to repress freedom, to substitute functional neurosis for pre-subjective psychosis and to virtualize its life is not something to be overcome, for it makes subjectivity itself possible. In order for the subject to exist, it must repress the indifference of primal freedom, banish freedom's anarchic openness from consciousness, and allow the absence it leaves in its wake (the real) to function as a ground.

Schelling's breakthrough to dialectical materialism is ostensibly recalled before it begins as Schelling falls back on esoteric notions of polarity and premodern sexual cosmology. What Schelling truly discovered, says Žižek, eluded him. The real is not stuff that is idealized but the gap or break in the symbolic that indicates the contingency of the ideal. The ideal generates the real as the condition of its impossibility. The two cannot be grounded in an indifferent absolute without obfuscating their intimate dialectical entanglement with each other. For this reason Žižek ultimately prefers Hegel to Schelling, albeit a Hegel also standing on his head, not the arch-rationalist herald of "the march of spirit" but the thinker of negativity *par excellence*, the one who carries forward Schelling's breakthrough to the essential role of the negative in the construction of identity (Žižek, 1996: 98). Žižek's Hegel is an atheist masquerading as a Christian – not because Hegel is hiding from the truth, but for the sake of performatively unmasking the dissimulation inherent in all theories of the transcendent. Schelling's failure in Hegel's eyes is not, as is commonly said, to have resolved the ideal–real dyad into a point of indifference between them – their indifference is Hegel's clue to their dialectical entanglement with one another; rather, Schelling's failure is to have hypostasized this point of indifference into the Godhead outside of all dialectical process.[32] Schelling's absolute indifference is an instance of Lacan's Big Other, the fantasy by which subjectivity both consolidates itself by negation of the real and conceals its own inherent negativity from itself (constitutive repression), only Schelling fails to recognize the vacuity of the construct. In Žižek's view, this Schellingian fantasy of transcendence is corrected by Hegel, for whom the dialectic of the ideal and the real is purely immanent. The Hegelian third (repeatedly misinterpreted by Hegelian rationalists as a purely affirmative synthesis that restores identity) replaces Schelling's indifferent absolute with a spirit that is eternally "out of joint" because it has absorbed the real into the ideal and rendered it a constitutive moment of itself.

Žižek calls the breakthrough that slips through Schelling's hands into Hegel's ready grasp *"die Grundoperation des Deutschen Idealismus,"* a single insight working its way through Kant, Fichte, and Schelling until Hegel finally gets it right, but one that can only be fully understood in light of Lacan: the notion of "the 'primordially repressed' *vanishing mediator* which generates the very *difference* between the Real and the Ideal" (Žižek, 1996: 112). In the Schellingian theogony the negative is the moving principle of life and mind: God introduces negativity, first potency, lack, so that something positive might come to be as a result of the effort to overcome it. But the something that comes to be is not simply a return to the God that posited the negativity in the first place; what "returns" is something *other* than God. Hence the negative is not merely cancelled; it is also preserved as the mediator of the next level of structure. Schelling, in Žižek's reading, misses the merely transitive significance of negativity and hypostasizes the negative into "the dark principle" essential to the luminosity of "the light principle." For Žižek this represents a regression to premodern dualistic cosmology. Hegel corrects Schelling in this respect, for the Hegelian dialectic abandons transcendence in favour of an immanentized absolute: that which moves the first moment into division is not its incompleteness when measured against the prior fullness of an absolute that is neither the one nor the other; rather, the movement is the logical result of the incompleteness of the first to itself. Hegel does not need a transcendent ground because Hegelian logic "moves": a principle can be "othered" in itself, contained within itself as its own negation.[33] The negative has no place outside the dialectic of the three principles: that which makes mediation possible, the negative, disappears in the mediation itself, proves itself to be not-different from what is mediated. Negativity drops out as a distinct moment in Hegel, shows itself to be nothing but the one side of the absolute in transition to the other side. Negativity is not overcome (as in the mainstream reading of Hegel) but revealed to be the truth of the whole.

Žižek concludes that the Schellingian absolute is an "idealist-ideological" fiction related to premodern banalities about the complementarity of light and darkness, or to Jungian "New Age" libido-theory. The Schellingian "idealist-ideological" dialectic insists on a conjunctive sense of the "and": darkness *and* light, feminine *and* masculine. The "and" here conjoins two really distinct and opposed structures, which can only be distinguished by positing the indifferent absolute. By contrast the Hegelian "and" is "dialectic-materialist" (or, we might add, nominalist): the Hegelian "and" is not a conjunctive that presupposes a disjunction, but an identifier. Darkness *is* (from a certain perspective) light; the feminine *is* masculine.

There is no assumed point of indifference behind the opposites but only the endless (and senseless) alternating of the one into the other.[34] When he refuses to draw the atheist consequences of his insights, Schelling becomes complicit in reason's substitution of a comforting fiction for the "horrible" truth of constitutive repression. Žižek sides with Hegel because the eldest of the Tübingen trio finally does away with the transcendent God and squarely faces the unconsoling fact of the insubstantiality and negativity of every identity, even the identity of the absolute itself.

Žižek reads Schelling against himself, like the psychoanalyst who does not place great stock upon what the analysand consciously intends to communicate but adverts to how he speaks ("the subject of the enunciation" by distinction from "the subject of the statement") and finds unintended significance therein.[35] For example, when Žižek re-describes Schelling's eternal cycle of potencies as "the chaotic-psychotic universe of blind drives" (Žižek, 1996: 13), he effectively pathologizes the Schellingian absolute. Schelling is unwittingly confessing the primal crime of subjectivity, the murder of the real, in the disguise of a grand narrative about the beginning of time; he is the Lacanian hysteric, telling the truth about himself by lying. Schelling describes eternity as "the original equivalence" of ipseity and alterity in the absolute, the original indifference of the absolute to the No and the Yes, which excludes time, events, and growth (Schelling, 1815: 9). Where Žižek sees this as the original psychosis of infancy, which must be repressed if ordinary neurotic subjectivity is to function, Schelling describes it as the bliss and harmony of heaven which must be left behind if life in time is to begin. In Schelling's understanding of it, eternity is not a being at war with itself, but just the opposite, a being free of contradiction and strife. It follows that the psychology of dissociation founded upon this metaphysics does not assume constitutive repression: the Schellingian self must divide if it is to grow and live, and division means that some aspects of the self inevitably sink back into unconsciousness as others take centre stage, but this dissociation is not subjectivity defending itself against horror by substituting the safety of the symbolic for the chaos of the real; rather, the dissociation is for the sake of becoming conscious in a new way, that is, for the sake of an increase in being.

We introduce the notion of positive and negative dissociation, which is only implicit in Boehme and Schelling, in order to amplify the therapeutical significance of Boehmian-Schellingian metaphysics. The tendency in psychoanalytical and psychotherapeutical literature is to speak of dissociation in a purely negative sense: to dissociate from x is to render x unconscious and so a threat to the ego. Lacanian psychoanalysis demolishes ego-psychology, but goes to the other extreme, into a merely negative theory of subjectivity as lack, constitutive repression, the self's necessary and tragic absenting of itself from itself. Positive dissociation is the growth in consciousness made possible by the contraction of some aspect of the individual's identity, which henceforth becomes the past, a dissociated other which is never "sublated" by consciousness (cancelled and preserved), but subsists in the self as a grounding potency. Positive dissociation is not *only* the production of unconsciousness but also and primarily the production of consciousness: to dissociate from x is to render x an object of consciousness or to make x conscious, for when x is attached to the I in such a way that the I has no distance from it, consciousness of x as such is not possible. Consciousness presupposes dissociation from that of which it is conscious. Negative dissociation is the dissociation that does not produce life and consciousness but the opposite, the dissociation from the dissociation growth is demanding of us, or wilful unconsciousness, the paragon of which is Boehme's figure of Lucifer. Boehmian-Schellingian dissociation is teleological, the dissociated parts of the self working together behind the scenes for the sake of the flourishing of the whole in which they inhere. Jason Wirth describes this as "the conspiracy of life": "the breathing out of the dark abyss of nature into form and the simultaneous inhaling of this ground, the retraction of things away from themselves" (Wirth, 2003: 2). The metaphor of "conspiracy" is perfect, for the dissociated parts of the self are really distinct and in no way determined to work together, and yet, when the Schellingian personality thrives, they surreptitiously collaborate in the production of consciousness.

Most problematic for classical Schellingians is Žižek's a-cosmic reading of the middle Schelling, which effectively divorces the middle from the early Schelling. Schelling published the *Freedom* essay in 1809 as an appendix to his first collected works without announcing any axial divergence from the thrust of his early work. It would seem that he regarded the *Freedom* essay as continuous with both the nature-philosophy and the identity-philosophy. In the 1827 Munich lectures Schelling summed up his philosophical career thus far as a sustained investigation into the being of nature without any breaks or reversals. There is no doubt that the phases of Schelling's work do not cohere into a system, but this is not to say that the work is marked by violent breaks. Even the 1809 personalist turn, with its sudden appropriation of Boehme, is continuous with the central aim of the early work, to overcome the modern divide between nature and spirit. Boehme's great achievement, doubtless aided by the fact that he did not read the philosophy of his contemporaries (which was moving via Descartes in the opposite direction), is to think matter and spirit as one. The point of Boehme's positing potency, drive, and desire in God is to set up divine archetypes for natural processes and thus to overcome the Jewish-Christian tendency to deny an essential connection between materiality and divinity. Schelling writes "ground or nature" (significantly re-phrasing Spinoza's *Deus sive natura*), and given that he spends most of his early career discussing "nature," we ought to take him at his word (Schelling, 1809: 27). The split-off part of God, the excised other of subjectivity, is nature in the full cosmological sense of the term, matter, potency, force, drive – the non-verbal material order that precedes and exceeds subjectivity.

For Žižek, by contrast, there is no nature in this cosmological sense, no "order" that precedes subjectivity. The notion of nature as the infinite material matrix of possibilities is the romantic fantasy produced by the constitutively repressed subject for the sake of sustaining its virtual existence, the subject in effect concealing its own virtuality from itself behind a cosmological screen. There is no productive cosmological polarity generating a hierarchy of being, no teleology directing the evolution of consciousness from the unconscious. Modern science, which discloses matter as the residue of an unthinkable accident, is the truth of matter, the truth that matter has no truth; there is no non-verbal order of things, no meaning or purpose served by life and the appearance of consciousness. In Schelling's later emphases on the violence of beginnings, the contingency of reality, and retroactively posited origins, Schelling ostensibly expresses this axiom of disenchantment without knowing it, like the Freudian dreamer enjoying his repressed secrets in a censored form acceptable to consciousness. Schelling, in Žižek's psychoanalytical reading of him, actually discovers that the nature which obsessed him in his early work is nothing but the trace of the repressed life of the pre-subjective subject, essential if the latter is to be conscious of itself, that is, he discovers the flaw in his early naturalism, but he disavows the discovery by constructing a meta-narrative of God's birth from ground. Hegel, by contrast, goes the full distance with the Schellingian breakthrough to the negative and makes the interplay of the virtual (self-posited) ideal and the equally virtual (self-posited) real the whole of reality, with no *telos* behind the show of the absolute's ceaseless activity of self-overcoming. As Freud's dreamer unconsciously generates an elaborate narrative to represent and at the same time conceal from consciousness a difficult truth, Žižek's Schelling constructs his theogony of ground–existence to express and conceal the truth of constitutively repressed subjectivity.

Psychoanalytical suspicion is a two-edged sword: on the one hand, it can give the analyst access to a repressed truth which the analysand unconsciously camouflages in everything he says; on the other hand, it places the analyst in a position of unimpeachable sovereignty over the analysand and precludes mutuality, the possibility that the analyst himself has something to learn from the analysand. Žižek might defend himself from such a critique by arguing that Lacanian suspicion does not mean that the analyst is always right, but rather, that the analysand is always wrong (Žižek, 1997b). But however implicated in the dissimulations of the unconscious the Lacanian analyst may be, one thing is never in question: the Lacanian theory of the unconscious. As a hermeneutical technique, suspicion can become a way of protecting the reader from thinking otherwise, a defence against the text, a way of reading which ensures that the reader is never touched by the world of the text. Such suspicion sometimes achieves distance at the cost of understanding and participating in the thought of that which is being interpreted, raising the reader above the text, which is at the same time rendered powerless. Such is Žižekian suspicion: Žižek has no more to learn from Schelling himself, Schelling as a thinker, than he does from Keanu Reeves; the *Freedom* essay is read with the same immovable cynicism and psychoanalytical sovereignty with which Žižek approaches the bits and pieces of pop culture that interest him equally. *The Ages of the World* is no different in principle from *Avatar*; both are symptoms of constitutive repression, to be decoded by the analyst-sovereign who alone maintains an unblinking gaze on the hidden truth of the matter.

Žižek's psychoanalysis of Schelling belongs to a long tradition of reading Schelling as a misguided genius, stammering and sputtering mostly metaphysical, theosophical, and mystical nonsense, but occasionally, in spite of himself, saying something of real importance, which he himself does not quite understand, but which more disciplined thinkers, say Kierkegaard, Marx, Heidegger, or Lacan, rescue for philosophy. Thus do Jaspers, Heidegger, Habermas, and Frank read Schelling: his undisputed importance for the history of philosophy lies elsewhere than he thinks or intends, respectively in existentialism, in the overcoming of metaphysics, or in setting the stage for Marx's dialectical materialism.[36] Jaspers puts the thesis of "Schelling's failure" succinctly: "Schelling was hardly aware of what he was driving at, and his meaning is only discoverable by those who have acquired Kierkegaard's light" (Jaspers, 1933: 160). Substitute "Nietzsche," "Marx," or "Lacan" for "Kierkegaard" in this sentence and you have respectively the verdicts of Heidegger, Habermas/Frank, and Žižek. Schelling on this view is not so much the philosopher of the unconscious as an unconscious philosopher.

Whatever the fruit Žižek's Schelling reading has borne (not the least of which is to have rescued Schelling for another generation of readers from the obscurity into which he habitually falls), I believe that philosophy and psychology need a deeper reading of Schelling, a more Schellingian reading of Schelling, a Schelling not selected, cut, and pasted according to pre-given criteria of psychological coherence, but one that can make available all of the psychological resources his thought contains. It is not my intention in this book to "set the record straight" about Schelling and the unconscious. There is nothing straight about Schelling's diverse output, pregnant as it is, no doubt, with multiple approaches to the unconscious: Freudian, Jungian, Lacanian, and perhaps others that have yet to be noticed. Nor is this book merely an exposition, unified through the notion of the unconscious, of Schelling's diverse career. This book puts a question to Schelling, a question that could not have been framed without the last hundred years of psychoanalysis, analytical psychology, and transpersonal psychology: how are we to understand the unconscious? Is it a clinical hypothesis or an ontological concept? Is it a social construction? Is it simply a vague philosophical term that was intended to compensate for the inadequacies of Cartesian psychology? Is the unconscious a psychic container of repressed experiences and desires or is it an image of God? Or is it merely a semantic remainder, the cut left in us by the advent of symbolization? Does it have a future or has the concept spent its force in the golden age of psychoanalysis, the second half of the twentieth century, with little relevance in an era of increasingly precise psycho-pharmacology?[37] This question, which we cannot hope to answer (our aim is only to set the stage for properly asking it), is put to one of the first to use the term "unconscious" (*das Unbewusste*) as a substantive – in any language.[38]

My aim is not to help Schelling discover what he really means to say, nor to force Schelling's text into producing something that is not native to it. I have no intention of improving Schelling or giving birth to Schellingian monsters. Nor do I believe that Schelling's text needs to be psychoanalysed if Schelling's contemporary relevance is to be rescued from his antiquated metaphysics and theology. At the same time, this book is not a work of pure exposition. I think of my approach as one of hermeneutical refraction: I wish to carry Schelling's thought forward into contexts that it does not and cannot anticipate: late psychoanalysis, analytical psychology, theories of schizophrenia. To be so carried forward it must be permitted to penetrate an atmosphere alien to its first construction. It will not remain what it was: like light that must change direction in order to penetrate certain media, so does the direction of Schelling's thought change in my reading of him. But rather than reading Schelling against Schelling, I propose that we read Schelling through Schelling, permitting Schelling's various writings on the unconscious to interpret themselves, the way the discontinuous pieces of the Jewish-Christian Bible are permitted to interpret themselves in the late Schelling's *Philosophy of Revelation*. Other possible levels of significance (allegorical, psychological, symptomatic) will be subordinated to the literal sense of Schelling's texts on the assumption that the sense of these texts does not lie outside of them, in an unnamed social context, or a psychology unknown to Schelling, or in Schelling's own neurosis; the key to the interpretation of any particular text lies in the corpus as a whole. The disjunctions in Schelling's writings in this reading are no longer problems but clues: by letting the texts lie side by side in all of their apparent incompatibility, as Schelling himself did, we will let their meanings emerge from the tensions that suture them together as a whole.

When Schelling is read in this way, interesting possibilities for understanding individual texts come to light. For example, Žižek's stark alternative between the *System of Transcendental Idealism*'s teleological unconscious, on the one hand, and the *Freedom* essay's self-constituting unconscious on the other, is shown to be a choice that Schelling himself urges us not to make. When we place the early Schelling in dialogue with the later Schelling on the unconscious, we see that two perspectives are possible: a realist perspective, which would see matter as prior to consciousness, a cosmological matrix of potency, and a transcendental perspective, which would see consciousness as prior to matter, positing it for the sake of its own self-definition. Both perspectives are justified because the unconscious decision to be a subject is at once a free decision of self-positing spirit and an event in the history of nature.[39] The unconscious as a natural stratum teleologically giving rise to self-conscious spirit is spirit described *ad extra*, from a third-person perspective. To the metaphysician's gaze, it can only appear as the material latency of spirit, which evolves into consciousness through a natural process of division and recombination, the way life evolves from the division of cells. The unconscious as contracted self and ejected past which founds the individual's identity is spirit described *ad intra*, from a first-person perspective, transcendentally experienced, not as some night of being that precedes the self (how could that be experienced?), but as the self's act of separation from that which it is not, the act that has always already occurred and is continually being repeated, which spirit experiences, paradoxically, as a free act. That this presupposes the self's being present at the moment of its coming into being is one of the temporal conundrums in which we inevitably entangle ourselves when we attempt to think freedom. Which view is more accurate? Both and neither, and here we return to the early Schelling's original impulse, to give both a transcendental philosophical account of the absolute (*ad intra*) and a natural philosophical account (*ad extra*).

When we interpret Schelling's various versions of the unconscious as stages in a developing theory, we discover an unusual convergence of metaphysical, psychological and theological positions. Metaphysically, Schelling is a co-inherentist. We coin the word to describe a position on the relation of mind to matter which is neither idealist nor realist and which cannot be identified with the psycho-physical parallelism of his followers (e.g., Gustav Fechner). For Schelling, matter and mind are really distinct but co-inherent: they are neither causally reducible to each other nor do they mirror each other; rather, matter co-inheres in mind as its substance and ground, and mind co-inheres in matter as its formal logical structure. Psychologically, Schelling is a dissociationist, in the lineage of Paracelsus, Boehme, Janet, James, Peirce, and Jung. For the dissociationist multiple identities are not a problem; everything depends upon the relations of the personalities to one another. In a positive dissociation, the other personalities are permitted their space of operation and become collaborators in the flourishing of the self; in a negative dissociation, the other personalities are denied consciousness and go insane, vying with each other for possession of the self and precipitating its breakdown. Theologically, Schelling is a Trinitarian, but not in the historical immanentist style of Hegel, rather in the transcendentalist style of Baader. The triad is not exhausted in the dialectical play of the three terms; a still point at the centre of the triad is constellated by the movement of the three terms, a point which is not one of the three terms but which subsists as the *arche* and *telos* of the whole. Finally, in this sympathetic reading of Schelling through Schelling, a coherent psychology of the unconscious comes into view, a speculative psychology of the unconscious, i.e., one which begins in metaphysics and finds confirmation in the empirical (by distinction from a metapsychology, which forms hypotheses on the basis of the empirical). Its fundamental thesis is as follows: negative, subject-oriented desire (neither death-drive nor narcissism but introverted life-drive) obstructs positive, object-oriented desire for the sake of a precarious production of that which is irreducible to both the ego and the other. Just as in the nature-philosophy negative force obstructs positive force so that infinitely productive nature (*natura naturans*) might be revealed, just as in the philosophy of freedom, ground obstructs existence so that love might be revealed, just as, in Schelling's late philosophy, first potency obstructs second potency (literally crucifies him) so that God might be revealed, the negative features of the human psyche, the inferior qualities, selfishness, vice, insurmountable neuroses, etc., are not accidents, absurdities or reactions of the subject to a universe that has no place for it, but conditions of the possibility of finite personality. Our vices fuel our virtues; our complexes are key to our character. Such a unique psychology – it shares features of Freudianism, Lacanianism, Jungianism, and even behaviourism, without coinciding with any of them – is relevant in its own right and on its own terms.

## Notes

1　While I believe there are only two main phases in Schelling's career, divided by what I call the personalist turn of the 1809 *Freedom* essay – an early Schelling, 1793–1809, and a later Schelling, 1809–1854 – I follow (roughly) Manfred Schröter and distinguish the stages of Schelling's publications and lectures as follows: the early Schelling (Fichtian writings, nature-philosophy, identity-philosophy, 1793–1806), the middle Schelling (philosophy of freedom, 1806–1821), and the late Schelling (philosophy of mythology and revelation, 1821–1854). The transitions are connected to decisive phases in Schelling's academic career. In 1806 he moved to Munich, began his bureaucratic career, and, more importantly, his extra-curricular collaboration with Baader. In 1821 he took up lecturing again at Erlangen (after a fifteen-year hiatus) and, resigning himself to the failure of *The Ages of the World* project, began to work on the philosophy of mythology and the positive philosophy, which occupied him almost exclusively in his final years teaching in Munich (1826–1840) and Berlin (1840–1846).

2　See Schelling (SSW 10: 176): "Any philosophy which does not remain grounded in the negative but tries instead to reach what is positive, the divine, immediately and *without* that negative foundation, will inevitably end up by dying of spiritual impoverishment."

3　In the 1927 lectures *On the History of Modern Philosophy*, Schelling concedes to Hegel that, indeed, logic is in some ways self-sufficient; it can, it seems, explicate the whole of the intelligible world as the implicit content of its innate "logical idea," but this whole of the intelligible is not the real, for it leaves out one thing, upon which everything else depends, its own existence: "Although the concept cannot be the *sole* content of thought, what Hegel asserts might at least remain true: that logic in the metaphysical sense which he gives it must be the real *basis* of all philosophy. What Hegel so often emphasizes might for this reason be true after all: that everything that is is in the idea or in the logical concept, and that as a consequence the idea is the truth of everything, into which at the same time everything goes as into its beginning and into its end. As far as this constantly repeated conception is concerned, it might be admitted that everything is in the logical idea, and indeed in *such* a way that it could not be outside it, because what is senseless really cannot ever exist anywhere. But precisely thereby what is logical also presents itself as the merely negative aspect of existence, as that *without* which nothing could exist, from which, however, it by no means follows that everything only exists via what is logical. Everything can be in the logical idea without anything being *explained* thereby, as, for example, everything in the sensuous world is grasped in number and measure, which does not therefore mean that geometry or arithmetic explain the sensuous world. The whole world lies, so to speak, in the nets of the understanding or of reason, but the question is how exactly it got into those nets, as there is obviously something other and something more than mere reason in the world: indeed there is something which strives beyond these barriers" (Schelling, 1833: 147). In other words, the real is not the rational and the rational is not the real. See also Schelling (SSW 14: 23; Hayes, 1995: 213): "If we say that reason is all being [*Seyn*] (and therefore, inversely, if all being is reason), it is very difficult to come up with the unreason [*Unvernunft*] which is needed for an explanation of the real world [*die wirkliche Welt*]. For anyone can see that alongside a great and powerful reason which seems to govern things in a certain way, a great and powerful portion of unreason is mixed in with all being."

4 See especially Habermas (1954) and Frank (1975).
5 See Schelling (1809: 228). On the influence of vitalism and vitalist theology on Schelling (especially Oetinger), see Schneider (1938), Benz (1955), and, more recently, Matthews (2011).
6 See Schelling (1809: 228).
7 See Schelling (1800: 211): "History as a whole is a progressive, gradually self-disclosing revelation of the absolute . . . a never wholly completed revelation of the absolute which, for the sake of consciousness and thus merely for the sake of appearance, separates itself into consciousness and unconsciousness, the free and the intuitant; but which *itself*, however, in the light inaccessible wherein it dwells, is eternal identity and the everlasting ground of harmony between the two."
8 Hegel's first major publication, *The Difference between Fichte's and Schelling's System of Philosophy* (Hegel, 1801), in which Hegel argues that Schelling's nature-philosophy is the crucial correction to Fichte's subjectivist tendencies, and, by implication, the presupposition of Hegel's own still-to-be-developed absolute idealism, is largely responsible for the memory of Schelling as merely a transitional figure.
9 See Schelling (SSW 6: 26): "Just as the essence of God consists in an absolute, immediately known ideality which is as such absolute reality, so the essence of the soul consists in a cognition that is one with the absolutely real, hence with God."
10 The reader is referred to several outstanding studies of this topic, for example, Fuhrmans (1940) and Tilliette (1970).

11 C.H. Eschenmayer, *Die Philosophie in ihrem übergang zur Nichtphilosophie*, published in 1803. For a summary, see Fuhrmans (1940: 31–32).

12 For a short summary of the middle Schelling's realist historical immanentism, which is so essential to the development of his psychology of the unconscious, see the appendix to this book.

13 See Kant (1798: 18).

14 On Bruno, see Yates (1964) and Couliano (1987).

15 See Schelling (1809: 259; 1813: 181–182).

16 "There is no dawning of consciousness (and precisely for this reason no consciousness) without positing something past. There is no consciousness without something that is at the same time excluded and contracted" (Schelling, 1815: 44).

17 Schubert was a student of Schelling's at Jena from 1801 to 1803, and maintained contact with him throughout Schelling's later career (Hanegraaff *et al.*, 2006: 1042). Troxler attended Schelling's *Würzburg* lectures (1804a) (Beiser, 2002: 689, n. 1). Carus had no direct contact with Schelling but aligned himself enthusiastically with Schelling's nature-philosophy (Bell, 2010: 163). Burdach was a biologist and physiologist also influenced by Schelling's nature-philosophy. On the Schelling school of dynamic psychology, see Orth (1914); Shamdasani (2003: 109–110, 125, 147, 164–167, 174–175); Ellenberger (1970: 202–210, 303–304, 685, 729); Ffytche (2008). Some of the main works of the Schelling school include Ignaz Paul Vitalis Troxler, *Ideen zur Grundlage der Nosologie und Therapie* (1803); idem, *Elemente der Biosophie* (1806); idem, *Blicke in das Wesen des Menschen* (1811); G.H. Schubert, *Die Symbolik des Traumes* (1814); idem, *Ansichten von der Nachseite der Naturwissenschaften* (1808); idem, *Ahndungen einer allgemeinen Geschichte des Lebens* (1806–1821); idem, *Altes und Neues aus dem Gebiete der inneren Seelenkunde* (1817–1844); idem, *Geschichte der Seele* (1830); idem, *Die Krankheiten und Störungen der menschlichen Seele* (1845); Karl Friedrich Burdach, *Der Mensch nach den verschiedenen Seiten seiner Natur* (1837); idem, *Blicke ins Leben* (1842–1848); Carl Gustav Carus, *Vorlesungen über Psychologie* (1831); idem, *Psyche. Zur Entwicklungsgeschichte der Seele* (1846).

18 Jung claims that his own view of the unconscious is less indebted to Freud than to Carus, the latter of whom was, in Jung's opinion, the first "to point to the unconscious as the essential ground of the soul" (Jung, 1952 interview, cited in Shamdasani (2003: 164)). Jung's misstep here is another example of his sloppy scholarship: it is not Carus who first grounds the soul in the unconscious, but Schelling. The first line of Carus's 1846 *Psyche* is nothing less than a summary of Schelling's early philosophy: "The key to an understanding of the nature of the conscious life of the soul lies in the sphere of the unconscious" (Carus, cited in Shamdasani (2003: 174)).

19 See McGrath (2011).

20 There are three endowed chairs dedicated to Western esotericism, at the Sorbonne, the University of Amsterdam, and the University of Exeter.

21 See Hanegraaff *et al.* (2006).

22 See Faivre (1994: 11–12): "The cosmos is complex, plural, hierarchical. . . . Multilayered, rich in potential revelations of every kind, it must be read like a book. The word *magia,* so important in the Renaissance imaginary, truly calls for that idea of a Nature, seen, known, and experienced as essentially alive in all its parts, often inhabited and traversed by a light or a hidden fire circulating through it. Thus understood, the 'magic' is simultaneously the knowledge of the networks of sympathies or antipathies that link the things of Nature and the concrete operation of these bodies of knowledge. (Let us think of the astral powers that

the magus brings to talismans, Orphism in all its forms, especially musical forms, the use of stones, metals, plants favourable to re-establishing physical or psychological harmony that has been disturbed.) Inscribed in this perspective, Paracelsism represents a vast current with multiple ramifications, from animal magnetism to homeopathy, by way of all the forms of *magia naturalis* (a complex notion at the crossroads of magic and science). More than the practices, properly speaking, it is knowledge – in the sense of 'gnosis' – which seems to contribute to establishing the notion of the esoteric attitude. This is knowledge in the sense Goethe meant when he had Faust say that he burns with desire to 'know the world/in its intimate context/to contemplate the active forces and the first elements.' To this is often added, fraught with implications for alchemy and for a *Naturphilosophie* of esoteric character, an interpretation of a teaching of Saint Paul (Romans 8:12–22), according to which suffering nature, subjected to exile and vanity, also waits to take part in salvation. Thus are established a science of Nature, a gnosis laden with soteriological elements, a theosophy which labours over the triad of 'God-Humanity-Nature' from whence the theosopher brings forth dramaturgical correspondences, complementary and forever new."

23 See Benz (1955, 1983); Brown (1977); Fuhrmans (1954); Gulyga (1989); Horn (1954); Matthews (2011); Schneider (1938); Schulze (1957a, 1957b); Tilliette (1970); Zovko (1996). Some recent attention has been dedicated to Hegel's involvement with the esoteric. See O'Regan (1994); Magee (2001).

24 S.J. McGrath, *The Esoteric Unconscious* (forthcoming from Routledge). Christian Kerslake has shown the generic relation of the esoteric to the Deleuzian unconscious. See Kerslake (2007).

25 See Žižek (1996: 75–77): "The 'unconscious' is not primarily the Real in its opposition to the Ideal; in its most radical dimension, the 'unconscious' is, rather, the very act of decision/differentiation by means of which the Ideal establishes itself in its opposition to the Real and imposes its order on to the Real, the act by means of which the Present differs from the Past – that is to say, by means of which the rotary motion of drives is 'repressed' into the eternal past. Is this not clearly indicated in Schelling's 'formula of the world' from *Weltalter* III? . . . the ever-increasing 'sublation' of the Real (B) in the Ideal (A), the progressive subordination of the Real to the Ideal, relies on the exception of a B which, as the excluded ground of the process of sublation, guarantees its consistency."

26 Detlev von Uslar is an exception. He describes Schelling as "the true discoverer of the unconscious" (Uslar, 1987: 115).

27 I owe this insight to William Davis, who delivered a paper entitled "Along the Borderlines of Modern Madness" at a conference at Oriel College, Oxford, on 16 September 2010.

28 The endlessness of personal individuation might be regarded as one of Schelling's earliest ideas. See Schelling (1799a: 19): "The originary strife of self-consciousness – which is for transcendental creation (spirit) precisely what the strife of elements is for physical creation – must, like self-consciousness itself, be infinite; therefore it cannot end in an individual product, but only in a product that always becomes and never is, and is created anew in each moment of self-consciousness."

29 Lacan's debt to Western esotericism is in need of scholarly attention. The connection between Lacan and Boehme has been noticed in the French literature. See Dufour (1998).

30 See Johnston (2008: 72). "As Žižek puts it, the Schellingian Real is the obfuscated originary/primordial underbelly of reality that nonetheless repeatedly

'insists' within the fragile, framed field of experience, an unruly protomateriality constantly threatening to irrupt within the domain of mundane reality."

31  In the *Religion* Kant gives his most developed analysis of evil and concludes that it cannot at root be an act of weakness or passion, for in both instances it would be heteronymous and hence non-culpable. "Every such action must be regarded as though the individual had fallen into it directly from a state of innocence" (Kant, 1799: 36). Evil cannot be externally motivated: it has no "final cause," it cannot be a means to some other end, for this too would abrogate the freedom without which it would not be evil. The consequence for Kant is that wicked people do evil in an act of pure autonomy which is formally identical to the act that is morally good.

32  See Schelling's letter to Eschenmayer of 10 July 1804 (Schelling, 1804b: 60–61): "Now and then, I may have made out that the *Absolute* is the *third unitive mode* or potency. I have, however, also expressly stated the opposite. . . . The Absolute for me is precisely that wherein those three unitive modes lie in equal measure and absoluteness . . . . Insofar as it dissolves all potencies into one and, because it comprehends all of them and is not a potency itself, is neither real nor ideal nor simply their unity but all of this, which means that it is nothing in particular . . . *this* Absolute = God."

33  See Žižek (1996: 103): "Schelling, in contrast to this (Lacanian and) Hegelian matrix of self-identity, insists on an irreducible and irrecuperable Otherness (in the guise of the obscure Ground which eludes the grasp of *Logos*, etc.); this, then, inevitably leads him to conceive the Absolute as Third with respect to the polar opposites of the Ideal and the Real, of *Logos* and its Ground: the Absolute is primarily the 'absolute indifference' providing the neutral medium for the coexistence of the polar opposites. Hegel's premise is that there is no need for this Third: an element can well be a 'part of itself,' that is, the encompassing unity of itself and its Otherness – that is what notional self-relating is about."

34  See Žižek (1996: 104): "'And' is thus, in a sense, *tautological*: it conjoins the same content in its two modalities – first in its ideological evidence, then in the extra ideological conditions of its existence. For that reason, no third term is needed here to designate the medium itself in which the two terms, conjoined by means of the 'and,' encounter each other: this third term is already the second term itself which stands for the network (the 'medium') of the concrete existence of an ideological universality. In contrast to this dialectic-materialist 'and,' the idealist-ideological 'and' functions precisely as this third term, as the common medium of the polarity or plurality of elements. Therein resides the gap that separates for ever Freud's and Jung's respective notions of libido: Jung conceives of libido as a kind of neutral energy with its concrete forms (sexual, creative, destructive libido) as its different 'metamorphoses'; whereas Freud insists that libido in its concrete existence is irreducibly *sexual* – all other forms of libido are forms of 'ideological' misrecognition of this sexual content. And is not the same operation to be repeated apropos of 'man *and* woman'? Ideology compels us to assume 'humanity' as the neutral medium within which 'man' and 'woman' are posited as the two complementary poles – against this ideological evidence, one could maintain that 'woman' stands for the aspect of concrete existence and 'man' for the empty-ambiguous universality. The paradox (of a profoundly Hegelian nature) is that 'woman' – that is, the moment of specific difference – functions as the encompassing ground that accounts for the emergence of the universality of man." It is interesting to note that one of the results of Žižek's reading of Schelling is an alignment of Jung with Schelling, and Freud with Hegel.

35 The subject of enunciation is the I who speaks; the subject of the statement is the I of the sentence. The I is not identical to itself – it is split between the individual I (the subject of enunciation) and the grammatical I (the subject of the statement). The latter is a necessary substitute for the former. Lacan refashions Descartes' maxim "I think, therefore I am" as "I think where I am not, therefore I am where I think not." The "I think" in the latter sentence is the subject of the enunciated (the Symbolic subject) whereas the "I am" is the subject of the enunciation (the Real subject). The subject is irrevocably split, torn asunder by the language without which he would not exist. See Lacan (1966: 517, 800).

36 See Jaspers (1955); Heidegger (1971, 1991); Habermas (1954); Frank (1975).

37 The unconscious as clinical hypothesis is a standard thesis in post-Freudian and post-Jungian literature. See, for example, Samuels (1986). The unconscious as ontological concept is a basic interpretation of German Idealism (Nicholls and Liebscher, 2010). The unconscious as repository of repressed memories and desires is the classical Freudian position. The unconscious as image of God, the harbour of "the Self," the unconscious centre of the psyche that directs and guides the soul into its individuation, is classical Jungianism. The unconscious as compensation for Cartesianism and, as such, reinforcement of Cartesian representationalism, is Michel Henry's theory (Henry, 1993). The semiotic theory of the unconscious is, of course, Lacan's. The unconscious as social construct is originally Foucault's thesis (Foucault, 1962) but it has now become a widespread postmodern view.

38 Schelling usually uses the adjective *bewußtlose* (conscious-less) to characterize mental acts that escape reflective consciousness. Sometimes he uses *das Unbewußte* as a substantive, for example: "This eternal unconscious [*Dieses ewig Unbewußte*], which as it were the eternal sun in the realm of spirits, hides itself by its own unclouded light" (Schelling, SSW 3: 600). The first to use "the unconscious" as a substantive appears to be Ernst Platner (1744–1818), successor of Leibniz in carrying forward Leibniz's idea of unconscious perceptions (*petits perceptions*). Platner coins the term *das Unbewusstsein* to explain how the soul, always active (otherwise it would cease to exist), continues to form representations in sleep but without being conscious of them (Platner, 1776: §11–19, §25). On the etymology of "unconscious," see Nicholls and Liebscher (2010: 20–21).

39 See Schelling (1809: 27): "In the circle out of which all things become, it is not a contradiction that what engenders one thing is itself regenerated by it. Here there is no first and last, because all things mutually presuppose each other; nothing is the other, and yet nothing is without the other."

# Chapter 2

# Tending the dark fire

## The Boehmian notion of drive

> If the all were only one, the one would not be revealed to itself.
>
> (Boehme, BSS 7. 3.22)

### The theosophical root of the unconscious

Where the role of romanticism and idealism in the history of the unconscious is not disputed, the influence of Western esoteric discourses in
particular theosophy is more controversial.[1] Theosophy enters the history of
psychiatry through the mediation of the German romantics and plays as
decisive a role in the development of the theory of the unconscious as do the
widely referenced remarks in Leibniz and Kant concerning "dark
representations."[2] The importance of theosophy for Schelling's philosophy,
especially that of his middle period, is well known in the German literature
and almost completely overlooked in the surge of recent English studies of
Schelling.[3] Schneider (1938) and Benz (1955) argue that Schelling is already
appropriating theosophical insights into the nature-philosophy of 1797–
1799. They suggest that the early Schelling's inspiration for problematizing
Fichte's subjectivism with a brazenly revamped nature-philosophy is
Oetinger's post-vitalist neo-Boehmian theology. According to Oetinger, the
common enemy of theology and philosophy is mechanism, which elevates
the lifeless causal interaction of discrete particles into an ontological
paradigm. Modern natural scientific discoveries, Oetinger argues, need to be
interpreted in a biometaphysical context that appreciates the absolute not as
first cause or highest being, but as self-revealing life. The then-new sciences
of electricity, magnetism, and chemistry, with their interest in the ability of
matter to act from a distance, exemplified for Oetinger a theological principle largely forgotten in modernity but central to the thought of Jewish
theosophy, Boehme, and the Renaissance Kabbalists: life is only possible in
the antagonism and resolution of polarities. Ostensibly baptized into
Friedrich Christoph Oetinger's speculative Pietism, Schneider argues that
Schelling was already sceptical of "the transcendental turn" – even when he

was actively contributing to the Fichtian idealist movement. Transcendental philosophy needed the complement of nature-philosophy because it inflated consciousness to a place that could only be occupied by life. If Schneider and Benz are correct, we could make an even stronger case for the theosophical root of the Schellingian unconscious and by implication the theosophical origins of the psychodynamic unconscious of the nineteenth century. We could then argue that both Schelling's early and middle concepts of the unconscious (which are distinct and responsible for different impacts on nineteenth-century psychology) are theosophical in origin.

The argument for the influence of Oetinger on the early Schelling is unfortunately largely speculative.[4] Because both Schelling's father and grandfather were pastors in the Würtembergian Pietist tradition (Benz, 1955: 41), it is assumed that Schelling would have read Oetinger's *Biblisches Wörterbuch*, a compendium of theosophy and biblical theology written as a study guide for lay people (Oetinger, 1776/1999). What we do know is that at the age of ten Schelling was sent to Nürtingen for Latin school, and lived for a time in the house of his uncle, who was known as a "fiery disciple of Oetinger's" (Schneider, 1938: 8). There Schelling met Phillip Matheus Hahn, the most important follower of Oetinger, who impressed the boy so deeply that he was inspired to compose his first poem on the occasion of the great theologian's death (Schneider, 1938: 8–9).

Schelling's early exposure to speculative Pietism does not prove that the young philosopher who turned abruptly from Fichte's transcendental philosophy to nature-philosophy was already formed in Boehmian theosophy. Much of what the early Schelling says about nature as a productive strife of opposing forces, about organicism, and about the unconscious activity by which consciousness generates itself is already anticipated or developed by Kant and Fichte.[5] What no one can deny is the influence of Franz von Baader on the middle Schelling. During the early years of Schelling's first Munich period (1809–1821), Baader exposed Schelling to an extensive theosophical and occult literature. While Schelling was aware of Boehme's significance and had most likely read him before 1806, it was Baader who showed Schelling that Boehme's theosophy could be brought to bear directly on contemporary philosophical problems such as theodicy, freedom and the relation of the infinite to the finite. Always reluctant to acknowledge his sources, Schelling admits his debt to Baader (Schelling, 1809: 35, fn.).[6] It is via Schelling's *Freedom* essay that theosophical themes first enter mainstream nineteenth-century philosophy (if they are not already there) and contribute, through philosophy, to the psychodynamic horizon of late nineteenth-century Europe.[7]

The Boehmian distinction between a contractive, wrathful dark principle and an expansive, loving light principle is the paradigm for Schelling's distinction between "ground" and "existence" in the *Freedom* essay and the doctrine of potencies in the *Stuttgart Seminars* and the *Ages of the World*.

In the second draft of *Ages*, the distinction is developed as the difference between universal being (*Seyn*) and determinate being (*das Seyende*) (Schelling, 1813: 126–143). Universal being is associated with potency, the pronominal, the non-subjective, that which *is* not (*das Nichtseyende*), i.e., that which withdraws into itself. Determinate being is associated with actuality, predicative being, the subject, that which exists, i.e., that which stands outside of itself. This distinction succeeds Schelling's earlier distinction between negative and positive natural forces. But something decisive happens between the early and the middle Schelling: universal being is associated with affectivity, with desire, longing, and passivity – that is, with qualities that metaphysics had typically regarded as secondary, derivative, and inferior. This is nothing short of a reversal of the historical relationship between act and potency – a century before Heidegger.

The *Freedom* essay is a decisive moment in the genesis of the psychodynamic notion of the unconscious. The genealogies of the unconscious that focus on the contributions of Leibniz, Kant, and the early Schelling are missing something crucial that comes to birth in late, theosophically influenced, German Idealism. The epistemic "dark side of the mind" is only one aspect of the unconscious, and from the perspective of psychoanalysis and analytical psychology, it is not the most important aspect. Subliminal perceptions and lost memories are only the surface of the unconscious; far more significant is the sense of a dark drive at the basis of personality. This thought is not a contribution of modern philosophy as such (it is foreign to Spinoza, Kant, and Fichte). Its origin is theosophy. The theosophical reversal of the Scholastic understanding of the relation of will to being is the key to this largely untold story. Scholasticism stipulates that a thing must first be before it can desire or be desired; theosophy holds, on the contrary, that drive for existence precedes being itself. In Luria, Boehme, Oetinger, and Saint-Martin, an alternative notion of personality takes shape, strikingly different from the model of representational consciousness emerging out of late Scholasticism, Descartes, and Leibniz. On the theosophic view, personality is primarily the product of drive and desire rather than representation and knowledge. Both the middle Schelling and Hegel thematize this model in modern philosophical terms, thereby freeing it from its visionary and gnostic frames. Schopenhauer and von Hartmann in turn secularize the Boehmian-Schellingian will by disentangling it from its religious frame. In this disenchanted form, the psychodynamic unconscious becomes a catch-phrase for late nineteenth-century medical psychiatry. For Charcot, Bleuler, the early Freud, and Jung, the unconscious is a technical term for the appetitive dimension of psyche – "eros," "the feminine," "the irrational" – which is the source of the creativity and life of the personality but also of its destruction and death. For these thinkers, handling this volatile "psychic energy" is the great challenge of human development. Those who cannot manage it – the "possessed," the split personalities, the hysterics and schizophrenics – are casualties of the precarious transition from primal will to consciousness.

The claim for a theosophical influence on Schelling has become unpopular in the last four decades. There are three main reasons for this. First, Schelling makes scant and ambiguous references to theosophy in his works and letters. The work of Schelling's that is most influenced by Boehme, the *Freedom* essay, makes no mention of him. Second, trying to make sense of the *Freedom* essay through Boehme is, we are told, like explaining the obscure through the obscure.[8] Third, imputing an influence of theosophy on Schelling has become a reason to dismiss him as an irrationalist, a mystic, and his philosophy, *Schwärmerei*. Theosophy is held to be based not on argument and reason but on ecstatic vision; Hegel's remarks on Boehme and esotericism have been decisive in this regard.[9] Thinkers interested in retrieving Schelling's more philosophically rigorous concepts and contributions to logic (Hogrebe, Frank, Bowie, Gabriel) see no good reason to pursue this line of research.

All of these reasons are weak grounds for dismissing the theosophical element in Schelling. There is ample proof for demonstrating that Schelling's reading of Boehme in the years 1806 to 1809 is the decisive explanation for Schelling's leap from the monism of the identity-philosophy to the esoteric theism of the *Freedom* essay and the *Ages of the World*.[10] That Schelling makes no mention of Boehme is neither here nor there; he had plenty of reasons not to. Explicitly referencing Boehme would not only have made Schelling seem dependent on Baader (famously named "Boehmius redivivus" by A.W. Schlegel), it would, as Hegel's equivocal remarks on Boehme suggest, have rendered his philosophical arguments suspect. If the unmistakable systematic parallels between Boehmian and Schellingian theogony are not already enough, Schelling's reference to Baader establishes the historicity of the Boehme–Schelling connection. Schelling salutes Baader for "emphasising" "the only correct" "concept of evil" (Schelling, 1809: 35). This concept of evil is also Schelling's, and is arguably the main theme of the *Freedom* essay: "evil resides in a positive perversion or reversal of the principles" (Schelling, 1809: 35). But Baader's concept of evil is Boehme's, as Baader would be the first to acknowledge. Schelling suggests that he and Baader are not inventing a new concept of evil but are contributing to an older tradition – that is, to the Boehmian theosophical account of evil.

The argument that Boehme is too obscure to explain Schelling is based on prejudice and second-hand accounts. If Boehme is obscure, it is not only because he is difficult to understand; it is also because no one bothers to read him anymore. Such arguments give scholars a licence to ignore the thought of a man who was read by all the major German romantics and idealists, and who was, to varying degrees, respected by them. Finally, the visionary or mystical elements of theosophy should not be taken for granted. We need not accept Boehme's word that his work is directly inspired by the Holy Spirit; this sort of religious acknowledgement was a common trope among alchemists and theosophists. Boehme makes a great deal more sense when he is reconstructed on the basis of his sources: Kabbalah, Paracelsus, and German theology. Schelling's dependence on Boehme renders Schelling's philosophy eclectic and unconventional, but not for that reason irrational.

There is no need for me to set the record straight on Boehme's influence on Schelling: Paola Mayer has already done so. Although her intention in *Jena Romanticism and Its Appropriation of Jakob Böhme* (1999) is to question the degree of Boehme's influence on German romanticism, she is driven by the facts of the case to argue that Schelling's *Freedom* essay is in its main moves Boehmian. Schelling, under Baader's influence, was reading Boehme as he wrote the essay. The characteristic innovations of the essay – the doctrine of the birth of God, the notion of ground, and the theory of evil – are, Mayer argues, entirely Boehmian in derivation. Mayer does not recognize the same degree of Boehmian influence in *Ages*, but it is not difficult to align the 1809 triad of ground, existence, and personality with the three potencies in *Ages* (they have for the most part identical properties). Making this conceptual alignment reveals that Schelling's doctrine of personality – arguably his most psychodynamically relevant contribution to the history of the unconscious – is derived from Boehme's theosophy.

It is in light of the importance of Schelling's reading of Boehme to the *Freedom* essay and the *Ages of the World* that Schelling's disclaimers concerning theosophy take on a new significance.[11] For Schelling, philosophy is the heir of theosophy. Philosophy, in a fuller sense than Hegel gives it, has available to it not only the insights of theosophy and religion but their distinctive modes of cognition: intuition, faith, vision. Schelling is not responding to wild accusations; rather, he is distinguishing his work from his sources, making clear how he is developing certain themes beyond the theosophical sources from which everyone at the time knew he originally drew them. Schelling's method is to translate theosophical insights into philosophical concepts, that is, to translate intuition and vision into discursive or "dialectical" terms, anticipating the method he will perfect in his late positive philosophy.[12] Schelling never abjures discursive reason: it remains essential to his method at all stages of his career.[13] From the early concept of "intellectual intuition" to the late notion of "the ecstasy of reason," Schelling maintains that discursive reason, although not the origin of philosophical insight, elaborates and demonstrates what has been cognized by other means.[14]

## Esoteric voluntarism

It is not easy to categorize Boehme: he does not fit well into the Neo-platonic lineage of German mysticism (Eckhart, Tauler, Seuso), nor is his work exclusively theological, for he has also made major contributions to nature-philosophy and metaphysics. He is associated with the reform of the Reformation, the upsurge of spirituality in seventeenth-century Protestantism that was largely a reaction to the return of dogmatic Scholastic legalism in the Lutheran Church (Sebastian Franck, Valentin Weigel, and Kaspar Schwenkfeld). It is not entirely certain whether Boehme influences or is influenced by the Rosicrucian documents anonymously published by Johann Valentin Andrea at the beginning of the seventeenth century.[15] Boehme belongs as much to the hermetic and alchemical tradition, which he received through his study of the writings of Paracelsus, as he does to the history of Protestantism. The Kabbalistic influence on his thought equally situates him in the tradition of the Christian Kabbalism of Johannes Reuchlin, Pico Della Mirandola, and Cornelius Agrippa von Nettesheim.

Boehme is at the centre of the theosophical counter-culture in modern Western Christianity. His speculative metaphysical theosophy is connected by way of innumerable tendrils to a variety of allied theosophical movements in the history of Western religion. The shoemaker from Görlitz was an autodidact. A contemporary of Descartes, he knew little about medieval or modern philosophy, nor was his knowledge of theology particularly wide. Relatively few were the materials he had at his disposal – the Luther Bible, a second-hand knowledge of German theology (Eckhart, Seuso, Tauler, the *Theologia Deutsch*), Paracelsian alchemy, and the Kabbalah – when he combined them into a totally original form. Boehme's many-sided writings revolve around a single thought: God is a will to revelation.[16] Nature is both the product of God's original revelation and a repetition of the internal dynamic of that revelation. For anything to be revealed to itself, it must become doubled, dividing into something that withdraws and hides itself and something that comes forward and shows itself. According to Boehme, withdrawal from relation is the root of evil, whereas self-showing (relatedness) is knowledge and love. But the self-showing is only possible on the ground of withdrawal. The condition of the possibility of self-revelation is therefore also the condition of the possibility of evil: life calls for a careful negotiation of the self-withdrawal necessary to self-manifestation, a tending of the "dark fire" of "the first principle." The dark fire must be held latent in love; in Schellingian terms it must always only ground, it ought never exist. But the dark fire cannot be put out save at the expense of life itself.

The motive of Boehme's vast output is to explain how evil could appear in a creation that is *ex Deo*, a direct expression of the divine life. Boehme speaks of seeing a disturbing coincidence of good and evil in all things in this world. He observes the suffering of the just and the apparent triumph of injustice – experiences that originally made him sick with melancholy.[17] Following the Kabbalah, Boehme argues that evil is rooted in a creative duality in God: the simplicity of the unground (*Ungrund*) supports a dialectical play of wrath and love, darkness and light, which Boehme describes as two conflicting wills, a self-assertive and a self-diremptive will. This polarity becomes concretized in creation as cold and heat, hard and soft, fire and water. In human beings and angels, these essential opposites are capable of being separated from one another. The separation of the self-assertive will (without which nothing could exist) from the self-diremptive will (which eternally tempers it in God) is the origin of evil.

Boehme is not without his contradictions, but certain recurring misinterpretations of his thought are not infrequent. The first misinterpretation to be avoided is the argument that Boehme "naturalizes" the divine, transposing upon the infinite the finite truths of nature, for example, the play of polarity (and therefore of potency). This argument misses what is for our purpose the most important feature of Boehme's methodology. Boehme does not configure the divine life on the model of the natural world, but instead conceives nature on an analogy with the human psyche, which he believes to be an image of God. In the tradition of Christian Kabbalism and Hermeticism, Boehme takes man, "the little world" (or "little God," as Boehme sometimes describes him), as his reference point both for his nature-philosophy and his theology. As his followers Saint-Martin and Baader make clear, the theosophical move is not to explain man through nature but to explain nature through man. We must, as Saint-Martin says, explain things through man and not man through things (*Il ne faut pas expliquer l'homme avec les choses mais expliquer les choses avec l'homme*).[18] This point is crucial for recognizing Boehme's importance to the history of psychology. Boehme's hermetic assumption of man as microcosm, combined with his Christian interpretation of the biblical doctrine of *imago Dei*, compels him to attend to himself, to his interior life, with an intensity and seriousness perhaps not seen since Augustine. The divine personality is conceived on an analogy with the human personality, which is understood introspectively. Nature is then interpreted in terms of the dynamics of personality on the biblical assumption that creation images the creator. The assumption is not that the structure of nature is mirrored in God, but exactly the opposite: the structure of the divine personality is mirrored in nature. The theosophical foundation of this assumption is primarily a theory of personality. What we might call "the Boehme school" (Oetinger, Saint-Martin, Baader, the middle Schelling) is united in holding personality to be a more decisive lens than act-potency through which to interpret the divine.

A second misinterpretation is that Boehme represents a regression to ancient Gnosticism.[19] This misinterpretation leads to the obscuring of one of Boehme's most distinctive contributions to the Christian tradition: his emphasis on embodiment as perfection. Nothing could be stranger to ancient Gnosticism than to hold such a view. While Boehme shares with Gnosticism a substantive and productive account of evil (to be elaborated below), he shares nothing of the Valentinian or Manichaean matter-vilifying dualism. On the contrary, Boehme's cosmology is one of the most affirmative philosophies of nature in the history of theology.[20] Personality is for Boehme essentially embodied. Boehme has little time for gnostic other-worldliness, or the milder (and more orthodox) Neoplatonic denigration of corporeality characteristic of Christian mysticism. Rather than turning away from the body, the appetites, and matter, dismissing them as less than real, Boehme turns toward the body as the visible manifestation of the inner life of God. Boehme's theosophy is charged with a sense for the divine source of the vitality, energy, and manifold physical qualities of the natural world. To call this "nature mysticism" is not precise enough: it is *life mysticism*, born of an alchemical conviction that the processes of transformation in the natural world are not accidental to the life of God. Nature is rather an outward sign (*signatura*) of the divine personality. The energetic, volitional, and corporeal side of the human being – passion, feeling, appetite, and will – has a divine significance: it mirrors the volitional side of God. Mastery of passion is no longer enough: Boehme calls for a total mobilization of all the natural drives of the human being, for their consecration toward a single transcendent goal. This positive approach to the body is at the heart of Boehme's most idiosyncratic concepts: the dark and reactive side of God; the quasi-material element in the divine ("harshness," "tone," "figure"); and, finally, his ambiguous use of the term "ipseity" (*Selbstheit*). For Boehme, body is the seat of ipseity. Without ipseity the body could not exist. Essential to embodiment is boundary, separation, enclosure from the environment. Boehme does not advise us to transcend the body, nor even to master it; the body must rather be tended to carefully so that it can become the medium of revelation.

A third misinterpretation of Boehme is that he is an unlearned mystic who gives spontaneous utterance to his visionary experiences. This argument is made not infrequently the ground for a philosophical dismissal of Boehme's ideas: the complaint is that private visionary experiences can never be grounds for philosophical claims. This judgement, which Boehme's rhetoric encourages, overlooks the dependence of Boehme's thought upon alchemical, Kabbalistic, and hermetic sources. Boehme did not undertake a formal course of study, but study he certainly did (van Ingen, 1997: 803). Already in his first work, the *Aurora*, a 500-page handwritten theosophical treatise first distributed among friends, Boehme shows a broad knowledge not only of the Kabbalah but also (and above all) of the text of the Luther Bible and the writings of Paracelsus.[21] His command of alchemical and esoteric lore becomes even more evident in his later writings, especially the text regarded as his most difficult, *De Signatura Rerum* (1622). Despite evidence of reading in his writings, Boehme insists that he did not learn his doctrine from books but that it was "shown" to him. In chapter 19 of the *Aurora*, Boehme describes a sudden experience of spiritual light by which he saw God in all things, in the lowest creature and the highest heavens

(Boehme, 1612: 19.13–14). This experience, he reports, filled him with a great drive (*Trieb*) to describe the essence (*wesen*) of God – but he could not immediately understand what he saw. Twelve years passed before he was able to put the experience into words. Is anything more than an *intellectual* experience of faith (however dramatic) indicated here, a life-changing understanding of the relation of all things to God? The experience drives Boehme into intense intellectual activity. Boehme does not describe dramatic visions, voices of angels, or other paranormal phenomena; he speaks instead of suddenly seeing everything differently. Worth noting in the *Aurora* passage referenced above is Boehme's own references to "compre-hending in reason" (*in meiner venunfft begreiffen*, as Boehme puts it in his baroque German) and "correct understanding" (*rechte verstand*). Whatever the transrational nature of Boehme's inspiration, the conceptualization of his vision is a work of reason. Against the tendency of recent literature to regard Boehme as an irrationalist, a writer of mystical expression in need of the clarification and conceptualization he later receives from the Idealists, Boehme's own self-understanding is otherwise.

Boehme's greatest contribution to the tradition is his esoteric notion of will, which should be sharply distinguished from the Aristotelian-Scholastic faculty of volition. Boehmian will is the drive that produces being; it is, as such, older than being. Boehme's notion of will has no direct relation to medieval philosophical debates concerning the relation of the psychological faculties to one another. Its roots are much more deeply buried in Western spiritual traditions: in Judaism and its notion of "the will of Yahweh," in the Kabbalah, and in alchemy. The creator does not choose among options; rather, his choosing makes the chosen first possible. The will in this tradition is the creative power to produce being. It is not ordered by reason, which judges the best among possible alternatives; it is prior to reasoning and judging. We should not call this will irrational; it is rather non-rational, pre-rational, the energetic ground of rationality. The unground, the abso-lute beyond predication and distinction, wills self-manifestation "prior" to its knowing what self-manifestation entails (division, self-return through another). The unground is neither ignorant nor psychotic (*pace* Žižek); it is unknowing and indifferent (non-dual). Knowledge, reason, order, and being depend upon this primordial drive – and not the other way around. Boehme's is not the ethical-epistemological voluntarism of the late Middle Ages; it is an onto-genetic voluntarism constructed on the basis of esoteric theology and nature-philosophy. Late medieval voluntarism is a doctrine of responsibility; Boehmian voluntarism is a doctrine of why there is some-thing rather than nothing. It is in the context of the reception of Boehme in German Idealism that the hold of Greek metaphysics on Western philos-ophy, and the priority of form over matter, is broken. Boehme reintroduces into Western metaphysics notions of personality and divinity that are fundamentally Hebraic, not Hellenic.

The apparent model for Boehme's theogony is the doctrine of *zimzum* in the Lurianic Kabbalah. According to the Renaissance Kabbalist Isaac of Luria, the infinite, *Ein-Sof*, contracts its being in order to create the nothing in which the finite can emerge.[22] The contraction is initially a negation, a withdrawal into self, a self-limitation and self-concealment. The negation is also an implicit affirmation, for it happens for the sake of letting another be, or better, letting otherness itself be. The first act in the Boehmian theogony is a negative moment of contraction: the unground negates its own infinity. In the wake of its infinity, two countervailing wills are introduced into being: a dark will asserts itself over and against a light will. The dark will finitizes the divine by withdrawing into itself and demarcating itself; the light will counteracts this contraction by self-donation and expansion, that is, by reversing the direction of the dark will. Only because the dark will has contracted the divine is it possible for the light will to establish expansion, love, and self-donation as laws of being. The dynamic of contraction and expansion, of something unfolding on the ground of something withdrawing and contracting, is carried forward as a basic principle of consciousness through Boehme, Oetinger, and Schelling.

Boehme's unground is the ineffable, non-dual, and incomprehensible darkness of the Godhead out of which the light of self-consciousness emerges through a dialectical interplay of opposites. The unground in itself "lacks" the duality necessary to revelation; Boehme repeats, like a mantra, that without distinction and duality there can be no manifestation. Without duality an eternal peace would reign in the Godhead, but the eternal nature of the Godhead would not be revealed. Duality emerges out of the non-duality of the unground in the form of hunger: the eternally quiescent nothingness of the Godhead suddenly gives rise to a second form of nothingness, nothingness as lack and hunger for something (*Begierde zum Etwas*), ultimately for a revelation of itself (Boehme, 1623b: 1.9)). Boehme's meaning cannot be that some external law of nature imposes necessity on the unground, as though the unground must allow for difference, or is coerced into differentiation as a condition of its becoming manifest to itself. The freedom of the unground is the foundation of Boehme's thought. It is more accurate to say that by dividing and mediating itself to itself, the unground establishes the law of revelation, consciousness, and personality; this law is mirrored on a lower level in the polarities that animate all living things. Why the unground wills self-revelation ultimately cannot be answered. To give an answer would be to ascribe a cause to that which has no ground, that which is absolutely unconditioned and free. Boehme says only that the unground churns with a drive (*Trieb*) for a relation with itself. The aseity of the divine is not contradicted by the unground's desire for a likeness. God does not need to be othered or revealed to himself; he chooses to be. The doubling necessary for revelation is not a perfection, not the actualization of a potency or the completion of the divine being. To put it in Deleuzian terms, the drive to revelation is not desiring-lack but desiring-production, the desire of the artist who wills the artwork not because he needs it to be complete but because he wishes that it be so for its own sake.[23]

What the unground "finds" (that is, generates for itself) is nothing other than its own search for a self, "the hunger, which is itself" (Boehme, 1622: 2.7). The "first principle" of "the eternal nature" arises, a will "that has nothing that it can will but itself" (Boehme, 1624a: 3.7).[24] By desiring itself the will makes itself into its own object. It longs for the fullness of self-manifestation, which it can only have insofar as it has another to whom it can show itself. Thus God must allow for another, wholly other than it, to which it can be revealed, and in being revealed, through which it can come to know itself. The first principle is sometimes described by commentators as the principle of egoity (Boehme does not use this Latinism, but rather *Selbstheit*), but in truth it is too unconscious to say "I." Better to describe it as a principle of "ipseity."[25] The unground desires to give itself a ground. Out of this desire emerges the dark principle, which Boehme calls by many names: "cold fire," "the centre of nature," "dark fire." It is composed of three qualities that perpetually struggle against each other. The three dark qualities image the three divine principles, but in an unresolved state. The dark fire is therefore pain, unappeased desire and anxiety. Boehme describes it as the corporeality of God (*Leiblichkeit*), but it is not in itself God. In order for God to be born and for self-revelation to occur, the dark fire must be "tinctured" by its opposite, the light fire.

In the second principle the countervailing opposite will opens itself up and affirms and mirrors all that is exterior, willing only that the other be. The second principle is "light fire," the principle of love and "alterity." The dark fire and the light fire are bound together by the law of being that binds all binaries to one another. Out of their antagonistic rotation around each other (a circular motion caused by alternating attraction and repulsion), a middle ground is described that is neither light nor dark but the centre that makes both possible: the third principle, which mixes the dark and the light.

The opposed principles must differ essentially from one another; they must be determined by opposed intentions. The "light fire" or "hot fire" is the antithesis of the dark and cold fire. Where the dark fire closes in on itself, the light fire opens out onto the other. The dark fire hungers only for itself; the light fire hungers for another. Out of the unground's drive for self-revelation, the basic polarity of life emerges: the No and the Yes; the dark principle of negation and contraction and the light principle of affirmation and expansion.[26] Oetinger will describe the first principle, in Newtonian language, as the centripetal force distinct from the centrifugal force of the second principle – or, in vitalistic terms, as the contracting force (*enziehende Kraft*) distinct from the expanding force (*ausdehnende*

*Kraft*). The first principle is a "shutting-in" (Boehme, 1624a: 3:3) or "a drawing-together" (*Zusammenziehen*) (Boehme, 1612: 13.55).[27] It holds itself within itself, resisting otherness, which it simultaneously posits as that against which it asserts itself, contracting into a hidden centre. To resist is a double intention: it is first of all to posit oneself as the point of affirmation, and negatively, to affirm the existence of that against which one posits oneself. The dark fire is thus the principle of ipseity or self, defined, as it must be, over and against the "other." The second principle is the principle of alterity or otherness, defined over and against "self."[28] The first principle, mirrored in creation, is the source of antipathy and individuation in nature. Recoiling from the other constitutes a centre of ipseity that resists universality and communicability. Without this No, nothing would be distinct from anything else.[29] The second principle is the source of sympathy and order in creation, drawing things together into wholes that exceed the sum of their parts.

Although the two fires continually struggle against each other, their relations are not unordered. The dark fire is the "root" of the light fire; the negative is clearly primary, the ground of the positive. But the light fire is the cause of the dark fire's becoming "perceptible." The "movement" described in Boehme's theogony is from the negative to the positive, from a primary shutting-in to a secondary opening-out. But we must be careful here not to assume any priority in time. The dark fire is never without the light fire, much as self is never without other. The first grounds the second, but the second defines the first.[30] The centripetal force is only what it is because it strives against its opposite and resists the centrifugal force pulling it outwards. Every expansion is made possible by a prior contraction. But every contraction presupposes an expansion.

The principles interpenetrate each other such that what is manifest in one is latent in the other, and vice versa.[31] To desire oneself is to negatively posit another; to desire the other is to negatively posit oneself. Boehme explicitly relates the two principles to the Hebrew attributes of God: the first principle is the wrath of God that contracts into itself, negates the other and asserts itself. The second principle is the love of God that expands, affirms the other and negates itself. Without the second, the dark fire would be narcissistic darkness, obscurity, and obduracy. But without the first, the light fire could not be. The psychological ramifications of Boehme's point will be further developed by Schelling and Baader: latent in love is selfishness, but held in potency, where it functions to support the outward kenosis; latent in selfishness is suppressed love.[32]

Boehme is most obscure about the function of the third principle in the divine economy. It is clear that it mediates the two, that it has something of the dark fire and the light fire in it, and that it represents the completion of the movement toward self-revelation which begins with the unground's decision to divide itself. Sometimes it is described as the fire of transformation by which the dark fire becomes a light fire. Other times it is described as a repetition of the transformation that occurs with the emergence of the second principle.[33] Boehme associates the third principle with the Holy Spirit for it proceeds from the duality of the first and the second principle. If one reads Boehme carefully one notices that the third principle does not add anything new to the drama that transpires between the first and the second principles but rather serves to mirror their ordered relationship. The third principle contains in a single principle the movement of the first principle to the second. If the first principle is the principle of contraction, and the second the counterbalancing principle of expansion, both made possible by and contradicting the first, we could say that the third is the principle of the proper movement between contradictory wills, the principle of the subordination of the first principle to the second. The third principle thus reveals the pattern of self-revelation already accomplished in the dialectical play of the first and the second principle. God reveals himself in the transition from the first to the second principle; the third is this revelation revealed to itself. If the opposition of the first and the second principle establishes ontological difference in the divine, the third principle orders that difference, or rather reveals the order that is the essence of the difference. The third principle is thus the new kind of unity made possible by difference. It stands in contrastive opposition not to either one of the preceding two principles, which it successfully sublates, but to the undifferentiated unity of the unground, which it others and distances itself from. For where the unground is indeterminate, undifferentiated and unrevealed, the third is determinateness, differentiated unity and dialectically mediated self-revelation.

Jungians note that Boehme's divinity has four terms (unground, dark fire, light fire, revealed God), and prematurely conclude that Boehme anticipates Jung's critique of the Trinity (Dourley, 2008: 58–74).[34] The Jungian interpretation raises a vexed question concerning the relation of the fourfold Boehmian divinity to the Christian Trinity. Although Boehme struggled with this question, he was never able to fully map his three principles onto the three divine persons of the Christian Trinity. As Koyré points out, one significant problem is that the principles are not in themselves persons; they only become persons, or rather produce personality, in interaction with each other (Koyré, 1929: 186–187). In the Christian Trinity, the persons, though constitutively related, are each persons in their own right insofar as each subsists in a unique relationship to the other two.[35] Boehme associates, without identifying, the first principle with the Father (who is wrathful, "jealous" and self-withholding), the second principle with the Son (who is merciful, loving and gives himself wholly to the Father), and the third principle with the Spirit (the mediator).[36] Is the unground, then, a prototype for an unnamed fourth person in the Trinity? Dourley would like it to be; he identifies the unground with the Mother

Goddess, the abyss of the divine feminine (Dourley, 2008: 63, 77–80). Setting aside the fact that none of Boehme's principles are persons, the unground could never count as a person (even in a revised version of Boehme's concept of God such as Baader's, Schelling's, or Tillich's) because there is no act that is distinctive of it, no act that can distinguish it from the three co-inherent acts constituting the divinity.[37] The unground is the common source of all three principles. The unground is not a fourth person of the Trinity for the same reason that the divine nature in orthodox accounts of the Trinity is not a fourth person. Non-duality, indifference, and indeterminateness are not positive features capable of lending the unground a distinctive personal identity. Indeed, Schelling will later explicitly develop the unground as the non-personal, or better, pre-personal element in the divine. The Schellingian unground (the Godhead in *Ages*) is absolute indifference (Schelling, 1809: 68), the "will that wills nothing" (Schelling, 1815: 24). As such the unground/Godhead stands in marked contrast with the three potencies, each of which are distinguished by their characteristic acts of will (willing self without other; willing the other; willing both self and other). A person in Trinitarian theology is constituted by its distinctive relations: the Father is uniquely unbegotten; the Son is uniquely begotten; the Spirit is uniquely proceeding. Since non-duality (indifference) is not a relational term, it does not distinguish the unground as a person with its own distinctive relational mode but rather makes the unground the divine nature common to each of the three persons of the Trinity. Looked at from another angle, if personhood in the Trinity is constituted by relationality (the Father is a person because of his relation to the Son and the Spirit and so forth), the unground is strictly speaking not related.

Baader's comments on the relationship of the fourfold Boehmian divinity to the Christian Trinity offer a significant alternative to some of Jung's clumsier remarks about the incompleteness of the Trinity and the need to supplement the three persons with a fourth figure (alternatively Mary, the eternal feminine or the devil, the excluded shadow). Baader would agree with Jung that every triad is completed in a tetrad. Baader follows Pythagoras and anticipates Jung in holding four, not three, to be the symbol of completeness. He would also agree that the archetype of the feminine must be located in the divine. But his solution is not to simply add the divine mother to the community of persons in God. For Baader, the fourth is not just one more in a sequence. Rather, the fourth has a special relationship to the three that precede it. The monad is unity; the dyad is opposition; the triad is the reconciliation of opposites. The tetrad, in Baader's esotericism, is the completed three-sided figure of the triad, which constellates a centre enclosed by three sides and three angles. The fourth is not one of the sides but the point in the middle of the triad, something Baader expressed by means of the diagram shown in Figure 2.1.[38]

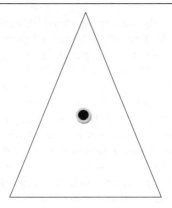

*Figure 2.1*

In Baader's reading of Boehme, the fourth has a passive function in relation to the activity of the three principles; it is not one of the principles of activity in the divine but the centre constituted by the interrelated activities of the three principles. When the three are active, the fourth is passive.[39] The point, which seems to have influenced the late Schelling's Trinitarianism (the three potencies held together by a common form that is not itself a potency (Hayes, 1995: 174)), is crucial for Baader's esoteric fusion of Pythagoreanism, Boehme, and orthodox Trinitarian theology. There is no fourth person required to complete the Baaderian Trinity; every triad is already a tetrad. The fourth is not simply another member in the series; we do not arrive at the fourth by adding $1 + 1 + 1 + 1$. The formula for the Boehmian-Baaderian quaternity is $3 + 1$. The centre of the triad is not in relational opposition to any one of the three principles but stands in contrastive opposition to the whole triune God, as that which does not act, that which is not expressed, that which is not revealed in activity but always disappears behind the revelation: the abyss of Aquinas's divine nature, the ineffable and infinitely unfathomable Godhead of Meister Eckhart, and the *Ein-Sof* of the Lurianic Kabbalah. The Boehmian-Baaderian fourth is not something that completes the other three by addition; as Friesen puts it, the fourth represents the "totality from which the other three arise" (Friesen, 2008: 23). Insofar as it is not an act that the three share but a common, non-active and pre-personal foundation, the Boehmian fourth indeed affirms something of the divine not typically asserted by orthodox Christian theology (although not as antonymic to Christian thought as Jung thinks it to be): passivity, emptiness, indeterminateness and capacity for determination. It is the essence of Boehme's Christianity to resist the tendency to expel such qualities from the divine, for the expulsion of potency from God alienates matter and body, and opens an unbridgeable gap between Creator and creature, rendering the latter at some level inexplicable in terms of the former. Far from implicating Boehme in the ancient Gnosticism that Jung privileges as compensating for the one-sidedness of Christianity, Boehme's quaternity (read through Baader) has the opposite effect of foreclosing gnostic derogation of material processes of birth, growth, and transformation.

The three principles constitute the architectonic of the eternal nature, the divine being, which emanates from the unground. Boehme develops, at great length, seven qualities manifest in the eternal nature: three dark qualities at work in the dark principle; three light qualities in the light principle; and one mixed quality mediating between the light and the dark.[40] The sevenfold eternal nature is the divine paradigm for the created order, which Boehme models on the *merkabah Kabbalah* and its biblical source, the vision recounted in Ezekiel 1. Like the *Sephiroth*, the eternal nature is the concretization of the divine in specific attributes, which, although they express and reveal God, can never exhaust him.[41] The seven forms of the eternal nature are the archetypes of seven qualities basic to creation: harshness (*Herbe*), bitterness (*Bittere*), angst (*Angst*), lightning (*Blitz*), light (*Licht*), sound (*Ton*), and figure (*Corpus*). The first three – harshness, bitterness, angst – are the contractive "wrathful" qualities of the dark fire. The last three – light, sound, figure – are the expansive "loving" qualities of the light fire. All that exists manifests the polarity of negative and positive at play in the divine nature. Everything has an interior that it conceals and protects from the outside, and an exterior that it reveals to the outside. The first three qualities are related to the concealing and self-withholding side of nature; the last three are related to the appearance and show of nature. The negative qualities are the ground of creaturely subsistence, and the positive, of creaturely identity. The negative qualities set everything in motion, for without negation, as Schelling will say, there can be no beginning (Schelling, 1815: 16); in Boehmian terms, the negative is "the foundation, through which the love becomes mobile" (Boehme, 1624a: 3.27). The three positive qualities – light, sound, and figure – are all related to embodiment. Boehme's point seems to be that the body is the externalization of the interior. Although it is not itself corporeal, the eternal nature is the model for all embodiment (*Leiblichkeit*), containing within it structures that will become physically sensible in temporal creation. The mediating quality, lightning – the flash of fire in the moment of transformation from dark to light (*Blitz*) – fuses the two sides. *Blitz* marks the moment where the concealed becomes unconcealed, where the contraction gives rise to expansion, and where the three dark qualities become the ground of the three light qualities.

Like the wheel of eyes in the first chapter of Ezekiel, Boehme's seven spirits are seven interlocking wheels revolving around one centre, that is, a sphere of wheels eternally circling a still point (Boehme, 1612: 13.72ff.). The tensions between the seven qualities, their sympathy and antipathy for each other (at one moment attracted, at another repelled), generate movement in the eternal nature. This movement is the archetype for all the changes and transformations in finite nature. The struggle and torment of the qualities, striving to become free from each other yet incapable of breaking the bond that ties them together, sets the wheel of birth into motion. The wheel has nothing quiescent about it; it is a wheel of anxiety (*Angst-Rad*).

Dourley contrasts Boehme's mysticism with Eckhart's. Whereas the direction of Eckhart's mysticism is a *reditus*, a return into the non-dual, unmediated point of origin of being (the *unio mystica* in which the mystic can no longer distinguish herself from God), the direction of Boehme's mysticism (if it can still be called that) is *exitus*, that is, away from the non-dual toward differentiation, personalization, history and mediation. The Eckhartian mystic seeks to be free of the duality necessary to consciousness. Boehme's God (and the Boehmian mystic) seeks to be free of the unconsciousness inherent in non-duality (Dourley, 2008: 86). Although Dourley confuses God's self-mediation through the immanent generation of the eternal nature with the repletion of this mediation in creation, Dourley's distinction between these two alternative spiritualities is spot on. The Eckhartian *reditus* is an introverted non-dual Christian mysticism, and the Boehmian *exitus* model, an extroverted Christian personalism. Not only does the distinction highlight Boehme's unique contribution to the Christian mystical tradition (which explains why Boehme and not Eckhart, who has equal claim to being the architect of the Germanic speculative tradition, is the true departure point for German Idealism); Dourley's distinction also shows that Germanic Christianity is both non-dual and personalist, affirming both the oceanic point of origin and the necessity of mediation through difference. One can find both these tendencies in Schelling. The Schelling of the identity-philosophy emphasizes non-duality and Eckhartian *reditus*; the Schelling of the *Freedom* essay and *Ages* emphasizes mediation, personality and Boehmian *exitus*.

## Lucifer, the first psychotic

Evil is always a possibility for created freedom: it is the refusal to participate in what Boehme calls the "play of love" (*Liebe-Spiel*), the universal order established by self-abnegation. As the product of freedom, evil is rooted in the dark fire; it is not "nothing," not an "illusion," but something that has come to be, like all things, *ex Deo*. The explanation of how evil can be rooted in God without God himself being the cause of evil is the fundamental question that drives all of Boehme's works. Evil has something divine in it that is twisted, perverted, turned into its opposite.

Boehme's concept of evil is built from two insights that are basic to his original vision and central to all his theology. The first insight concerns the mixed nature of the order of creation. There is no evil in Boehme's God, nor is there any integration of good and evil in Boehmian theosophy; the tension between good and evil is only resolved by decision, i.e., by the final and definitive separation of good from evil. Nonetheless, everything finite is a mixture of good and evil; after the fall, we cannot, with Augustine, simply say, "being is good." It is not enough to follow the Scholastics in distinguishing moral evil from natural evil, to attribute moral evil to the abuse of freedom and to dissolve natural evil into the privations necessary for every grade of being to be filled. The world strikes Boehme as both a wonder through which the glory of God shines in the most insignificant things, and a harsh and cruel place, a world of pain and unjustified suffering that no moral God could will directly. Boehme is troubled by the discrepancy between the evil of which men are capable (pride, wrath, greed, and so on) and the evil they suffer (sickness, natural disasters, old age, and death). For Boehme, we find ourselves not only in a morally fallen order of existence but in an ontologically disordered creation.

Boehme's second insight is to recognize in moral evil a drive that is in itself divine. This is going further than saying that the being of the devil, insofar as it is created by God, is good; Boehme says, with the Kabbalah, that God has within him a capacity for violence which stands eternally tempered and transformed by mercy, a "tart, terrible sharpness." This is the first of the seven qualities, harshness (*Herbe*). Considered alone, it is a negation of life, like winter without the promise of spring (Boehme, 1612: 13.55–56). In God it is never separated from the other qualities. The dark fire in God is essential to his being; it is the principle of divine movement, life, and individuation, which can never be separated from the light fire that tempers it. But in his creation, which is free on the angelic and human levels, a one-sided upsurge of wrath over love is possible. In the first creation, the creation of the angels (which precedes the creation of the earth), the angels are given a choice: they may join the harmony of heaven and mirror the divine personality by participating in the play of love and effectively laying down their lives for each other – or not. The choice is between order and chaos, between life and death – for there is no other way to be a person than to participate in the eternally self-abnegating personhood of God. The fallen angels' refusal to submit to the divine order is ultimately a decision to self-destruct. By tearing the wrathful qualities out of alignment with the merciful qualities, the rebel angels create a self-imploding anti-nature and become subpersonal. On the occasion of their fall, the three forms in the demonic realm do not issue into the second triad, which tempers and transforms them. Rather, the fire of transformation becomes a destructive blaze: everything conflicts with everything else and war irrupts within heaven (Boehme, 1612: 13.37–50).

Lucifer was raised above all angels, ennobled with the most beautiful and powerful body in all the heavens, "the morning star," singled out by the

Father to freely become his perfect image, the pinnacle of his self-revelation, the first incarnate Son. But seeing how beautiful he was, Lucifer became entranced with himself. He fell in love with his own image and desired nothing other than that he alone should be all in all, that there should be nothing above him. He willed only himself, and the principle of darkness – the perpetually sublated harshness of the Father – possessed him, upsetting the balance (*Temperatur*) of his own nature and disrupting heaven. The dialectic of the three principles was thus truncated and became demonic; the principles clashed with each other in a way that produced not harmony but terrible discord, the sound of a being at war with itself. The result was not aggrandizement but diminishment: Lucifer became less than what he was, losing his divine stature and corrupting his own essence. His nature changed: he was rendered sick, distorted, uncoordinated, insane, hating God and himself, lashing out in rage at everything good and true. The first principle wars against the second, and refuses the move into the ordered relationship of the two in the third; in effect it refuses the otherness without which it cannot be free. The finite destroying itself by wilfully asserting itself against the infinite is Boehme's figure for evil.

Boehme's figure of Lucifer must not be misinterpreted as a figure for individuation, an emancipated personality, or a proto-existentialist who achieves a higher level of selfhood by overcoming authority and breaking with the system. Although the figure inspired the ambiguous anti-hero of Milton's *Paradise Lost*, who elicits our sympathy for courageously setting out where none in heaven had ever dared go, asserting the rights of the individual over every system of government, even God's, there is nothing sympathetic about Boehme's Lucifer: he is a coward whose narcissism and resistance to growth cause a diminishment of being and twist the created order into the production of monsters, disease and death. Boehme's innovation is to take the biblical figure of Lucifer, the antagonist of *Job*, who seems to play an important role in God's court (Job 1: 6–12), or the tempter of the Gospels, who appears to have been created precisely to test us and so drive us to perfection (Matthew 4: 1–11; Mark 1: 9–13), and re-conceive him within a dynamic ontology in which personhood is not ready-made but must be achieved through a difficult process of self-birthing. Invited to give birth to God's Son, i.e., himself, Lucifer resists and gives birth to an abomination. Called to become something more than he was initially created, called to become the Christ by ordering the forces inside of him, subordinating his ipseity to love, or in Schelling's terminology, subordinating the first potency to the second potency (which does not destroy the first potency but perfects it), Lucifer devolves under the pressure of his narcissism. He does not simply forsake his place at God's right hand because he prefers "to reign in Hell, than serve in Heaven" (Milton, 2003: 1.263); he does not make a mistake in judgement elevating a lesser over a higher good; he does not choose something good in itself, say free will, or individual autonomy, over the good prescribed to him; rather, his act is entirely negative: he refuses to recognize otherness. Rather than risking everything on a new value, he prefers the safety of his "animal" selfhood to the risk and pain of personal transformation.[42]

Without making God responsible for evil, Boehme posits a substantial material structure to evil. Evil is not merely a *privatio boni*; the inversion of the three divine principles in the free-falling creature gives rise to an alternative nature, a being that should not be, and which, moreover, has perverse productive power. The primordial fallen being, Lucifer, does not impotently rage, parasitically incapable of producing genuine effects and living off of the life of the good; rather Lucifer has productive if not creative power. He can, in Boehme's account, produce significant alterations in the structure of beings, alterations which cannot be entirely qualified as negations or privations. For Boehme the catastrophe of Satan is the source not only of sin but pestilence, sickness, natural abominations and disasters. Evil is more than a moral negation of God; it is also an ontological negation of material balance, a recombination of natural elements to produce something God does not intend. Lucifer's rebellion changes the structure of nature itself: God's first creation, the angelic order, which was free of ontological evil, was destroyed by Lucifer and the rebel angels; God's second creation, the earth, was disfigured from the beginning by the interference of Satan in the process of its creation.[43] Adam was meant to take Lucifer's place, to become the new morning star, the image of the Father, but he succumbed to the temptation of the serpent, and the tragedy of the first fall repeated itself. Christ redeems both orders: first, he does what Lucifer ought to have done and becomes the true Son of God; second, he redeems material creation and restores humanity's lost image of God.

Granted that it has been redeemed, there is nonetheless some sense to the proposition that for Boehme material being as it exists ought not to have been. If we call "gnostic" any theology that holds creation to be to some degree God's antithesis, the negation of not only his infinity but also his goodness, then it is undeniable that Boehme approximates something like what O'Regan calls a "gnostic return" (O'Regan, 2002). However, Boehme's point is not the Manichaean one, that material creation is in itself evil, as though matter could only exist as the negation of God, but rather the more subtle claim that creation as it has historically unfolded includes elements that are indeed evil and not the direct product of God's design. Boehme does not maintain that materiality, temporality and embodiment are evil; how could they be since they mirror divine processes? His point is that material being has fallen under a spell and is now subject to productions and processes that are not directly of God. When Schelling suggests in the *Freedom* essay that material creation is the result of a moment of madness in the divine life (the madness of genius), God letting the devil loose, so to speak, allowing his "nature" or "ground" to move independently of his "heart" or "love," for only in this way can individual beings come to exist in their own right, emancipated as it were from the infinite, he is articulating this Boehmian point (Schelling, 1809: 45). Creation in the *Freedom* essay is God bringing goodness out of a perversely disoriented material order, a world infected by evil which he himself unleashed for the sake of making possible his masterstroke of redemption.[44]

In Boehme's theosophy, the harshness of the Father, the first of the seven forms, is the principle of the materiality and individuality (ipseity) of things. Without it a thing could not hold itself together and be differentiated from other things. Ipseity is not evil in itself: if things did not assert themselves against the infinitely attractive power of God and against all other created things, they could not be. God invests his creatures with a will to selfhood, a contracting principle that protects each being from its environment and encloses it around a pulsing middle point that animates the whole organism with an overpowering hunger to live, to preserve itself, to be what it is and nothing else. Suffering arises from the apparently inevitable conflict between individual essences (not only between individual beings but between principles within a single being). Sickness, pain, and death have their roots in a conflict of wills, a collision of self-asserting forces. Health is a precarious *détente* between warring elements, a momentary image of the eternal balance between contraction and expansion achieved in the heart of God. At the centre of everything is strife and struggle; if there were no such oppositions, nature could not be, for only in movement is there life and only in opposition is there movement, or as Boehme puts it, nature is only made manifest in war (Boehme, BSS 6: 2.4). Everything wills only the likeness of itself; because the will comes into conflict with counter-wills, it suffers sickness and pain (*Wehethun*). And yet if it was not opposed by others, it would not be. It would seem that the price of the material revelation of God is sickness, pain, and death. However, Boehme repeatedly argues against those who interpret him as saying that God wills evil.[45] Boehme insists that evil need not be, that the wrathful qualities of God have within them the seeds of health, love, and peace. Neither can we say that the historical development of evil out of fallen freedom is necessary for the sake of goodness, for at no point is Boehme's God subject to historical necessity.

If O'Regan is right and there is indeed an instance of gnostic return in Boehme (O'Regan, 1994), it lies in Boehme's contention that Lucifer's rebellion plays a role in the creation of the world. Lucifer falls before the world is created; he is therefore capable of interfering with God's plan. The serpent is in the garden before Adam and Eve: for Boehme this means that the world comes to be in a malevolently altered form; it not only shows forth the glory of the creator, it is also marred by the monstrosities of Lucifer's interference. Between God and the creation he intends stands Boehme's figure of Lucifer, who maliciously interferes with the production of beings and twists what God makes into perverse forms that God never intended. This heterodox cosmogony is the source of Boehme's bizarre view that some creatures are simply evil, e.g., toads, goats, and things that crawl on the ground. In the *Freedom* essay Schelling incorporates Boehme's position into a theology of the "happy fault," as the ancient Catholic Church put it in the *Exsultet*:[46] the world, Schelling recognizes, is not simply good and reflective of the goodness of the creator, it is historically fallen and disfigured by sin, but the fall is part of the plan. God in his goodness cannot will that something imperfect and fallen should exist in place of the perfect and whole; what he wills is that an intermediary cause (ground) become a collaborator in creation. Ground freely actualizes evil. God proves that his allowing this to happen was not an act of imbecility or madness by bringing an even greater good out of the fall than would have otherwise existed: the redeemer, whose infinite selflessness brings about the redemption of the world.

Whatever Boehme's intentions, his work is rife with ambiguities. It is not clear, for example, whether Lucifer's fall is necessary to the revelation of God, as Hegel will argue.[47] God allowed Satan to persist in being when he could have destroyed him. Why does he let him live? Is something not revealed in Satan that would otherwise be concealed? Does the conflict with Satan not fully unconceal what is hidden in God, hidden even from God himself? Boehme never fully answers these questions. The weapon Lucifer wields against God is the one given him by God himself – Lucifer encloses himself in the dark centre of ipseity, which had been granted to him so that he might freely become who he was created to be (Boehme, 1624a: 7.1). Entranced by his own magnificence, Lucifer withdraws from the reality of God into the dark ground and resists the movement into light; he refuses to become transformed into the Son of God, wishing instead to be himself God, in other words, he denies the whole of which he is a part and wills himself to be the whole (Boehme, 1612: 13.32). The dialectic of love, the play between the two principles, ought to lead to the subordination of the No to the Yes; the first principle ought to lower itself and become ground of the second, much as the Father lowers himself in allowing the Son to be. But Lucifer refuses to submit, and that which should become ground elevates itself as a whole.[48] Lucifer goes mad striving to overthrow the order of principles; he wills chaos, even though doing so can only be accomplished at his own expense.[49] The result is an unleashing of things that should not be: powers that are eternally hidden in God, in whom they function as the ground of love, are dislodged from their proper context just as neutrons detached from uranium in fission become powers of destruction.[50] The devil is individuation gone awry, the principle of self become a principle of absolute separation. Far from being a romantic anti-hero, Boehme's Lucifer is a figure of insanity. His defection from the good has no reason and can have no reason, for it is free and self-destructive at the same time. Boehme sometimes describes Lucifer's sin as an act of self-displacement, the prince of the angels losing his bearings, his proper position in the order of things: Lucifer is "driven" from his "place" at God's right hand (*aus seinem Loco getrieben*) (Boehme, 1612: 13.53, 1624b: 2.8). Boehme's use of the Latin for "place" (*Loco*) is not unrelated to the Spanish expression *volverse loco* ("to go crazy"). Lucifer forsakes his place in the divine order and in the same moment loses his mind – he is a forerunner of the Lacanian psychotic who has lost his place in the symbolic. Better, he is the paradigm of what we call negative dissociation, the dissociation from the dissociation life is demanding of us. Lucifer is called to dissociate from the dark principle, which is not to repress it but to posit it as the ground of his being, to become conscious of it and at the same time other than it. He refuses to so transform and chooses instead to remain enmeshed in the first principle; he effectively wills unconsciousness over consciousness, self over love, himself alone rather than himself participating in the divine order, and this drives him mad.[51]

Boehmian evil is the dark fire misdirected, misused, removed from "the general circulation of the conspiracy of life" (Wirth, 2003: 163) and allowed to consume the soul in a holocaust of narcissism. What the inflamed self destroys is first of all the soul in which it rages: evil is intrinsically suicidal. But before extinguishing itself (its logical outcome), it attacks all health and life outside of it. Boehme's devil is no Jungian hero who transforms himself by breaking with the system; he is rather the miserable shut-in who refuses to transform. He is the personification of the No to love, the resistance to life and growth that is latent in the ground (where as potency it serves the subsistence of being) become perversely manifest and carried to its extreme at the price of the wholeness of its host. Lucifer is the first psychotic – only he goes mad voluntarily. Nothing could be further from Boehme's thought than the Hegelian notion that Lucifer's corruption is necessary. Lucifer freely falls, and God brings goodness out of the catastrophe. When Boehme is consistent, he insists that God does not need Lucifer's fall in order to achieve goodness or self-revelation, nor does he pre-determine Lucifer to fall; he could have achieved his ends otherwise, yet he wills that his design be accomplished collaboratively, even if his creature abuses that generosity. Lucifer's self-disruption infects the whole created order, from the physical level, where we see life corrupted by disease and death, to the psychic level, where self-division and madness disfigure personality.

## Sophia, the mirror of God

The dialectical play of the three principles does not conclude the drama of divine self-revelation; it achieves the self-actualization of the divine personality, with the ordered relation of the two aspects of wrath and mercy, but the full showing of God requires a further step. The interaction of the three must be reflected back to God before he can be said to be fully revealed to himself. Boehme personifies this reflection in Sophia, the divine feminine or the mirror of wisdom (*Spiegel der Weisheit*), associating her with the Hebrew myth of a feminine helper pre-existing creation, playing before the throne of the almighty, and assisting God in his design of the world (Wisdom 7–8).[52] In the nothing of the unground prior to the birth of God, a will arises that longs for itself without knowledge of itself because it exists without the duality necessary for knowledge. The will's longing generates an image of itself, an image that reflects its longing back to itself, an image of longing itself. Sophia is the mirror in which the divine image is generated: she is at once the medium by which the divine longing is made manifest to God and the manifestation itself which satisfies the longing.[53] The unground's non-agonic self-differentiation occurs when the will to self-knowledge first generates this mirror of itself, thus Sophia is the principle of differentiation in the divine; in her mirror the archetypes of all things possible first appear.[54] Boehme describes the mirror of Sophia as a swirling play of unfixed forms, of colours and sounds that come and go without cohering into anything actual or solid. Gazing at her, God not only knows himself for the first time, he knows all that he might do. He thus dissociates from the unground and identifies with the image reflected back to him, the image of a creator, a God who is no longer isolated in his immovable perfection but self-related and revealed in his productions. For Boehme, the pre-existence of Sophia proves that God does not need creation in order to know himself; he is already differentiated and revealed within himself before he creates the world. Thus Boehme is not strictly speaking a historical immanentist, as Baader, in his polemic with German Idealism, points out (Baader, BSW 13: 66). The mirror of wisdom is not yet creation, the images reflected therein are unstable and indistinct, a dreamlike play of possibilities. Everything that God could will, God "imagines" in Sophia, and his imagination, the "magic act par excellence," translates into images the infinity of his mind (Koyré, 1929: 347).

Although Sophia is a fourth term in Boehme's divine economy, the explicitly feminine figure that in some sense "completes" the Trinity, it is nonetheless important to the logic of Boehme's Trinitarianism to distinguish Sophia from the three divine persons. Sophia is to be associated with the unground rather than the three principles for she is as undetermined as it is: of itself her emptiness produces nothing and engenders nothing (Koyré, 1929: 345). Like the unground, Sophia has no act proper to her: she neither begets nor is she begotten. Her role is to be the passive double of the whole of the divinity, reflecting the begetting of principles and returning the image of the generative forces back to them (Faivre, 1994: 212). She is "pure virtuality," reflecting God's unconsciousness back to himself, showing him his unrevealedness, and in that act, revealing him (Koyré, 1929: 346). Boehme's figure of Sophia has a relationship to the alchemico-

Aristotelian notion of prime matter, the eternal substance which is itself without form but which enters into the formation of everything, but she is even more clearly a personification of Plato's *Khora*, the space or "receptacle of all becoming" within which the forms are differentiated (*Timaeus* 49a). Like both of these, Sophia is not a principle of form but of difference; she introduces plurality into unity (O'Regan, 2002: 237, n. 9). Most importantly, Boehme brings to theology an insight whose origin is alchemical and hermetic: the male–female, active–passive polarity characteristic of created nature is original to God. The archetypally feminine attributes – passivity, receptivity, emptiness, boundlessness – are every bit as divine as the masculine attributes of activity, form, and definition which are typically associated with God. As the mirror of God's mind, Sophia is not a dislocation or repression of the divine but a recapitulation of the unity of the unground – with a decisive difference: the unity of the unground is undifferentiated and unconscious; the unity of the three active principles reflected in Sophia is differentiated and self-conscious.

Both Schelling and Lacan make use of the Boehmian metaphor of the mirror in their psychologies. We will discuss them in order, beginning with Schelling. Like all of his borrowings from Boehme, Schelling's appropriation of the Sophia figure is unacknowledged and concealed behind a veil of metaphysical terms that are foreign to Boehme, even if the sense of the whole in which they inhere is thoroughly Boehmian. The Sophia figure can be teased out of Schelling's *Freedom* essay in the passages in which Schelling gives primacy to the feminine, for example: "Man is formed in the maternal body; and only from the obscurity of that which is without understanding (from feeling, yearning, the sovereign mother of knowledge) grow luminous thoughts" (Schelling, 1809: 29). It is not just man who takes form in the "maternal body," God, too, is formed in the primordial feminine, which Schelling, in the next line, explicitly identifies with Plato's *Khora*:

> Thus we must imagine the original yearning as it directs itself to the understanding, though still not recognizing it, just as we in our yearning seek out unknown and nameless good, and as it moves, divining itself, like a wave-wound whirling sea, akin to Plato's matter, following dark, uncertain law, incapable of constructing for itself anything enduring.

In this phantasmagoria of possible forms, like the dreamer emerging from the depths of dreamless sleep into the play of the dream, Schelling's God first apprehends himself as God:

> But, corresponding to the yearning, which as the still dark ground is the first stirring of divine existence, an inner, reflexive representation is generated in God himself through which, since it can have no other

object but God, God sees himself in an exact image of himself. This representation is the first in which God, considered as absolute, is realized, although only in himself; this representation is with God in the beginning and is the God who was begotten *in* God himself.

(Schelling, 1809: 29)

Schelling locates the archetype for all natural becoming as well as for the birth of personality in the autogeneration of the self-aware God from the mirror image of himself. In the second draft of *Ages*, God's vision of the contents of his mind is explicitly identified with the Old Testament figure of wisdom: "Wisdom played before the Lord, filled with childlike presentiment, and he saw in her what will one day be, as if it were a golden future in a youthful dream" (Schelling, 1813: 165, n. 2).

When Lacan studied Boehme with Koyré in the 1930s, he appears to have grasped the Sophia-figure as a premodern myth that unlocks the secret of Freudian metapsychology.[55] Whether Schelling is a mediator of the Boehmian Sophia tradition for Lacan is not known, but given Lacan's appetite for German philosophy, we cannot rule out the possibility. For Lacan, the role the mirror plays in the genesis of personality is exactly the opposite of the role it plays in Boehme and Schelling. Whereas for the latter two, Sophia effects an *increase* in reality (even if concealment inevitably accompanies the revelation), an entering into functional relation with self (consciousness of the unconscious), for Lacan the mirror facilitates the psyche's flight into the unreal or the symbolic. For Lacan, what comes to shape in the mirror – the ideal order where the subject enjoys an identity that differentiates him from other subjects and from the environment, and where language and symbolization put at his disposal endless possibilities not only of expression but of meaning-construction – is fundamentally an illusory order, a phantasmic other to a disowned life. The infant seeks release from the chaos of its uncoordinated body by disidentifying with its felt experience and re-identifying itself with the unified but alienated body revealed to it in a mirror.[56] The structure of Lacan's mirror stage formally repeats Boehme's theory of the divine non-agonic self-mediation: Sophia allows Boehme's God to disidentify with the undetermined unity of the unground and re-identify with the personality structured by the dialectical interplay of the three principles and reflected back to him as a glorious whole in her mirror. Where the analogy between the two theories breaks down is in the necessity that drives the Lacanian infant into the disidentification: the psyche that fails to so disidentify goes mad. Boehme's theogony, like Schelling's, is a creative product of free decision, not a coping mechanism; the unground projects itself onto the mirror of wisdom for the sake of revelation and the production of love.

The title page from the 1730 edition of Boehme's *Sex puncta theosophica* (Boehme, BSS 4), illustrated by Michael Andreas, gathers together the multiple levels of structure in Boehme's model of reality which we have outlined above (see Figure 2.2). On one level, we see the Triune God (S for *Sohn*, H for *Heilige Geist*, and V for *Vater*); on another level the two opposing spiritual drives: the first principle (dark), ipseity or contraction into self, and the second principle (light), alterity or expansion into otherness. On a third level, the image shows Boehme's doctrine of the three worlds, heaven, hell and earth, which correspond to the three divine principles. The dark sphere represents the first principle, the dark fire of centripetal ipseity. The flaming triangle reflects the tripartite structure of the dark principle, which encloses within it three dialectically related divine qualities: harshness, bitterness, angst. The light sphere is the second principle, the light fire of centrifugal love. The inverted triangle represents the tripartite structure of the light fire, which concretizes itself in the dialectic of light, tone, and figure. Between the two is the *Blitz*, the crack of lightning that transforms darkness into light. On either side of the middle sphere (the third principle) are the symbols of the sun and the moon, representative of the polarity carried forward into the created order, where it becomes embodied as day and night, form and matter, spirit and soul, fire and water, masculine and feminine. The triangle on the left is an alchemical symbol for the masculine; the inverted triangle on the right is an alchemical symbol for the feminine. The outermost circle, the container of the three principles, is the unground, "the eternal freedom," God "beyond nature and creature." The two rings of eyes gazing into each other represent Sophia, the mirror of wisdom, eternally mediating God to himself. Sophia does not have a term or a figure associated with her in the dialectic itself; rather, she encircles the dialectic of three principles/worlds/divine persons and reveals it to be a self-contained and perfect whole.

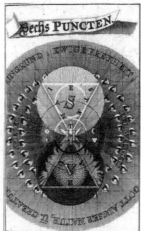

*Figure 2.2* Engraving by Michael Andreas of the title page of *Sex puncta theosophica* from the 1730 edition of Boehme's collected works

Let us abstract the psychodynamics from Boehme's theogony. The first principle of personality is the dark principle of the soul, which Boehme calls *Selbstheit* and which we translate as "ipseity." The dark principle is necessary to the unfolding of the second and third principles. It becomes pathological when separated from the second principle, but when it operates in conjunction with the second principle, ipseity is the source of all of the energy of the personality. Somewhat innovating on the logic of Boehme's terms, we have called the second principle of personality "alterity." Boehme sometimes speaks of it as "the light of knowledge" (*das Licht der Erkenntinis*). It is clearly associated with the divine logos of John's Gospel, with word, symbolization, etc. What Boehme means here by "light of knowledge" is not "reason" as distinct from "will" but the capacity of the soul to know something other than itself – that is, the intentional, expansive, self-diremptive and exteriorizing side of the soul. The second principle is every bit as volitional as ipseity, although it does not will itself: it wills the other. The fullness of self-manifestation is in the third principle, which, anticipating Schelling, we call personality. There is something still unconscious in the second principle, something not fully self-revealed. Love of the other can be as unconscious as narcissism. Ipseity is oblivious to the other; alterity is oblivious to self. The second principle knows the first principle but it does not yet know itself. In the third principle, the ordered relation of the first to the second principle becomes conscious and a doubling occurs: fully revealed personality is related to itself or self-conscious.[57]

## Schelling's appropriation of Boehme's dark principle

Schelling lifts the notion of evil as "inflamed I-hood" (*entzündete Ichheit*) directly from Baader (Schelling, 1809: 35, n.; Baader, BSW 3: 269–276, 1: 33–38). For Baader, who follows Boehme on this point, ipseity is not in itself "wrong," not some false identity that needs to be excised from the soul. Boehmian "transformation into Christ" is not a *unio mystica* wherein the self disappears into God. Rather, the dark ground is the point of gravity in the creature, essential to its remaining distinct from God. Baader interprets this to mean that without a healthy sense of self, the soul has no substance – or, to use another Kabbalistic metaphor, without the contraction into self, the soul would have no space in which to become what it is or give itself away.[58] Boehme does not identify the transformed soul with God; rather, the transformed soul becomes *gelassen* (surrendered) to the divine will, which reigns in the soul while remaining distinct from the creaturely will. The significance of this difference from mainstream ascetical-mystical Christian literature must not be overlooked: what Nietzsche sought in the Greek-heroic tradition can be found in Boehmian Christianity: healthy self-assertion, the Yes function of all that lives, is encouraged here rather than suppressed or denied.

Baader's image of sin as "inflamed selfhood" (*entzündete Ichheit*) is meant quite literally. The word *entzündete* is used to characterize an infection. The "inflamed ego" is sick, a life in which the life principle has become a death principle. Sin is to the soul what sickness is to the body. A tumour is life (the reproduction of cells) gone wild, vitality no longer in sync with the health of the whole, which sickens and eventually kills the life it is meant to serve.[59] The dark ground is meant to serve the life of the soul, to ground the soul's relations to others and its surrender to God. In sin ground steps out of the centre, where it ought to remain hidden and subordinated to the life of the whole, and wills to be itself the whole. The Baaderian-Schellingian dark ground is not properly characterized in Freudian fashion as infantile pleasure drive; nor does it harbour a death-drive, a will to the cessation of willing; it is the drive for self without other, a tenacious, unreflective, unconscious introversion natural to every individual being. Without transformation or moderation (because moderation transforms it), ground renders the soul insane. The dark ground struggles against itself, for by willing itself it wills in spite of itself the other against whom it demarcates itself; it posits the other in the very act of willing itself. Ground ought to disappear in use, so to speak, allowing itself to be mediated by "the periphery," by consciousness, understanding, universality, and love. Instead, by inflating itself to the whole compass of the soul, it finds itself in endless antagonism with the principles of understanding and love.

Boehme's theosophy is already a psychology before Baader and Schelling get to it, a point that emerges clearly in scattered passages from Boehme, such as the following, which are charged with psychodynamic insights, however cloaked they are in esoteric imagery:

> For no creature can be born and subsist solely from the divine love-desire, but it must have in itself the fiery triangle in accordance with painfulness; that is, it must have an individual will, which goes forth as an exspirated power and as a ray from the whole will, out of the temperament of the primal unfathomable will, the Word of power separating itself in fire, and passing out of the fire again into the light. Here the angels and the soul of man have their origin, namely, from the fiery enkindling of the beginning of the eternal Nature; and here this ray of the fiery kindling must unite itself again to the constitution of the light, that is, to the whole. And then it eats of the holy tincture of the fire and the light, *i.e.* of the spiritual water by which the fire becomes a kingdom of joy. For the spiritual water is a daily mortification of the fiery enkindling, whereby the fiery kindling along with the fire of love becomes a temperament; and then there is but a single will therein, which is to love all that has its subsistence in this root.
>
> (Boehme, 1623a: 2.38–39)

"The divine love-desire" and "the fiery triangle in accordance with pain-fulness" are the opposite vectors of desire necessary to life, the basic ontological polarity of love and wrath, light and dark, light fire and dark fire. No creature can be born or subsist solely in the love of God because in the Godhead there is no distinction, no space that could permit another to be. This is the nub of Boehme's answer to the question of evil, the single question behind all of his works: evil exists because God has something in him that is not identical to his love, something that makes creation (ontological difference) possible, but that also makes evil possible.

The dark fire is "a fiery triangle of painfulness" – a triangle because it mirrors (in darkness) "the Ternar" or triadic structure of Boehme's Lutheran God – described alternatively as the "dark cold painful fire" (Boehme, 1623a: 6.9), "the origin of eternal nature," and "the cause of all being" (Boehme, 1623b: 6.14). Within the dark fire are the first three "dark" or wrathful qualities, warring against each other without resolution, in pain because the pleasure of resolution is reserved for the second triad, the triangle of love or the three light qualities, from which the wrathful qualities are eternally separated by the crack (*Blitz*) of the mediating quality. The tension generated in this eternal antagonism makes "subsistence" and onto-logical difference possible. Individuality is pain, separateness, and antagon-ism, but the pain is only for the sake of the pleasure of union. The dark fire empowers beings with "an individual will." In the angels and in human beings, this individual will becomes freedom as Schelling defines it, the capacity for good and evil. "The temperament" in the above passage refers to the functional relation of the opposites to one another in God: wrath never without love, the dark fire eternally transmuted into the light fire or love-desire. The temperament emerges "out of the primal unfathomable will," out of the unground, the Godhead beyond Trinity, beyond person-ality, i.e., the divine unconscious.

All rational creatures are hence commissioned with a task, a quest, the goal of which is to actively realize through free decision their potency for love: "this ray of the fiery kindling must unite itself again to the con-stitution of the light, that is, to the whole." When this happens – and it can only happen freely – a Eucharist occurs: "the fiery kindling" (the dark fire) "eats of the holy tincture of the fire and the light." In other words, the dark fire is transmuted. Out of the *coniunctio* of fire and light "the spiritual water" is produced "by which the fire becomes a kingdom of joy." The tempering of the dark fire of individual will is individuation and sanc-tification: "a single will" emerges from the *coniunctio*, but as Schelling makes clear, it is not a singularity that excludes duality; rather, it is a singularity that unites that which could be apart but *wills* not to be. The single will wills one thing, "love" for "all that has its subsistence in this root." But since everything that exists has its subsistence in this root, the single will loves everything.

The key to Boehme's metaphysics, to the theogony as much as the esoteric psychology, the ascetical-mystical theology as much as the philosophy of nature, is this original notion of the productive negative. Dark fire burns without illumination; it is a fire that consumes itself, feeds off itself, and generates its own heat. It can be the ground of infinite productivity, but on its own, it is impotent. Left to itself, without the tempering qualities of its opposite, light fire, dark fire can do nothing other than burn. In the Paracelsian alchemical tradition some of the properties of Boehmian dark fire are fore-shadowed by "sulphur," the caustic, acerbic, self-consuming power that, when combined with "the dry water" of mercury, constitutes the basic creative binary in all living bodies. Dark fire is that which burns in the heart of nature. If Boehme had known about nuclear physics, he would have doubtlessly identified dark fire with the power locked inside the atom. Dark fire is energy that needs to be transmuted by the "crack" of lightning (*Blitz*) before it becomes light, but even so transformed dark fire does not disappear; rather, it withdraws into the light, burning steadily there, the root and source of its power and heat.

## Notes

1 See Nicholls and Liebscher (2010); Faflak (2008a, 2008b); Marquard (1987, 2004). By and large most genealogies of the unconscious focus on the influence of the post-idealists (Schopenhauer, Nietzsche) on psychoanalysis. See Gödde (1999); Zentner (1995). On Schelling's role, see Vater (1978); Žižek (1996); Snow (1996: 119–140); Buchheim (2004); Ffytche (2008, 2012); Marquard (2004); Neugebauer (2007). Mills (2002) has made a case for Hegel's role in the development of the Freudian unconscious. Schelling is widely recognized for having been the first to posit a single ground of matter and mind, which cannot itself be conscious. See Whyte (1960: 125); Uslar (1987: 115). There are no recent studies of the influence of theosophy on the development of the unconscious. Neither Ellenberger (1970) nor Shamdasani (2003) have anything to say about theosophy. One finds scattered remarks in studies of Western esotericism connecting various strands of the esoteric tradition to Freud, Jung, or Lacan. See Drobb (2000a: 43–47); Faivre (1994: 107); Goodrick-Clarke (2008: 245–248); Dufour (1998); Hanegraff (1998): 482–513.

2 Leibniz speaks of perceptions that occur without our being aware of them (*petits perceptions*) (Leibniz, 1765: 55). Kant develops this into a theory of "dark representations" that do not cross the threshold of consciousness (Kant, 1798/ 1978: 18). The concept of unconscious representation is generally held to be the beginning of the concept of the unconscious. See Nicholls and Liebscher (2010: 4–13); Shamdasani (2003: 170). Michel Henry argues that the concept of the unconscious emerges in modern philosophy as a compensation for the Cartesian-Kantian substitution of image (representation) for reality, the revenge of life on subjectivism. See Henry (1993).

3 The new appreciation for Schelling in the English-speaking world begins with Bowie's solid presentation (1993). Notable contributions include: Beach (1994); Žižek (1996); Snow (1996); Beiser (2002); Norman (2004); Wirth (2003, 2004); Grant (2006); Laughland (2007); Lauer (2010); Shaw (2011); Matthews (2011).

With the exception of Beach (1994) and Matthews (2011), Boehme and theosophy are scarcely mentioned in these works. Brown's study (1977) remains the standard reference in English for theosophy the Boehme–Schelling relationship. This eliding of theosophy in recent Schelling scholarship is a reversal of the mid-twentieth-century trend. The classic German studies were clear on the theosophical origins of Schellingian philosophy. See especially Fuhrmans (1954) and Habermas (1954). A trickle of works have appeared in English on Boehme and his relation to German philosophy (Weeks, 1991; Magee, 2001; O'Regan, 1994, 2002). The best work on Boehme is still found in the French literature (Koyré, 1929; Deghaye, 2000).

4  Matthews has made a good case for an influence of Oetinger on the young Schelling via Philipp Matthäus Hahn. See Matthews (2011: 39–68). An 1809 letter from Schelling to a pastor-friend of his father's (Christian Gottlob Pregizer) makes an important reference to Oetinger. Schelling is quoted as writing to Pregizer, "The time is come, when that which Oetinger long since understood will be realized in a universal, living and determinate way" (Schelling, cited in Schneider, 1938: 10). Schelling's letter to Pregizer is lost, but Pregizer was so struck by Schelling's statement that he cited it in full in his reply. In 1806 Schelling directed Baader to Oetinger, writing to his father that Baader had discovered "our Oetinger" and requesting his help in acquiring copies of Oetinger's works (but not his father's copy, which Schelling reserved for himself) (Schneider, 1938: 9). Schneider concludes that the middle Schelling understood himself to be transposing Oetinger's theosophical vision into the dialectical language of discursive reason. To provide proof for this claim, Schneider looks at how much of the language of the *Freedom* essay, which has usually been attributed to Schelling's innovations on Boehme (*Licht/Finsternis, Abgrund, der Band der Kräfte, lebendige Bewegungskräfte*), repeats phrases directly from Oetinger (Schneider, 1938: 10).

5  The question of the influence of theosophy on Kant's philosophy of nature and Fichte's philosophy of subjectivity – the two mainstream sources of the early Schelling's philosophy – cannot be explored here. Suffice it to say that such an influence is not only possible but likely. The influence of theosophy and alchemy on Newton's physics is an old story.

6  Zovko argues that Schelling could not complete *The Ages of the World* because he realized, midway through, that it was too close to Baader's neo-Boehmian enterprise (Zovko, 1996: 110–121). Baader, who had criticized Schelling's nature-philosophy in print, openly approved of the turn in Schelling's thinking signalled by the *Freedom* essay (Zovko, 1996: 104). He was in discussion with Schelling throughout the period in which Schelling struggled to bring *The Ages of the World* to birth (Zovko, 1996: 121).

7  Schelling was not breaking new ground with his 1809 turn to theosophy; a retrieval of Boehme was already on the agenda of many of the early romantics (Tieck, Novalis, Schlegel) (Korff, 1956: 2; Fuhrmans, 1954: 114ff.). See especially Fuhrmans (1954: 120). Schelling had participated in the early romantic theosophical craze; he read Boehme with Tieck as early as 1799 and asked for help in acquiring Boehme's books in an 1802 letter to A.W. Schlegel (Benz, 1955: 29).

8  In 1956 Wilhelm Wieland attacked the "appalling custom" of explaining Schelling with reference to Boehme. The theosophical reading of Schelling "made a thoughtful appreciation of these matters much more difficult, if not impossible" (Wieland, 1956: 23). Dale Snow concurs and adds that "explaining a little-known thinker in terms of one still less well known" is a dead end (Snow, 1996: 147).

9 See Hegel (1807: 7–8): "Only what is completely determined is at once exoteric, comprehensible, and capable of being learned and appropriated by all. The intelligible form of science is the way open and equally accessible to everyone, and consciousness as it approaches science justly demands that it be able to attain to rational knowledge by way of the ordinary understanding." Hegel's remarks on Boehme in his *Lectures on the History of Philosophy* are even more telling. "We now pass . . . to the *philosophicus teutonicus*, as he is called – to the German cobbler of Lusatia, of whom we have no reason to be ashamed. It was, in fact, through him that philosophy first appeared in Germany with a character peculiar to itself" (Hegel, 1896: 188). Worthy of note here is Hegel's condescending and apologetic tone; presumably some among Hegel's contemporaries (perhaps Hegel himself) were "ashamed" of Boehme.

10 Mayer has compiled the evidence and concluded that there is "a substantial reception of Böhme's theosophy in the *Freiheitsschrift*." That the conclusion runs counter to the thesis of her book (Mayer argues that Boehme is far more marginal to romanticism than previously thought) only makes it more convincing. "Here, for the first and only time, a member of the Jena circle appropriated an entire doctrine central to Böhme's system, that is, appropriated both the content and the terminology in which it was originally clothed" (Mayer, 1999: 198).

11 Schelling made several efforts to differentiate his work from theosophy at different times in his career. See Schelling (1815: xxxviii–xxxix). See also the introduction to Schelling's *Philosophie der Offenbahrung* (Schelling, SSW 13: 121–124). Here Schelling notes that while Boehme is "a wonder," a revelation of the depths of the German spirit, and the first thinker to explain myth through psychology, theosophy remains unscientific and un-methodological. Despite his intentions to do otherwise, Boehme cannot think God as free. Positive philosophy speaks scientifically about what theosophy struggles in vain to say.

12 See Jacobs (2001: 153).

13 The emphasis on discursive reason, on logic, and argument distinguishes Schelling from his romantic peers, e.g., Novalis and Hölderlin. On this point see Beiser (2002: 467).

14 "We do not live in vision. Our knowledge is piecemeal, that is, it must be generated piece by piece, according to sections and grades, all of which cannot happen without reflection. Therefore, the goal is not reached in simple vision. For there is no understanding in vision in and for itself . . . . Hence, everything must be brought to actual reflection in which it could reach the highest presentation. Here runs the boundary between theosophy and philosophy, which the lover of knowledge will chastely seek to protect" (Schelling, 1815: xxxviii–xxxix). This disclaimer is no doubt written for those critics who suspected him of "mysticism." The critics assume theosophy to be subrational; Schelling reverses the assumption and gives theosophy primacy over formal, logical, and merely discursive philosophy. The latter organizes and represents; the former intuits the real: "Theosophy is much ahead of philosophy in depth, fullness, and vitality of content in the way that the actual object is ahead of its image and nature is ahead of its presentation . . . . The theosophical systems have the advantage over everything else hitherto current: at least there is in them a power, even if it does not have power over itself, while in the other systems, in contrast, there is but unnatural and conceited art" (Schelling, 1815: xxxix).

15 See Weeks (1991: 117–142).

16 Oetinger describes Boehme's God as *ens manifestativum sui*.

17 "I fell into a very deep melancholy and heavy sadness, when I beheld and

contemplated the great deep of this world . . . . I found to be in all things, evil and good, love and anger, in the inanimate creatures, viz. in wood, stones, earth and the elements, as also in men and beasts" (Boehme, 1612: 19.5–6).

18 Cited by Baader (BSW 11: 233).

19 Boehme most likely knew nothing about ancient Gnosticism. Recently the Notre Dame theologian Cyril O'Regan has argued that Boehme's theogony is an unconscious return to Valentinian Gnosticism. See O'Regan (2002). For the opposite view, see Koslowski (2001).

20 This is one of the reasons that Oetinger, who is a critic of both modern philosophy and Patristic theology, takes Boehme so seriously. For Oetinger, any philosophy or theology that denigrates the body or even makes it a mere means to a spiritual end, as many orthodox theologians do, is to be rejected. "Embodiment is the end of all God's work" (*Leiblichkeit ist das Ende der Werke Gottes* (Oetinger, 1776, pt 1: 223)).

21 For political reasons, Görlitz in the seventeenth century was a hotbed of religious diversity, a place where alchemy, Kabbalah, and the reform of the Reformation were widely discussed. Kasper Schwenckfeld, Valentin Weigel, and Paracelsus were known in the circles in which Boehme moved. Van Ingen maintains that Boehme knew of these movements as well as the German mystics and the *Theologia Deutsch*. See van Ingen (1997: 803–805). On the intellectual culture in Görlitz in the seventeenth century, see Weeks (1991: 13–34).

22 On Luria and *zimzum*, see Scholem (1974: 128–140); Drobb (2000a: 121–154). Cf. Schelling (1815: 15–17). While Boehme left no notes on his sources, the parallel between Boehme's doctrine of the primary negation (Boehme's first principle) and the notion of *zimzum* is too close to be accidental. On Boehme and the Kabbalah, see Schulze (1955); Häussermann (1966/1967, 1968/1969, 1972); van Ingen (1997). Marcus Pound has drawn attention to the parallel between Lurianic Kabbalah and Žižek/Lacan. See Pound (2008). It is likely that Lacan picked up the idea of *zimzum* from Koyré's *Böhme* (1929). See Dufour (1998).

23 This point is often missed in the interpretation of Boehme. Casual readers tend to conflate Boehme with Hegel and attribute historical immanentism, the position that God only knows himself through the history of man, to Boehme. Historical immanentism is first sketched in outline by Schelling in the *System of Transcendental Idealism*, but the full elaboration of the thesis is the work of Hegel. For Hegel, God needs creation, specifically human reason and history, in order to become God, that is, absolute thought thinking itself. Boehme makes no such claim. Dourley (2008) repeatedly says that an identification of human with divine self-consciousness is Boehme's great contribution. "Though Tillich draws on Boehme extensively in his understanding of the distinct moments in Trinitarian life, he draws back, as we have seen, from the conclusions of Boehme and Jung who are explicit in their positions that the creative source of human consciousness must create human consciousness so that it can itself become conscious in the consciousness of the creature" (Dourley, 2008: 100). More careful readers of Boehme (Friesen, 2008; O'Regan, 2002) follow Baader and Koyré in arguing that for Boehme, God's self-revelation is always already achieved prior to God's creation of the world. Creation is a free repetition of the drama of the self-mediation of the absolute; it adds nothing to God. The objection is sometimes made to this authentically Boehmian position that creation on this view is arbitrary, adding nothing significantly new to the absolute. But one could just as well put this point positively: creation is "play," a free act in which God allows the life he has unleashed within himself to become

concrete. The latter is Schelling's view on the issue in the *Philosophie der Offenbarung*, although Schelling is far from clear about it in the earlier *Freedom* essay. The point is closely related to the question of the necessity of evil in Boehme, which Dourley also obscures. Unlike Hegel and Jung, and in accordance with Schelling and Tillich, Boehme does not hold actual evil to be necessary to God's self-revelation. Both arguments, that human history is necessary to God's self-knowledge and that actual evil is necessary to God's perfection, violate the founding presupposition of Boehme's thought: the freedom of the divine.

24 Schelling repeats this transition from "a will that wills nothing" to "a will that wills something" in the third draft of the *Weltalter* (Schelling, 1815: 12–26).

25 This is a term with a rich history in twentieth-century phenomenology. Boehme's first principle is close to Michel Henry's notion of an immediate presence of the self to the self, which is absolutely interior, prior to consciousness, and can never be made visible. See Henry (1993: 38). Ipseity is not to be confused with "ego."

26 Cf. Schelling (1815: 9).

27 "The No is therefore called a No, because it is a desire turned inwards, as shutting in to negativity" (*Und heisset das Nein darum ein Nein, daß es eine eingekehrete Begierde ist, als Nein-werts einschliessend* (Boehme, 1624a: 3.10)).

28 "And the Yes is so called because it is an eternal outgoing and the ground of all being, pure truth. For it does not have the No before it, rather the No first arises in the outflowing will of acceptance" (*Und das Jah heisset darum Jah, daß es ein ewiger Ausgang, und der Grund aller Wesen ist, als lauter Wahrheit. Denn es hat kein Nein vor ihme, sondern das Nein urständet erst in dem ausgeflossenen Willen der Annehmlichkeit* (Boehme, 1624a: 3.10)). To be precise, Boehme does not speak of alterity, difference, or otherness. Rather he associates the second principle with the divine logos, which expresses and reveals; with light, which is expansive and generous; with the second person of the Trinity, who does not will anything of his own, but wills only what the Father wills, etc. The opposition to the first principle, which is clearly defined as a self-centred revelation-resisting drive, is my warrant for describing the second principle as alterity or otherness. The term is less than precise: the opposition of the two principles, and not the second principle alone, constitutes Boehme's notion of ontological difference. But where the first principle resists difference, the second wills it. Boehme's point is that difference is dyadic, it requires two, a No and a Yes. What the No negates, Boehme tells us, is the opposition and duality of which it is a part. It posits the other negatively, by willing that it *not* be.

29 "The individual will takes form in the No, as in the fierce fire-nature" (Boehme, 1624a: 12.4). "The coherence and solidity [*die Zusammenziehung und Haltung*] of a body consists in the austerity [of the bitter quality]" (Boehme, 1612: 13.57).

30 Cf. (Schelling, 1809: 237).

31 "There is an eternal contrariety between darkness and light; neither of them comprehendeth the other, and neither of them is the other; and yet there is only one essence, being or substance, wherein they both subsist. But there is a difference in quality and will; yet the essence or substance is not divided, but a principle maketh the division. So that the one is a nothing in the other, and yet it is there, but not manifest in the property of that thing wherein it is" (Boehme, 1624b: 2.10). Cf. Schelling (1815: 18).

32 See Fuhrmans (1964: 155).

33 Boehme's third principle does not map precisely onto the third moment in Hegel's logic. For Hegel, the resolution of the opposites happens in the third moment; for Boehme, the resolution already occurs in the second moment.

34 See Jung (CW 11: 243–285).

35 Aquinas, I *Sent.*, d. 23, q. 1, a. 4. See also Augustine, *De Trin.*, VII, 6, 11.

36 This would be one of the decisive places where Boehme contradicts the Patristic and orthodox Trinitarian tradition. For Boehme, the word, or second principle, perfects the divine. What is expressed by the first principle is partial, one-sided and calls forth this correction. For the orthodox Trinitarian tradition, the second person of the Trinity does not add something that is lacking to the first person. The Father does not need the Son in order to be complete. See Thomas Aquinas, *Super evangelium Joannis*, Chapter 1, lectio 1: "But the Word is not said to be with God (*apud Deum*) as though the Father were perfected by the Word and enlightened by it. Rather [the Word] is with God in such a way that it [he] receives the divine nature from the one who speaks the Word, from whom he has it that he is one and the same God with him (*a quo habet quod sit idem Deus cum eo*)." Cited and translated by Robert Sokowlowski (2008: 290). One could argue that Boehme is not speaking of the Father and the Son when he speaks of the counterbalancing and complementary vectors of desire in the first and second principles. But there is plenty of evidence to show that this is precisely how Boehme understands the Trinity, as though one of the persons makes up for what is wanting in the other.

37 On this point see Betanzos (1998: 91ff.).

38 See Baader (BSW 3: 266).

39 See Franz von Baader, "Über das Pythagoräische Quadrat in der Natur oder die vier Weltgegenden" (Baader, BSW 3: 247–268); Grassl (1993); Friesen (2008).

40 Different and conflicting accounts of these seven properties appear in Boehme's writings, so a definitive list is not possible. I follow Oetinger's list as given in Großmann (1979: 311).

41 Boehme seems to have reduced the ten *Sephiroth* to seven, two triads and a mediator. The relation of the seven qualities to the unground is the same as the relation of the ten *Sephiroth* to *Ein-Sof*. In both economies, they express and reveal the divine while personifying unique attributes of divinity. These personifications of divine attributes or "spirits" then become templates for natural properties. "From this eternal Nature the visible world also sprang and was created, as a representation of what is inward" (*ein Gegenwurf der Inwendigkeit* (Boehme, 1624a: 3.20)).

42 "Now of all God's princes, Lucifer had the most beautiful and powerful body in heaven, and the light that he had always born in his body was one with the heart or son of God. As he saw, however, that he was beautiful, and felt his inner birth and his great force, so did the spirit that he bore in his body, his animal (psychic) spirit, son or heart, displace itself, so as to wilfully triumph over the divine birth, and elevate itself over the heart of God" (Boehme, 1612: 13.31–32; translation mine).

43 See Koslowski (2001: 209).

44 Hegel, by contrast, remains generally gnostic on creation, closely associating finite being with evil: creation for Hegel is the negation of universal being necessary if the latter is to emerge from abstract substantiality to subjective life: only if being dies to the empty universality of the creator prior to creation and enters into particularity will it pass from the abstract and unsustainable position of being-in-itself to the ontologically richer position of being-for-itself. Just as finitude is an essential moment in the dialectic of being, so is evil necessary to the dialectic of goodness. See Hegel's 1817 *Enzyklopädie* (Hegel, 1989, vol. 13, §468). See also the 1827 *Lectures on the Philosophy of Religion* (Hegel, 1988: 432–452).

45 See for example Boehme (1623a: 1.25).

46  *O certe necessárium Adæ peccátum, quod Christi morte delétum est! O felix culpa, quæ talem ac tantum méruit habére Redemptórem!* ("Oh happy fault, Oh necessary sin of Adam, which won for us so great a redeemer"). *Missale Romanum*, 1970.

47  On this question, Hegel, Schelling, and Baader each have different answers. For Hegel, evil is a necessary moment in the unfolding of the absolute. For Schelling, actual evil is contingent and anarchic and not-necessary to God's self-revelation, but God uses it to reveal himself. For Baader, evil occludes rather than accomplishes the revelation of God. On these alternative receptions of Boehme, see McGrath (2006).

48  "He [Lucifer] wished with the No to rule over the Yes, for the No had elevated itself in him and despised the Yes. Because power of separation and form lay in the No, the creaturely will desired to rule in the No, as in the source of transmutation, and broke itself off from the unity of God and went into the receptivity of the properties" (Boehme, 1624a: 7.6).

49  Cf. Schelling (1809: 250): "For all evil strives to return to chaos, i.e., to that state in which the initial centre was not yet subordinated to light."

50  "And forthwith properties were manifested in him, namely, cold fire; also sharpness, sourness, hardness, the bitterness, stingingness, hostility, anxiety and painfulness of fire. Hence he became an enemy of all love, humility and meekness; for the foundation of the wrath of God had taken captive the false will" (Boehme, 1624a: 7.7).

51  "When something or someone falls out of the conspiracy, they become inflamed with sickness and fever, as 'inflamed by an inner heat'" (Wirth, 2003: 2).

52  See Boehme (1623b: 1.6–7). On the role of Sophia in Boehme, see O'Regan (2002: 33).

53  "This unfathomable, incomprehensible, unnatural and uncreaturely will, which is one only and has nothing before it nor after it; which in itself is but a one, which is as nothing and yet is everything, – this will is called and is the one God, which seizes and finds himself in himself, and begets God from God . . . . He wills in himself nothing more than just to seize and find himself, go out from himself, and with the outgoing bring himself into an intuition; by which is understood the triad of the Deity together with the mirror of his wisdom of his seeing" (Boehme, 1623a: 1.4).

54  The agonic mediation of God is the revelation of himself achieved through creation; but it is preceded by a non-agonic (i.e., non-temporal) mediation of God to himself in eternity. I owe this distinction to O'Regan (2002).

55  See Dufour (1998).

56  Subjectivity necessarily denaturalizes itself in Lacan's mirror stage. The pre-subjective mind of the infant seeks release from the chaos of its uncoordinated body by disidentifying with its lived experience and learning to identify with the unified and defined body revealed to it in the mirror. Mommy and Daddy help it along by pointing at the reflection and chirping brightly, "It's you!" This misidentification marks the child's entrance into consciousness, first into "the imaginal," which is for Lacan the base stratum of consciousness upon which the full network of the symbolic order rests, and later into "the symbolic," the world of meaning substituted for "the real." The child's identification with the coherent image of itself in the mirror is a repression of the lived experience of its own body. Repression is thus the condition of the possibility of subjectivity – repression not only of basic sensations, but of anything that challenges or threatens the ideality around which the psyche must consolidate its virtual identity. The child, liberated by the mirror from the coil of appetites and drives

that compose its awkward and disobedient body, is henceforth an "I," an "immaterial subject" able to author its actions and enjoy an interior life about which it can then communicate to other subjects. See Lacan (1966: 93–100).

57 "For [Boehme] to *be* means to realize one's potentialities actively, dynamically, and realization means manifestation, uncovering one's essential nature and deploying all inherent possibilities. The perfect being is the one in whom this self-realization is most complete. Essential nature becomes conscious of itself within us in order to be revealed. Being as personal is thus the highest form of being because it achieves self-realization and self-revelation. Only by defining itself and manifesting itself is self-realization and self-revelation fully achieved." (Koyré, 1929, cited and translated in Waterfield, 2001: 36).

58 Cf. Schelling (1815: 57).

59 "Since nature cannot find the potency that helps it and transfigures it into something higher, it must burgeon into a malformed life because the drive toward progression does not cease and because nature can neither abide nor go beyond itself" (Schelling, 1815: 43).

# Chapter 3

# The night-side of nature

## The early Schellingian unconscious

Nature's highest goal, to become wholly an object to herself, is achieved only through the last and highest order of reflection, which is none other than man.

(Schelling, 1800: 6)

Within nature there was something nameless and frightful; something toward which, with a dreadful desire, she sometimes felt drawn and sometimes repelled.

(Schelling, 1810b: 21)

In stark juxtaposition, the two citations above display an ambiguity that divides Schelling's early and later approaches to nature. Insofar as nature is the code-word for the Schellingian unconscious, the ambiguity runs through his notion of the unconscious. The early Schellingian unconscious, developed in the nature-philosophy and the identity-philosophy, is impersonal and immanent. It is not yet the dark side of God unveiled in the *Freedom* essay, not the underside of the personality of the *Stuttgart Seminars*, not the doorway into the spirit-world of *Clara*; rather, the early Schellingian unconscious is the collective intelligence running through all of matter, and insofar as we too are material, running through us as well. It is the spirit in nature, or better, the spirit of nature, nature spiritualized and given subjectivity, but of an impersonal quality, like the subjectivity of a plant or an irrational animal. In the Boehme-influenced middle works, beginning with the 1809 *Freedom* essay, Schelling's thought takes a decisive turn towards transcendence, and at the same time, towards the personal. The early notion of nature as the dynamic polarized matrix of being is not abandoned but qualified. For the later Schelling, nature is no longer the one and the all, rather, de-centred from the place of prominence once granted it, nature becomes the dark ground of spirit, its whole *raison d'être* focused in its precarious teleologico-volitional subordination to the personal. In the 1810 unfinished dialogue, *Clara*, a text strongly marked by the middle

Schelling's turn to transcendence, nature is characterized as a fallen order which fills us with equal parts wonder and horror, the monstrous product of the failure of the dark ground to adequately found spirit. The split in nature, its antagonism to its own truth, cuts through the self: the Schellingian personality is divided against itself. The dark ground is not the self-equilibrating cosmos of the nature-philosophy but the unruly, dangerous, even sick underbelly of being, as likely to drive us mad as to launch us into a personal relationship with God.

Schelling always insisted on the continuity of his early and later philosophy; we can only conclude that the ambiguity noted above is not simply a matter of a change in view but rather of a long developing insight into a real ambiguity in nature, and by extension, in the unconscious. Nature, Schelling tells us, is both home and horror, both cosmos and catastrophe, and any theory which would emphasize one side of the antithesis over the other is *ipso facto* inadequate to the phenomenon.

## Schelling between Fichte and the early romantics

The romantics had a love-hate relation with Fichte: they loved his subordination of theory to praxis and, above all, his suggestion that the self does not coincide with finite self-consciousness but is rather rooted in an unconscious and infinite act of self-positing; they hated his utilitarian approach to nature and his Enlightenment agenda of totalizing reason. Schelling spoke directly to these concerns.

To the first point, once the I is no longer merely a mirror of the external world nor simply a synthesizer of sense data but a producer of reality, thriving in conflict, setting up resistance so that it might have something to strive against and overcoming opposition with its endlessly productive energy, a path opens to the reconsideration of all areas of philosophy, from logic to aesthetics. The Fichtian self posits itself by positing a not-self and finding itself in it; the product of this act is consciousness, but the positing itself is unconscious. The unconsciousness of the ground of the self remains for the most part unthought by Fichte, and it is here, on the dark side of Fichte, that Schelling, Novalis and Hölderlin find their point of departure for the exploration of the irrational, the mysterious, the world of feeling, intuition, and dream.

To the second point, Fichte's reductionist and instrumentalist view of nature is intolerable to early romanticism. For Schelling, nature cannot be reduced to a mere "not-I" required for the self-mediation of the ego; its inexhaustible productivity mirrors the infinity of the absolute I. Untameable and autonomous, nature is serene and deadly, gentle and violent, mercilessly tearing down what is and perpetually producing the new. Returning to Spinoza's substance metaphysics, the early romantics (the Schlegel brothers, Novalis, the early Schelling, Schleiermacher) see nature not merely as product (*natura naturata*) but also as producer (*natura naturans*), restlessly generating new forms, none of which satisfy an apparently infinite need for self-expression. All natural forms are provisional mediums of the inner infinity of an eternal life, which never rests in the creation of any one form but endlessly overpasses what it has produced by producing something new. The early romantics understand self-transcendence to be the essence of life and the soul of man to be a restless striving for self-differentiation. Everywhere the romantic turns he finds himself engulfed by infinity — and nothing could be more to his liking.

Schelling, appointed in 1798 at the age of 23 to the University of Jena, quickly rose to prominence as, if not the ringleader of the Jena romantics, their philosophical spokesman, and soon thereafter, as the foremost thinker in post-Kantian German philosophy. Treatise after treatise flowed from his pen as though he was himself the incarnation of Fichte's infinitely productive I. After a brief honeymoon, in which Fichte assumed that Schelling would be his disciple, Schelling began to construct a new kind of realism from within transcendental idealism (which he had mastered by the time he was 23).[1] For Schelling, Fichte's invaluable breakthrough to the unconscious is mitigated by his lack of insight into the independence, the power, and the spiritual dynamism of nature. The outcome of Fichte's *Science of Knowledge* is an all too familiar narrative of man as master of nature, albeit with a transcendental twist: where Enlightenment man confronts an intelligible order not of his making, Fichtian man is the giver of sense to nature, the source of the meaning and coherence of a material world that needs to be wholly alien to spirit (not-I) in order that spirit can realize itself as the infinite activity of overcoming opposition.

Schelling's relationship to the Jena circle, and to literary romanticism in general, was ambivalent from the beginning. Sharing their enthusiasm for emancipated individuality (the French Revolution) and, its mirror, an infinitely productive and unfathomable material nature, Schelling parted company from the Schlegel brothers and Novalis on the subject of religion. The Jena circle was passionate about mysticism and non-institutional spirituality, receiving Schleiermacher as their prophet and priest. Schelling was at best sceptical about romantic spirituality, at worst, he mocked it. The early Schelling is a philosopher of immanence with little taste for the mystical transcendentalism of, say, Novalis. Schelling's 1799 satirical poem, "Epikurisch Glaubensbekenntnis Heinz Widerporstens," expresses the irreligious and resolutely materialist quality of his nature-philosophy. But even where they most agreed, on the subject of nature, Schelling's approach was quite different from that of the Jena romantics. As Gulyga puts it, while the Jena romantics longed to be mystically united to nature, Schelling tried to understand it (Gulyga, 1989: 108). Nevertheless, Schelling was granted full admittance into the circle and eventually stole the heart of its darling, Caroline Schlegel.

Schelling's first independent move as a young philosopher is to correct Fichte's reduction of nature to a mere screen upon which the ego comes to know itself, and to make a case both for the spirituality of nature and for its irreducibility to consciousness. This is the theme of his first treatise in nature-philosophy, the 1797 *Ideas on a Philosophy of Nature* (SSW 2: 75–343). The work was soon followed by a short introduction to nature-philosophy (Schelling, 1797), and two further major treatises, *On the World Soul* (Schelling, 1798), which caught the attention of Goethe, and *First Outline of a System of the Philosophy of Nature* (Schelling, 1799a). In the latter two works, nature is described as a dynamic self-evolving system, an organic whole internally directed to self-manifestation, which it achieves when self-consciousness emerges. The development of nature is fuelled by the tension between polar forces, the endless conflict between centripetal and centrifugal tendencies, contractive and expansive forces, repulsion and attraction. The duality of forces explains both the infinity of nature's activity and the generation of an infinity of finite products. The expansive force of nature is only sustainable insofar as it is checked by an opposing contractive force; the former is the source of the energy and mobility of nature, the latter, the source of the subsistence and concrete particularity of natural entities. What Fichte says of the I – that it is nothing other than its own activity – Schelling says of nature.[2] The early Schellingian notion of nature must not be confused with the sensible order. Sensible forms are only the surface show, the finished product, *natura naturata*. Nature itself (*natura naturans*) is invisible and hidden from empirical view. It is not a thing and cannot be known as a thing. Schelling introduces something like an ontological difference between nature and natural things: nature never appears as a thing, but it never exists without things, which simultaneously reveal and hide it. What is needed is a specifically transcendental approach that will intuit the hidden structure that makes both forms of nature and forms of consciousness possible.

Beiser distinguishes three phases of Schelling's early nature-philosophy. It begins with a Fichtian phase, in which transcendental philosophy retains the primacy over all other areas of philosophy: nature, as spirit's posited other, is understood in terms of a priori organizational patterns implicit in subjectivity. Very soon thereafter Schelling enters a post-Fichtian phase, culminating in the *First Outline of a System of the Philosophy of Nature*, in which nature is no longer explicated through spirit but is thematized on its own terms. More than merely a concrete externalization of subjective principles, nature is a parallel revelation of the absolute. The parallelism of transcendental philosophy and nature-philosophy finally gives way to an anti-Fichtian phase, culminating in the monism of the identity-philosophy: nature is configured as the absolute itself, not only the hidden ground of the external world but the ground of spirit as well, in no way reducible to transcendental fore-structure or dependent on human subjectivity (Beiser,

2002: 483). In a reversal of the position taken in the 1797 *Ideas*, transcendental philosophy is subordinated to nature-philosophy in the 1799 *First Outline*, which breaks up Kantian subjectivism by emphatically affirming an intelligible universe the structure of which subsists independently of consciousness and categorical perception.[3]

## Divided desire and infinite productivity

Despite the progressive turn away from transcendental philosophy, Schelling never abandons the transcendental method vouchsafed to consciousness by virtue of its capacity to self-reflect. Reflection may be ultimately inadequate to grasping the absolute but it remains the principal tool of philosophy. Philosophy must use it until it can no longer proceed and reflection itself begins to reveal its own limits. Spinoza's lack of a transcendental method causes him intractable problems. He grasps the ideal only in contradistinction to the real; both are merely given for Spinoza without any clear sense of why they are given, that is, of why the ideal–real opposition exists in the first place. In Schelling's view, Spinoza's crucial insight into the correlativity of the ideal and the real should have led him into "the depths of his self-consciousness." Instead Spinoza literally loses himself in the object (Schelling, 1797: 186–187). Even in the 1799 *First Outline*, where Schelling attempts to explain everything on the basis of natural laws alone, transcendental method remains central: Schellingian natural laws are not empirically deduced; rather, as self-explanatory principles, they can only be transcendentally deduced. "What we call reason is a play of necessary, unknown natural forces that are higher than us," Schelling writes, but this never becomes a licence for him to abandon transcendental method (Schelling, 1799a: 31). It is precisely because reason is a play of the unknown natural forces responsible for everything that it has access to them.

Schelling's transcendental deduction of natural laws proceeds on the assumption that the subjectivity that intuits their necessity is equally their product.[4] When we no longer assume a mind–matter dichotomy but rather assume that mind and matter are two sides of one preconscious reality, the a priori ceases to be purely reflective of subjective conceptualizations and mind-dependent patterns of organization. Fichte had shown that if one takes away the ghost of a thing-in-itself which forever relativizes a priori judgements, the categories of reason become categories of being. Schelling's and Hegel's "objective idealism" is founded upon this move. But where Hegel hitches the Fichtian revolution to a rationalist trajectory, Schelling sees in it the undermining of every rationalism: no longer a secure possession of the self-reflecting subject, the a priori is the ground that always recedes from the reflective gaze; instead of serving as the transparent logical pre-structure of the Cartesian "I think," the a priori coincides with the unconscious, or at least that part of it that can be indirectly deduced. Material nature now tells us as much about the structure of the subject as the structure of the subject tells us about nature. The theory of infinite drive manifesting itself in natural polarities is not a scientific hypothesis based on empirical facts, but a metaphysical hypothesis based on transcendental facts.[5]

Schelling's application of transcendental method to nature-philosophy is worth dwelling upon because it underscores the role of psychological introspection in Schellingian nature-philosophy, indeed the origin of the latter in the former. Without introspection nature-philosophy is scarcely possible:

> The positive force first awakens the negative. Therefore in the whole of nature no one of these forces appears without the other. . . . In our experience there are as many singular things (likewise particular domains of force) as there are different degrees of negative reaction. The common attribute of everything earthly is this, that it is opposed to the positive principle that streams from the sun. In this primordial antithesis lies the seed of a universal world-organization. This antithesis is merely postulated by the doctrine of nature. It is not capable of empirical but only of a transcendental deduction. *Its origin is to be sought in the primordial duality of our spirit.*
>
> (Schelling, 1798: 91, italics mine)

It is not that we understand nature on the *analogy* of transcendental patterns of consciousness, or vice versa; it is rather that the dynamic of production through polarity, which is empirically and externally experienced in natural processes, is transcendentally and internally experienced in consciousness. Where early psychoanalysis *hypothesizes* the laws of psychic energy on the analogy of physical energy, Schelling assumes the non-difference of psychic and physical energy: what we deduce about mind through introspective or transcendental methods holds true for matter because only the identity of mind and matter can explain both. The dynamic play of polarities, which is the secret of natural productivity, is hidden from both empirical cognition and reflection, but the hidden side of nature is also the hidden side of the subject. Subjective idealism mistakes the *ratio cognoscendi* of nature-philosophy for a *ratio essendi*: because the subjective idealist understands himself and nature through consciousness, he mistakenly assumes that consciousness is the foundation of reality.[6] When mind and matter are quantitative differentiations grounded in a third term, access no longer indicates a founding relationship.[7]

Allied to Schelling's transcendental restoration of the non-subjective intelligibility of nature is his ontological extension of Kant's notion of teleology. The teleological structure of nature in Kantian philosophy is merely regulative, not constitutive; nature appears teleological because only thus can the mind understand it. Nature in itself should not be assumed to be teleological, purposive and designed. While on first glance this sounds like sensible scepticism, what troubles Schelling is how Kant denies the existence of the organism as such, for the *telos* that makes the organism an organic whole is assumed by Kant to be merely a regulative idea, i.e., a subjective imposition on sense data. In short, there is no genuine life outside the human experience of it, or at least none that we can know. The experience of life as such, self-organized being, every part of it teleologically oriented to the whole of which it is a part, and every whole in turn oriented to nature itself as part to whole, cannot, in Schelling's view, be explained by Kantian subjectivism. The organism cannot be reduced to the sum of its parts because it is only the life of the whole which explains the existence of the parts. The parts cannot be simply efficient causes of the whole, for were they not guided to a single end, the organism would never have come to be. The notion of the organic whole is a conceptual structure, and as such, ideal – this much of Kant Schelling agrees with – but subjectivity experiences this structure as given in matter, it does not impose it upon it. A flower, a tree, or a bird, reveal themselves to us as life unfolding out of itself, life living on its own terms, in no way merely the effects of a subjective synthesis of sense data. As Schelling puts it in a trenchant phrase, "It organizes itself" (Schelling, 1797: 190). We experience *telos* in nature because we must think teleologically about nature, but teleology is not only regulative, it is also constitutive. The mystery resides in the fact that teleological form is not arbitrary, imposed, or merely projected: it manifests itself in our thinking because nature actually is so designed.[8]

This notion of constitutive teleology allows Schelling to expand Kant's nature-philosophy into what Grant describes as "a properly dynamic, field-theoretical theory of nature" (Grant, 2010: 65). Every finite organism is related to every other upon which it to some degree depends such that nature itself must be regarded as a self-enclosed whole, an organism in its own right, a being which is the cause and effect of itself. Such organization is not explicable physically or mechanistically; only the hypothesis of a single principle of life explains it (Schelling, 1798: 68–69). We are to overcome the mechanist–vitalist dichotomy and the related separation of the inorganic from the organic by understanding the universe itself as a living whole, an unconscious subject which intends the anorganic as the condition of the possibility of the organic. The visible divisions of being into anorganic and organic, mineral, vegetable, animal, nature and spirit, are surface divisions of a single life. The species of minerals, plants and animals are so many different degrees of the organization and development made possible by the interplay of the a priori coordinated dualism of positive and negative force, attraction and repulsion, expansion and contraction. Nature is a hierarchically organized living whole, beginning with the lowest and

simplest forms and rising through increasingly complex levels of organization until it reaches self-consciousness, each higher level presupposing and
depending upon the lower. The difference between mind and body is one of
degree, not kind: spirit is the highest degree of organization of forces active
in matter; matter is the lowest degree of organization of forces active in
spirit. The decisive question becomes: what is the organizing principle
behind the dual forces of nature? The answer Schelling proposes underscores the unity of nature-philosophy with both the transcendental philosophy that preceded it and the philosophy of freedom that succeeded it: the
principle is self-manifestation. Nature is driven to reveal itself, a goal it can
only fully achieve if it gives rise to self-consciousness.

Nature in itself is a primordial unconditioned unity which divides itself
into opposing forces in order to become manifest. One force is expansive
and directed outward to infinity, the other is contractive and directed
inward to a single point. The opposed forces collaborate in striving to bring
about a return to the original unity and, at the same time, in blocking that
return by producing finite beings. The end result is endless manifestation
and concealment, ceaseless activity, which consists in tension (blockage of
flow) and release (freeing of flow). Nature is never more active than in this
self-opposition between production and product, flows and forms. Just as
the Fichtian subject posits the object as the resistance point it needs in order
to actualize itself as an act of infinite striving, nature posits itself by setting
up an infinity of points of resistance, productivity congealed into products,
which it then continually destroys. The infinite activity of nature manifests
itself to the degree that it is "inhibited" by individuals: the expansive power
of *natura naturans* is infinitely countered by the contractive power of *natura
naturata*. An endlessly expansive force can only sustain itself by limiting or
inhibiting itself. "Where there is no unity of form, there is also no real
opposition, and where there is no real opposition, there is no productive
power" (Schelling, 1798: 225). The duality of expansive and contractive
drives pushes nature forward into ever new productivity, just as the
expansion and contraction of the heart muscle keeps the blood flowing
through the body. The flow asserts itself against the obstructing products
by sacrificing each individual to the species and generating an infinity of
new products.[9]

The positive force in nature is a collective power distributed throughout
the universe, attracting matter to matter and impelling individual beings
towards self-transcendence. It is in a certain sense external to the organism,
agitating it into extroverted appetitive activity and meeting resistance in a
negative force internal to the organism. The latter preserves the individuality of the organism.[10] The negative force is not another form of
object-oriented desire. It does not have an object as such; it is rather the
negation of the positive force, which it presumes, the resistance to
attraction and the forward movement of life. The positive and the negative

forces are mysteriously coordinated: the positive self-transcending force is held in check by the negative self-withdrawing force such that living beings develop definite boundaries and individuate. But the negative self-withdrawing force, which strives towards equilibrium, is continually frustrated as the organism is, despite itself, enticed into appetitive activity. The coordination of these two opposed forces indicates the single principle operative in both them, present everywhere but never determined or individuated. The unifying principle of nature is not a force, for a force cannot exist without an opposing force, and the principle is not one of a pair of opposites but the common ground of all opposites. It is, Schelling says, in a somewhat sudden exposure of his esoteric proclivities, that which ancient philosophy called "the world soul" (Schelling 1798: 67).

Of most interest to the history of dynamic psychology is the language Schelling employs to describe this animating principle behind all natural polarity: he calls it "drive" (*Triebe*), or more precisely "developmental-drive" (*Bildungstrieb*) (Schelling, 1798: 216–217), later "infinite drive" (*unendliche Trieb*) (Schelling, 1799a: 47). The soul of the world is a drive to self-manifest which is universally distributed in nature. It presupposes a material upon which it works even if it itself is not bound to any particular matter. It is not a determinate drive, not sex drive, nor is it associated with any other qualitative determination; it is, Schelling adds, a *qualitas occulta* (Schelling, 1798: 219).[11] The developmental drive directs the traffic of nature, subordinating the individuation of matter, without which it could not live, to the higher end of life itself. "The restless universal drive" (*der rastlose Umtrieb*) is the cause of the movement of life, first out of itself, and then back on itself, a circular movement in which it is impossible to determine what is earlier and what later: the rotation of processes – which will return as the three potencies in *Ages of the World* – makes of every organism a closed system in which everything happens at once, and which mechanism is helpless to explain because there is no order of causality here, no before and after (Schelling, 1798: 237). The drive is not blind but intelligent in an unconscious way (Schelling, 1798: 253). It must be ubiquitous, even though it is only effective where it finds a determinate receptivity. It must be formless since it can take on any form. It is identical with the innermost essence of the living being, "an ever active drive of internal feeling" (Schelling, 1798: 255), and, at the same time, "the common soul of nature" (*die gemeinschaftliche Seele der Natur*) (Schelling, 1798: 257).

The drive keeps nature itself alive by engendering a basic instability of forces: nature cannot rest either in the single product or in plurality and diversity, but must *endlessly* seek to return to unity, which means it must also endlessly disrupt that unity by pluralizing. The conflict between the two forces is a disequilibrium which the organism naturally tries to overcome, but the achievement of equilibrium would represent the end of life. Everything finite resists change and development to some degree and organizes itself around a static centre, a knot of inert identity; at the same time it harbours within it an impulse toward infinite development that impels it out of itself in the direction of endless self-differentiation. If these opposed tendencies were equal, they would cancel each other out; therefore, disequilibrium must be built into the equation. Life is disequilibrium, not balance. "The immediate goal of nature . . . is the process itself, nothing other than the constant disturbance and restoration of the equilibrium of the negative principle in the body: what develops out of this process [the individual animal] is accidental to the process" (Schelling, 1798: 203).

The highest expression of material nature is the animal: here alone does life in the proper sense – that which moves from within – appear. The universal force of attraction animates the animal within a coordinated system of living beings; the negative force individuates it, enclosing life within a certain configuration of determinate matter. Life itself disturbs the animal, drives it outside of itself in actions of reproduction and nutrition, continually upsetting the animal's internal balance, which the animal pursues in everything it does, but which, if it were to definitively achieve it, would bring about its death. The aim of the animal's life is individuation, which is reached, Schelling adds, in sexuation (Schelling, 1798: 222). The division into sexes is the "last stage of individuation," "the one and the same homogeneous principles externalizing into two opposed principles," and in effect repeating the condition of the animal's genesis, the antagonism of opposites (Schelling, 1798: 224). After the division, the equilibrium is restored via the production of the offspring. Sexuation serves a double purpose of life and death: it is the means of inhibiting *natura naturans* (through the production of *natura naturata*), but also serves the end of freeing the flow and destroying *natura naturata*, for the result of sex is not the self-preservation of the propagating individual but the propagation of the species, not the survival of the reproducing organisms but their sacrifice and overcoming. Despite its resistance to diversity, each thing enacts the pattern of infinite production by tirelessly seeking to reproduce itself.[12] At the moment of its most profound individuation in sexuation, the animal begins to dissolve again back into the universal – it births its own replacement.[13]

Isn't Schelling saying the same thing that Freud will say a century later, that the goal of life is death? Hasn't Schelling broken through to the death-drive with his notion of a negative force that resists the positive force, with the result that the individual organism wills in effect its own death?[14] Passages such as the following seem to suggest this Freudian reading: "The same forces which have for a time maintained life finally destroy it too" (Schelling, 1799a: 68).

The activity of life is the cause of its own dissolution. It is extinguished as soon as it begins to become independent of external nature, i.e.,

unreceptive to external stimulus, and so life itself is only the bridge
to death.

(Schelling, 1799a: 69)

But on closer reading there is no true analogy with Freud. First of all, for
Schelling, it is the erotic principle, distributed throughout a living cosmos
(as opposed to being concentrated in an atomistic ego, as in Freud), which
if unchecked by the negative force, the *principium individuationis*, the No of
the individual to endless exteriority, would bring about the total death
of nature.

It indeed sounds paradoxical, but is no less true, that through the
influences which are contrary to life, life is sustained. – Life is nothing
other than a productivity held back from the absolute transition into a
product. The absolute transition into product is death. That which
interrupts productivity, therefore, sustains life.

(Schelling, 1799a: 62)

The negative force is not a resistance to life but a will to individuation, a
will to concrete, determinate existence, which, by blocking the ecstatic flow
of *natura naturans*, congeals *eros* into a finite being and prevents it from
totally emptying itself into *natura naturata*. For Schelling, curiously, it is
the positive force which appears to intend death for its aim is to return to
the original unity of the absolute. The negative force prevents the return by
blockage and individuation of a finite centre of force. The *reditus* of *natura
naturans* counteracts the will to live of the organic product; it "labors to
destroy" the individual (Schelling, 1799a: 41). But the positive force cannot
be said to aim at death in anything other than a superficial or descriptive
sense, for the drive toward unity never exists alone; it only exists as
endlessly counteracted by the drive toward multiplicity. Both efforts are
coordinated in the overarching *telos* of nature, to become manifest.

   Life, Freud notes, in one of his least original thoughts, is a disturbance of
equilibrium.[15] At the same time that it is externally stimulated into the
activities that constitute life, the organism longs to return to the peace of
the inorganic; it is internally driven to free itself from the tension of erotic
excitation. Freudian *eros* is a natural impulse to differentiate, a will to
exteriority, a world-building drive, opposed by an antithetical drive that
aims at the restoration of a primitive stage of inorganic equilibrium.[16]
Freudian *eros* is fundamentally egocentric object-oriented energy rooted in
the ego; while it impels separate parts of living matter to one another and
holds them together, it is hardly a universally distributed energy that animates all of nature, as is Schelling's positive force.[17] The difference is
decisive for it marks the exact place where Freud departs from organicism,

asserting instead the arbitrary and ultimately tragic nature of individual life. The Freudian death-drive is not a principle of individuation, as is Schelling's negative force; it is rather a reactive entropic drive that compels the arbitrarily existing organism to retreat from the horror of life and return to the more primitive state of matter out of which it inexplicably emerged. Freud effectively brackets teleology and abolishes organicism, refusing to see the dual drives as anything other than reactions of matter to the accident of life.[18] The consequence of Freud's concentration of *eros* in the ego is that the human being no longer belongs to a greater whole, but is ultimately an absurd eruption of self-reflective and self-interested life in a mindless universe.

Schelling, like Boehme and Oetinger (among countless other organicists), insists on the place of the individual organism in the world-whole and the positive and productive role of the negative individuating force in the drama of life. For Schelling, the "reservoir" of *eros* is not the ego but the universe itself. The negative force is not an anti-life-drive but a finitizing drive which contracts universal *eros* into the individual so that life itself might be sustainable, might be lived by *someone*, rather than dissipate in an endless exteriority. Schelling's negative force is not narcissistic in the Freudian sense because it does not have the ego as its object, nor is it perverse or undeveloped, primitive or regressive. The Schellingian negative force does not desire death; it rather resists the other for the sake of life.

This axial difference between Freud and Schelling can shed light on the Freud–Jung dispute on the question of libido. For Freud, libido is not a neutral or formless energy; it has a predominant form: sexual. Art and religion are therefore not essentially different expressions of *eros*; they are, rather, necessary substitutes for sex desired without limit. Hence the Freudian analysis of dreams, myths, art, and religion always seeks to uncover the sexual drive that has been disguised and at the same time expressed in the image. The dream is not fully analysed until all of its complex imagery has been unmasked as subtle subterfuges by means of which the psyche satisfies its need to express an essentially simple drive in images acceptable to the dreamer. Thus also are artworks to be interpreted, thus is religion to be interpreted, ultimately civilization itself is to be interpreted as an elaborate substitute for sex, a system of libidinal control, i.e., sublimation/repression. Just as the ego forbids the expression of certain excessive sexual desires by generating an image that seems to be about something else, the dream, but which in essence is formally identical with the sexual desire, so does civilization forbid us our sexual excesses while offering us a substitute in the form of art, philosophy, cuisine, drugs, religion, etc.

For Freud, sexual libido is formally identical to artistic and religious libido: what the artist, the mystic, the philosopher desires is originally sexual. Jung objected to this reductive approach, which seemed to him to exaggerate the significance of the sex drive and underestimate or deny altogether the other forms that psychic energy can take. For Jung, libido has no predominant form; it is not structurally or qualitatively determinate; rather it is a neutral energy that animates the psyche and can take any number of different forms. The difference from Freud does not consist in Jung's claim that libido takes many forms – of course Freud agrees on this point; the difference consists in Jung's claim that these alternative forms of libido are irreducible to each other, the differentiations of libido are to some degree not merely manifest but essential. Artistic, religious, and sexual libido can be irreducible to one another, really different determinations of libido for Jung, because Jungian libido in itself is, to use the Schellingian-ism, indifferent to art, religion, and sex (Jung, CW 8: 3–66). Jung's hypo-thesis of libido as a general, indeterminate *élan vital* is based on precisely the same Neoplatonic logic which we have identified as essential to Schelling's thought: any set of beings that are differentially related must share a common ground which is not identified with any one of them. If any two entities are opposed, then they must be both related and different; that is they must manifest opposed configurations of some common element. For Schelling, nature is oppositionally different from spirit; positive natural force is oppositionally different from negative natural force; object is oppositionally different from subject; an individual entity is, in its indi-viduality, oppositionally different from any other individual entity. There must be some common ground which relates all beings and orders of being while being different from each of them. This common ground is the absolute, which is indifferent to the various forms it takes, that is, it is indifferent to nature, spirit, you, me, etc. This does not mean the absolute is *the same* as (formally or structurally identical to) each of its manifestations. *Indifference is not sameness.* Because the absolute is indifferent to the nature which it grounds, there is no contradiction in it also grounding nature's opposite, spirit. To return to the nature-philosophy, Schelling's negative and positive forces are not different expressions of the same energy, with which both are structurally identical (like Freudian libido), but different forms (determination, potentizations) of one self-identical being, which, in its indeterminacy, is indifferent to both.

Freud's life- and death-drives are not essentially differentiated, but rather only manifestly different, that is, in content different but formally the same. There is nothing wholly other to *eros* expressing itself in death-drive; death-drive is just the diminution of *eros*; *eros* become uninterested, losing steam, entropically bottoming out. Hence there is no need to posit a third term beyond the opposites of life-drive/death-drive, and Freud's libido theory does not lead to metaphysics, as Jung's does. Schelling's opposed natural forces, by contrast, like Jung's various forms of libido, are essentially or formally different, that is, they are wholly different directions of force or will: the positive force wills the one; the negative force wills the many; the two opposed intentions are directed, however, by a deeper *telos:* that spirit should become visible. To return to Jung, cultural forms are formally different manifestations or determinations of libido, which must therefore be understood as in itself formless, indeterminate and indifferent to the many forms it can take. This metaphysics of libido situates Jungian libido theory squarely in the Schellingian trajectory.

Notwithstanding his refusal of teleology, Freud's "speculative biology" is situated squarely in the German philosophical tradition, a point of which Freud seems to have been to some degree aware.[19] There has been much said about the unfortunate translation of *Trieb* in Freud as "instinct" by Strachey. For our purposes, the problem is not that, as Lacan would have it, the translation naturalizes the Freudian drive – Freud's naturalism strikes us as an essential feature of his thought. The problem is that the translation conceals the continuity of Freud's metapsychology with German philosophy. *Trieb* is the centrepiece of the German idealist and post-idealist traditions. Boehme's meaning when he speaks of the *Trieb* which impels the unground to divide itself into opposing directions of will would be entirely obscured if we translated *Trieb* as "instinct." Similarly when the early Schelling speaks of the primordial movement towards self-manifestation which coordinates all natural forces, the world soul, as *Trieb*, he is plainly not speaking of instinct. Schellingian *Trieb* is instinct-like in as much as it is unconscious intention, but it is prior to instinct and more basic than any object-oriented intention; it intends the infinite; it is the will that is responsible for the existence of animals and instincts, the will that is no longer associated with the subjective capacity to choose but which the middle Schelling identifies with primal being (*Ursein*). When one includes Fichte, Schopenhauer and Nietzsche in this heritage, one can say without exaggeration that classical German philosophy (pre-idealist, idealist and post-idealist) is *Triebsmetaphysik*.

The speculative biology of *Beyond the Pleasure Principle* underscores the intimate historical and systematic relationship between nature-philosophy and psychoanalysis. But Freud's is a nature-philosophy without *telos*. The first organisms arose out of the inorganic because of some external event, an accidental cosmic excitation (Freud, 1922: 47–49). They lived for a short time and then returned to their former inorganic state. For no reason at all these primitive organisms were compelled to repeat the conditions of their birth, to recreate the tension of external excitation and the pleasure of release from tension, a compulsion that is countered by the opposite drive, to return to the inorganic. In Schelling, by contrast, we are working in a theologico-metaphysical key: the emergence of the polarity of forces which makes life possible is no accident but the means towards the self-revelation of absolute life.

## Non-duality

Schelling's identity-philosophy – both the culmination and the heir of his nature-philosophy – is a metaphysical elaboration of idealism without a subject, knowledge without consciousness. The project, which occupied Schelling for six of his most productive early years, aims at nothing less than the abolition of the Cartesian ego, the object-intending self-reflective subject ostensibly at the foundation of all human experiences.[20] At the high point of the identity-philosophy, the 1804 Würzburg lectures, Schelling puts it thus:

> In truth, there does not ever nor anywhere exist a subject, a self, or any object or nonself. To say I know or I am knowing already [posits] the *proton pseudon*. I know nothing, or *my* knowledge, to the extent that it is mine, is no longer true knowledge. Not I know, but only totality *knows* in me.
>
> (Schelling, 1804a: 143)

This is strictly speaking monism, which Schelling will later describe as "negative philosophy," i.e., philosophy of essence, philosophy in abstraction from the real. At its foundation is the doctrine of the non-dual absolute. But the entry-point of the identity-philosophy is the notion of intellectual intuition, a term first defined by Kant as knowledge without sensory perception (according to Kant, impossible for a finite subject), re-defined by Fichte as the subject's inalienable transcendental experience of its own activity, and further revised by Schelling as non-dual knowledge, absolute knowledge, knowledge in which neither a subject knowing nor an object known can be distinguished from one another.

Intellectual intuition is one of the more obscure and variously interpreted notions in German Idealism. The tendency in recent literature is to downplay its mystical overtones, to emphasize intellectual intuition as the early Hegel does as an exoteric principle of knowledge, universally distributed among human beings, reason's distinctive act. Schelling sometimes describes intellectual intuition prosaically as the intellect's act of seeing the part in the whole and the whole in the part: reason's grasp of the thing in its concrete universality.[21] In contrast with the discursive understanding, which subsumes particulars under universal categories, intellectual intuition operates independently of the principle of sufficient reason. It does not deduce or explain what it knows by reference to other things: the intelligibility of the known shows itself all at once, as it were. This is, in Heideggerian language, the aletheic moment in the German Idealist theory of knowledge, the contemplative act of seeing the thing in the light of its essence. Beiser wishes to assure us that there is nothing mystical about this (Beiser, 2002: 582). Unfortunately, the matter is not so simple. Intellectual intuition is not a cognitive act of consciousness, not a particular mode of the subject's cognizing an object. Nor is it, as in Kant's conception of the faculty of reason, a synthetic act that knits particular conceptions into a coherent whole, which is a functional prerequisite of all rational activity. In intellectual intuition a subject is no longer distinguishable from its object. There is therefore no act of seeing or cognizing as such: this is not an I enjoying an immediate grasp of the essence of an object, for what the I "sees" in the intuition is that it is identical with its object.

"Intuition" signifies immediacy between knower and known. In a sensible intuition there is no gap between sense organ and sensation: the sense organ sensing *is* its sensation. Just so in intellectual intuition, there is no gap between the intellect and the absolutely intelligible; they are, to use Schelling's preferred term, "indifferent." Intellectual intuition, therefore, could never be reflective; it is not a self-conscious act, not a representation accompanied by "I think." It is not the subject's cognitive "grasp" of the absolute. In intuition, a subject does not stand over and against an object. In any subject–object relation, neither the knowing nor the known are absolute. Intellectual intuition is a non-dual state of knowing, which is just as accurately described as a state of being, the non-objective condition of the possibility of reflectively cognizing an object, and the a priori horizon of identity within which things can show themselves as what they are. Ordinary consciousness only functions by exiling itself from this unity; the reflective I is, to use the Lacanianism, a barred subject, a constitutive lack. Consciousness departs from the non-dual absolute for the sake of knowledge, and thus finds itself always deprived of the final term of all of its intentional acts – the unconditioned – by virtue of a foundational, self-constitutive negation.[22]

In the *System of Transcendental Idealism*, Schelling argues that since the unconditioned is not a thing, the only candidate for what it could be is the self, "that which is intrinsically non-objective" (Schelling, 1800: 27). Here Schelling picks up on Fichte's notion of intellectual intuition as the self's grasp of itself as spontaneous activity. But for Schelling, intellectual intuition is not self-consciousness, not what Descartes defines and Kant and Fichte elaborate as the condition of the possibility of experience. The self is pure act. It only becomes an "object" of knowledge when it catches itself in the act of knowing. The object known is in intellectual intuition the subject knowing, or "a knowing that is simultaneously a producing of its object" (Schelling, 1800: 27). Since the subject only *is* insofar as it acts, and since its act is to know itself, the self itself is "a permanent intellectual intuition" (Schelling, 1800: 28). But the intellectual intuition is in no way subjective or purely introspective: the essences of things are co-known in the act of the subject knowing itself. Clearly, this subject is not the ego of self-consciousness; it is identical to the universe, containing within itself the forms of all things. Schelling is making something close to the Vedantic point that Atman (the self), in its original state, is identical with Brahman, the ultimate reality in Hindu metaphysics.[23] But Schelling's approach to non-duality is not Vedantic or in any way informed by non-Western sources (Schelling does not seem to have shared the early romantic passion for the East). Schellingian non-duality is in fact wholly Teutonic in origin, having much in common with Meister Eckhart's claim, "The eye through which I see God is the same eye through which God sees me; my eye and God's eye are one eye, one seeing, one knowing, one love" (Eckhart, 1955: 216). Schelling appropriates into philosophy the mystical thesis at the foundation of German thought, the primordial identity of the activity of the soul with God. Intellectual intuition, however, is not a graced moment of *unio mystica*. It is – Schelling is as emphatic on the point as is the early Hegel – reason's distinctive act, even if common law thinking is continually forgetting it. Is this a domestication of mysticism or a destruction of rationalism? In any event, it is clear that intellectual intuition is never a conscious act. Consciousness presupposes the subject–object duality; it defects and departs from intellectual intuition in order to be. Much as in Lacan's developmental psychology, in which the symbolic order that gives the ego a position in language is attained at the price of the infant's identification with its life, Schelling's theory of consciousness renders the "I think" an achievement of individuation at the expense of being: the "I think" becomes a subject, distinct from the object and other subjects, at the price of the fullness of the intuition, "I am." Michael Vater has it exactly right: "Intellectual intuition is an *unconscious* principle of consciousness" (Vater, 1978: xxiii). It is an absolute knowledge hidden in the subject's unconscious, that undifferentiated unity that consciousness has always already left behind but that continues to make possible everything the ego knows. As such, it is never directly defined or reduced to a reflectively known content. It can, however, be expressed: art is "intellectual intuition become objective" (Schelling, 1800: 229).

The inception of Schelling's philosophy of art is the sixth and final part of the 1800 *System of Transcendental Idealism*, the famous conclusion in which Schelling discusses for the first time the unconscious as a peculiarly human experience of the hiddenness of the mind to itself. He had begun to lecture on the philosophy of art the year before and would intermittently continue to do so for the next two decades. To understand the exalted role art plays in Schelling's early philosophy one must keep the epistemological situation in view. The task left to Schelling by the transcendental philosophies of Kant and Fichte is to think necessity/objectivity as also the product of spiritual activity, as the other side of the self-identical spirit. Both Kant and Fichte vigorously assert the freedom of consciousness, but only by extracting the transcendental subject from all objective context, leaving the subject isolated in a purely internal realm of ideal freedom, and the object, an inassimilable residuum outside of subjectivity, either an unthinkable thing-in-itself in Kant, or a *factum brutum* in Fichte. The early Schelling wishes to build a true system of nature and spirit, and a system requires that all diverse elements be derived from a single principle. If the principle is substance, objectivity, or the "nature" investigated by empirical natural science (the causal network of ironclad necessities), the inevitable result is Spinozism and its transcendentally inadequate denial of the freedom of the subject. But Fichte fares no better, for by making the founding principle the freedom of the self-positing subject he merely carries out a reverse reduction, rendering the other of subjectivity nothing more than the appearance of givenness for the sake of the self-mediation of subjectivity, a result that is every bit as inadequate for Schelling as Spinozism, but inadequate to a different set of facts: where Spinozism violates the facts of moral consciousness, Fichte violates the facts of the natural sciences, especially the biological sciences, the starting point of which is the autonomy and integrity of the mind-independent organism. Schelling's solution to the conundrum is the notion of absolute indifference: the duality of subject and object is underwritten by a non-dual origin, which is neither free, subjective and conscious, nor necessary, objective and non-conscious. The absolute unity of subject and object shows itself in that which is objective in the subject, the inner necessity and unconscious compulsion that guides the subject's decisions and productions, and equally, in that which is subjective in the object, the design and purpose exhibited in nature, which appears to be the product of conscious intelligence, but plainly is not and cannot be. But it is not enough to assert that nature and consciousness are two sides of the absolute; the identity must be *demonstrated*, a demonstration which faces a considerable (for Kant, and, for Fichte, impossible) task of grasping the subject and the object as identical in their primordial origin, or to put it yet more formally, to grasp freedom as necessity and necessity as freedom. To achieve this, the two primordially opposed activities, the free activity of consciousness and the necessary activity of nature, must be experienced by the philosopher as a single phenomenon.[24]

On strictly transcendental grounds this is impossible, for something could only become an object for consciousness by falling outside the subjective activity of consciousness, that is, by being experienced as necessity. The unconscious activity by which objects are generated for consciousness is, according to Kant and Fichte, the unsurpassable limit of consciousness. I grasp an object as given, and the condition by which it appears to me as such is precisely that I oppose it to myself, distinguish its substantial being from the spontaneous self-generative being of consciousness. On the other side, the freedom of the subject could never be experienced as an object, for it has no phenomenality in the causal nexus, it is always and only interior. By calling subjectivity's other "the unconscious," Schelling's work is half done, for by unconscious Schelling does not mean simply without consciousness, wholly other than spirit and subjectivity, but rather, spiritual activity which is not self-aware. Schelling assumes that the alienation of spirit from nature is to some degree mere appearance: everything that is, in whatever mode, is the product of spiritual activity. But the contradiction of subject and object on the phenomenal level remains: if it is experienced as object, it is experienced as necessity not freedom. The contradictory characteristics of spirit could only co-exist in a temporal succession, a succession which is not a simple juxtaposition, but a dramatic manifestation of identity. The manifestation could only occur at the point where one of the opposed activities is caught, as it were, at the moment where it turns into its opposite, a point of time outside of time. The intuition of the identity of subject and object must begin in consciousness and end in the unconscious, the moment where productive activity congeals into product and freedom becomes necessity.

Reflection is barred access to these depths of the absolute yet it finds traces of it everywhere. In the *System of Transcendental Idealism*, Schelling outlines three theatres of unconscious production: nature, history, and art, but it is art alone, the art-product and its peculiar conditions of genesis, which reveals the original unity of subject and object. To be sure, what is coming to manifestation in art is not different from what is at work in nature and history. Schelling's nature-philosophy had already established how visible nature (*natura naturata*) exhibits features typical of rational beings, but without consciousness: design, teleology, purposiveness without a purpose, et cetera. Plants reach toward the sun without conscious deliberation; insects carry out complex operations without reflection; birds "know" how to build their nests without returning to themselves through the "I think" of self-consciousness. Like the shoot reaching through the soil to the sun, nature reaches unconsciously toward consciousness, an end it achieves in man. However, this teleological view of nature is not an intellectual intuition: nature can just as easily be seen as pure external causality, just as the ends of history, the progress assumed to be directing otherwise random events, always remains merely a hypothesis and never becomes an experience. Historical events, which the early Schelling is convinced progressively converge on an ideal of human harmony, are providential acts of deliberating agents, but they can be equally seen as random and absurd. In the art product alone, intellectual intuition becomes concrete. The consciousness of the artist in its unity with the art produced concretizes and externalizes the absolute in a singular fashion: the unity of subject and object at the foundation of all culture and nature.

The convergence of unconscious processes with goal-oriented activity makes art an inverse image of nature: natural entities appear deliberately designed but are unconsciously produced; artworks appear unconsciously produced but are deliberately designed. Art and nature are therefore complementary revelations of the indifference of consciousness and unconsciousness in the absolute. A human being is never more natural or effective than when she acts intelligently but without purpose, for reflection is then no longer permitted to obstruct the creative flow of *natura naturans*. Later Schelling will describe this as a "lively understanding," "a controlled, restrained, and coordinated madness" (*beherrschter, gehaltener, geordneter Wahnsinn*) (Schelling, 1810a: 233). In the *System of Transcendental Idealism*, he calls it simply "genius," the division in the self, the coincidence of conscious and unconscious production, of freedom and necessity, exhibited in the conflicted subjectivity of a great artist. The genius does not know what he is doing and yet he surrenders to the flow of inspiration in a self-forgetfulness conditioned by intense concentration and succeeded by the production of an artwork, which not only transcends the mind of the artist and expresses his time, it transcends the power of any finite inter-pretation. Possessed by art, the artist is like a somnambulist, not in command of her cognitive faculties, and this is precisely what makes her a medium of intuition. The artist is not quite in a trance: her technique is conscious and deliberative, but what she produces exceeds her design, thus the production of the artwork as such is unconscious. The secret to artistic creativity is the artist's generosity to the unconscious: the artist keeps a light hold on the reins of consciousness, and the veil that separates ordinary consciousness from "that unalterable identity, on which all existence is founded," is momentarily lifted (Schelling, 1800: 222).

> Just as the man of destiny does not execute what he wishes or intends, but rather what he is obliged to execute by an inscrutable fate, which governs him, so the artist, however deliberate he may be, seems nonetheless to be governed, in what is truly objective in his creation, by a power which separates him from all other men, and compels him to say or depict things which he does not fully understand himself, and whose meaning is infinite.
>
> (Schelling, 1800: 223)

The subjectivity of the artist is not enough to prove a genius at work – a conflicted mind coupled with artistic ambition is a common enough human trait – the subjectivity of the genius must be corroborated in the produced object, which proves by its intrinsic qualities that it is a work of timeless artistic value. The artwork is inexhaustibly significant, "capable of being expounded *ad infinitum*, as though it contained an infinity of purposes" (Schelling, 1800: 225); it is nothing short of a revelation, a symbol of the identity of universality and particularity, of subject and object, and of consciousness and the unconscious in the absolute.

The relationship of philosophy to art in Schelling is complex, and Schelling's position changes somewhat between the *System of Transcendental Idealism* and the major work of the identity-philosophy, the 1804

Würzburg system (SSW6.71–576). In 1800, Schelling is clear that art achieves something which always eludes philosophy: adequate expression of the intuition of the absolute. It is not as though the artist knows something that the philosopher does not; rather what philosophy "knows" in an inarticulate way, the original unity of subject and object, which is the intellectual intuition at the foundation of all authentic philosophy – and one who lacks it cannot be taught it – the artwork makes manifest in a concretely existing work. Philosophy thus understands the artwork intimately, perhaps better than the artist himself, but philosophy is not art. The philosopher could not do better than the artwork; he cannot systematically and conceptually define what the artwork depicts, and herein lies the decisive difference with Hegel: philosophy is always a less adequate expression of the absolute than the artwork. If the philosopher were to adequately express the intellectual intuition which lies at the basis of all of his reflections, he would have to himself become an artist and produce an artwork.

The *System of Transcendental Idealism* was followed a year later by the *Presentation of my System of Philosophy*, a 100-page treatise published in Schelling's self-edited *Zeitschrift für Spekulative Physik* (SSW 4: 105–212). Here Schelling replies to critics who cannot discern any systematic unity to his various writings that their miscomprehension is due to the originality of his thought. Schelling claims that he has overcome the idealism/realism dichotomy which so trenchantly divides modern philosophy into contesting camps, on the one side, "criticism," on the other, "dogmatism." Fichte's transcendental philosophy is a subjective idealism; the entry point and foundation is the self-reflecting subject. Nature-philosophy, by contrast, is an objective-idealism; its foundation is not reflection but material production. Both transcendental philosophy and nature-philosophy remain one-sided perspectives on a whole that has not yet been adequately expressed in philosophical form. Now Schelling wishes to move beyond all one-sided systems and construct an absolute system of philosophy, one that can contain all opposed starting points, ideal and real, subject and object, by giving priority to none of them – in the *Presentation of my System* he no longer believes philosophy is incapable of expressing intellectual intuition. The absolute system, or the system of the absolute, privileges neither being nor thought: both are grounded in an original identity which is neither thought nor being, the "total indifference of the subjective and the objective" (SSW 4: 116). The indifferent absolute is not the cause of the universe but the universe itself, which has no cause and is no longer to be flattened into an order of causality. The universe is rather the manifestation of a hierarchy of potencies (quantitative differentiations in a univocal order of being), all of which exist simultaneously in the absolute. The mistake of idealism is to have given primacy to one potency (the ideal) and made all others causally dependent upon it. The later Schelling will retain this insight into the logical simultaneity of potencies, tracing time and historical development to a non-logical break with the absolute, a fall or a decision. In 1801, however, time and history itself are denied any real existence.

Schelling's identity-philosophy can be summed up in the following four claims: (1) Only one indivisible being exists, the universe itself; all apparent differences in being (subject–subject, subject–object, object–object) are merely quantitative variations of ontological intensity in the manifest absolute; (2) The universe is identical with reason; the absolute is identical with knowledge of the absolute; (3) The absolute infinitely knows itself by positing itself as subject and object; (4) Time and development are mere appearances; all potencies exist simultaneously and eternally in the absolute.[25]

The duality which was the central theme of nature-philosophy is now traced back to an original identity of all opposites, negative–positive, subject–object. Subject is distinguished from object not on the basis of qualitative differences but on the basis of degrees of identity. If qualitative differences were real, opposition would exist in being, and the absolute would not be self-identical. Since the absolute must be self-identical, differences cannot be qualitative. Subject (the ideal) and object (the real) are not essentially different forms of being; they are rather different degrees of the same being, with subjectivity predominating in one, objectivity in the other. The subject–object difference is essential to the existence of the absolute – it can only be in itself if it posits itself as both subject and object – but the difference is not itself an essential difference. The same being is posited in the one case as subjectivity or mind, in the other case as objectivity or matter.

The 1801 doctrine of identity is illustrated in the following diagram (SSW 4: 137), the early Schelling's complete schema of the absolute:

$$\frac{\overset{+}{A = B} \qquad \overset{+}{A = B}}{A = A}$$

A=A, the absolute in itself, posits itself as A=B with a surplus of A, or subjectivity, on the one side, and as A=B with a surplus of B or objectivity on the other side.

Schelling insists in 1801 that this Neoplatonic monistic system was the philosophical presupposition of his early works on nature-philosophy and transcendental philosophy (SSW 4: 107–108). In his later works, which depart so dramatically from monism, Schelling defends the rationality of the identity-philosophy while just as emphatically insisting on the necessity of going beyond it towards a philosophy of history. But the latter does not substitute another form of metaphysics for identity-philosophy, rather the system unveiled in 1801 remains for Schelling the only sound metaphysics, even if it itself proves to be wholly inadequate to reality. Hegel's alternative, which presumes to absorb history into metaphysics and identifies the absolute with human self-consciousness, is, for Schelling, a confusion of things that must be held apart. We must not mistake Schelling's notion of absolute knowledge with self-consciousness; Schelling's absolute is as much unconscious as it is self-consciousness, or rather it is neither. If the absolute is to be absolutely knowing it must be expressed as the perfect adequacy (identity) of subject and object, or A=A. But such an adequation must distinguish what it identifies; thus the distinction between subject and object, consciousness and unconsciousness, A and B, is one which is posited by the absolute itself. The difference cannot therefore be a difference in essence; but neither is it merely a subjective appearance of difference; it is rather a difference in intensity. What is given in surplus in one potency is deficient in the other and vice versa. Mind is being which lacks objectivity (materiality, determinateness); matter is being which lacks subjectivity (relation to itself). The absolute in itself can ground both because it is indifferent to both; it is as indifferent to matter as it is to mind.

What advance does Schelling make on the notion of the unconscious in the identity-philosophy? Consciousness is disidentified from knowledge and so renders knowledge itself an essentially non-conscious state. If I think *I know* something, say a particular state of affairs, I thereby prove that I know nothing. Because subject–object duality is essential to consciousness, the absolute in itself (knowledge) never emerges into the orbit of consciousness at all. Schelling's argument is alarmingly simple. To know (in a finite sense) means to identify a subject with an object (A is B). How is this identity to be conceived? If it is the identification of the subject with a pre-existing object – if the subject is a passive mirroring of the object, as in naïve realism – then the thing-in-itself rears its ugly head: the object is not known in itself; only its effects on the cognitive faculties of the subject are known. If it is the identification of a subjectively constituted object with the subject, as in subjective idealism, nothing is really known at all. But we can only deny an identification of subject and object at the expense of denying knowledge altogether. Schelling's extraordinary conclusion is that knowledge is not an *identification* of subject and object but their *original and indissoluble identity*. To make any knowledge claim, Schelling concludes, no matter how trivial ("it is raining"), is to implicitly affirm this absolute identity of subject and object.[26]

All of the tortured arguments of empiricism and rationalism, which seek to explain how the subject climbs out of itself and reaches the object, are therefore dead-ends. Reason is not the faculty of an individual subject standing over and against other individuals and peering out at an objective order through the spectacles of the senses. Rather, the subject is merely the organ of the absolute's self-recognition (Schelling, 1804a: 149).

Consciousness, already displaced from the centre by nature-philosophy, is wholly demoted by identity-philosophy: it is now associated with error, illusion, and unreality.[27]

The challenge in interpreting Schelling's identity-philosophy is that it seems so antithetical to the philosophy of freedom that succeeded it. All is one; difference is illusion. There is only one timeless being, and it is the universe. Within the absolute there are no essential distinctions. Schelling's conclusion is as non-dualist as the Hindu Vedanta: metaphysically speaking, particulars do not exist; the experience of multiplicity is the result of a fall from intellectual intuition. Viewed in the light of the works that followed, the identity-philosophy seems to be a sustained *reductio ad absurdum*. The conclusion Schelling draws in *Philosophy and Religion* (written the same year as the Würzburg lectures) is that if there had not been a breach in the absolute, there would be no things, no finite reality, and no philosophers who could search for knowledge of the absolute. Since it is clear that things and philosophers exist, there must have been a breach. In the light of the philosophy of freedom to which it gave rise, the point of the formal metaphysics of the identity-philosophy is to make clear that, (1) time could only be a fall from eternity (as Schelling first argues in *Philosophy and Religion*); (2) consciousness could only be a negation of identity; and (3) God could only reveal himself in the finite by doubling himself, on the one side, disappearing into the ineffable, and on the other side, entering into self-division, contraction, and process. The question that remains open in *Philosophy and Religion* is: why would God allow this break to occur? The answer Schelling first ventures in the 1809 *Freedom* essay: so that the absolute might become a person.

Each of the above three theses made Schelling receptive to the theogony of Jakob Boehme, which he studied carefully in his first Munich period (1806–1809), an experience which has justly been regarded as the key to the personalist turn in Schelling's thought. For in Boehme, as in the Lurianic Kabbalah, the absolute itself does not *enter* into the finite order but absents itself from it, withdraws into inaccessible depths so that the play of multiplicity can occur. To be sure, a stratum of non-duality remains in Boehme's model of God, and in Schelling post-1809: the unground does not enter into the interaction of opposites that makes self-revelation possible, much as in the later Schelling, the Godhead is not one of the three potencies. Boehme's unground generates an "eternal nature" composed of contesting wills – the archetype for all natural polarities – but it is not identical with it. But let us go back to the moment before Schelling's turn. What Schelling carries out in the identity-philosophy is effectively an analytic of the deep unconscious and an argument for why it must be understood as non-dual. In its most profound depths, the Schellingian unconscious is neither personal nor collective, neither spiritual nor natural, neither subject nor object. Schelling's non-dual absolute resonates in crucial ways, backward toward Boehme and

Eckhart and forward toward William James, Henri Bergson, and the later Jung, theories which deny the irreducibility of the subject–object distinction. The unconscious as subject–object identity is the act of absolute knowledge upon which consciousness depends, and which it is continually and inevitably losing. Forgetting the absolute – and this is the link between identity-philosophy and the philosophy of freedom – is the condition of the possibility of being a conscious subject.

## Postscript to nature-philosophy: melancholy, death, and the longing for being

Schelling's most romantic piece of writing, the unfinished dialogue *Clara*, it is assumed to have been written in 1810, shortly after the tragic death of his first wife Caroline, and thus belongs to his middle period.[28] While Schelling's theme is still nature – specifically the forms nature takes after death – the personalist ontology informing the dialogue is founded in Schelling's celebrated *Freedom* essay published the year before. The text expresses the crucial transition in Schelling's thought about nature, the qualification of his early pantheistic optimism by a religious sense for the fallenness of being. *Clara* thus serves as a fitting *Schluss* to his early philosophy – in both senses of the term: a conclusion and a ninety-degree turn. Nature for Schelling in 1810 can no longer be thought merely as self-revealing cosmos, it is also the residue of a spiritual catastrophe, not only home but also horror. Older than being is ground, a dark centre of possibility which longs for existence in itself, but which can only exist as the subordinated foundation of something other than itself, a self-immolation which it continually resists. This primordial contradiction rooted in the personality of God renders the ontology of the middle Schelling dynamic, unresolved, shot through with tension, feeling, and movement. The unfinished manuscript contains some of Schelling's most lyrical remarks on the subject of melancholy (*Schwermuth*) and "the irreducible remainder," the chaos that is older than order and which haunts the sensitive individual with a persistent sense of loss, horror, and longing. Like Heideggerian *Angst*, Schellingian melancholy is a mood with ontological significance; it discloses the historical truth about being: nature is not only potentially infinite, it is also actually fallen. Being endlessly longs for itself, it restlessly reaches for a completeness that appears to forever elude it. Craving (*Begierde*), longing (*Sehnsucht*), and need (*Sucht*) are therefore characteristic features of all that lives.

At this stage in his life, Schelling, already famous for his numerous treatises on nature-philosophy, the philosophy of art, and identity-philosophy, was more than casually involved in what we would now call occult research.[29] He was an avid reader of the growing literature of animal magnetism; he was studying theosophy, especially Boehme's alchemical psychology; he was experimenting with séances and spiritualism with his close friend and Munich colleague, Franz von Baader. None of this was as eccentric in the early nineteenth century as it now sounds. Early psychiatric research suggested that through natural unconscious states (sleep, dream, trance), the individual is liberated from mundane consciousness and, if not returning into the bosom of absolute knowledge, experiencing the relativity of the ordinary by venturing into other worlds. Animal magnetism seemed to many to offer evidence of a substratum of clairvoyance (*Hellsehen*) in the unconscious psyche – perhaps even evidence of the soul's potential to survive death. Schelling followed these developments with great interest. "Magnetic sleep" for Schelling demonstrated that we all pass into clairvoyant states every night, altered states of consciousness in which we can see not only the past and the future but also the eternal present, the spirit-world, the order of beings who have passed beyond death into the afterlife.

Freidemann Horn has shown the great extent to which the text of *Clara* is influenced by Schelling's readings of the Swedish mystic Emanuel Swedenborg, to whom Schelling seems to have turned out of existential despair that death had placed an insurmountable gulf between himself and his beloved (Horn, 1954/1997). Two Swedenborgian theses attracted Schelling: Swedenborg's claim that death represents not a diminishment of individual identity but an intensification of it; and, related to this, Swedenborg's conviction that romantic love survives death, for the identity of the individual depends on its relation to who or what it loves.[30] "The soul is surely not where it is, but where it loves" (Schelling, 1810b: 57).[31]

Schelling declares in *Clara* that his intention is to counteract the modern split of nature from spirit and "show the natural field's transition to the field of the spiritual world" (Schelling, 1810b: 4). He does not wish to develop a purely "spiritualistic," gnostic, or theosophic alternative to modern philosophy – that would have only entrenched the modern separation of nature and spirit by retreating from science into the world of "pure spirit." Rather, he wishes to rethink nature in such a way as to make possible a more holistic philosophy of spirit and continue the project of nature-philosophy by demonstrating "an upward growth of nature into the spiritual world" (Schelling, 1810b: 5). The story begins on All Souls' Day with the priest and the doctor coming into town to pick up Clara, who has just buried her beloved Albert. The scene is gloomy and gothic: a dark fall day, the cemeteries busy with locals visiting the graves of their departed family members and friends. The three interlocutors (and an unnamed clergyman) exchange remarks on the Catholic celebration of the feast and discuss the legitimacy of attempting to foster a connection with the spirit-world through religious ritual. Clara offers the hypothesis that grounds the whole dialogue. "Perhaps . . . the lower cannot act on the higher, but it is more certain that the higher can act within the lower, and thus the thought of some community [with the dead] would not be so inconsistent" (Schelling, 1810b: 12). *We* may not be able to re-establish the lost connection with the spirit-world through any ritual or natural act, Schelling (through Clara) says, but it is not so certain that the spirits, presumably enjoying a higher state of existence, cannot act on us. If we, the living, cannot communicate with the dead, cannot bring them back into contact with us, perhaps the dead can nonetheless communicate with us. Perhaps they do so all the time. The point here is that lack of consciousness of communication with the dead should not be taken as evidence that there is no communication. The priest suggests that the loss of contact between the living and the dead is symptomatic of a general "conflict and contradiction with nature" that has damaged all being (Schelling, 1810b: 14). "A deep depravity has taken root in man's nature such that he no longer has the capacity to draw purely from one or the other source of life [nature or spirit-world]." The doctor counters, in Paracelsian fashion, that a correspondence still exists between the larger world, the cosmos, and the smaller world, the human being (Schelling, 1810b: 19). "It seems to me," he says later, "that her [nature's] feeling for man is essentially one of friendship and often of sympathy" (Schelling, 1810b: 26). Between the pessimism of the priest and the cheery optimism of the doctor, Clara offers a mean:

> I am often terrified of these links . . . and of the thought that every-thing is related to man. Indeed, if another power within me didn't balance out this horror of nature, I would die from the thought of this eternal night and retreat of light, of this eternally struggling being that never actively is [*dieß ewig ringende, nie seyende Seyn*].
>
> (Schelling, 1810b: 19)

In *Clara*, Schelling offers what initially appears to be a basically Neoplatonic view of the human being as tripartite: a material principle, the body, is connected to an immaterial principle, the spirit, through the intermediary of the soul, which partakes of both matter and spirit (Schelling, 1810b: 35–41). In fact, Schelling inverts the Platonic hierarchy under the influence of Swedenborgian spiritualism. Soul is not universal but particularized by virtue of its participation in body (this much is Neo-platonic), but soul is nevertheless higher than spirit, for that which unites opposites is higher than either opposite (Schelling, 1810b: 34). Although in one way, soul is lower than the spirit, for it partakes of body, in another way, soul is "of a higher lineage than spirit and body" (Schelling 1810b: 35). This peculiar argument allows Schelling to argue for a doctrine of personal immortality, the only kind of immortality that can console a bereaved lover. Where the standard Neoplatonic doctrine of immortality would have the universal and intellectual part of the human being survive death, the immortal soul in Neoplatonism being somehow a universalized individual (like an angel in medieval theology), for Schelling, it is the singular soul that survives death, the soul of the person which remains eternal and unchanged in the individual, while body and spirit are constantly changing. And since soul is nothing without body and spirit, the immortal soul possesses some type of body in the next life, just as it possesses some type of intellect and will, albeit transformed and elevated. Spirit on its own is "rather repellent," Schelling argues; soul is "a milder essence," that part of the individual which "we love above all; that draws us, as it were, in a magical way" (Schelling 1810b: 33, 35). All three powers must be active in the living person, just as all three divine potencies in the middle Schelling's theology are essential to the divine. "The whole person thus represents a kind of living rotation: wherever one thing reaches into the other, neither of the others can leave, each requires the other" (Schelling, 1810b: 35). The soul, however, has pre-eminence over spirit and body; it is the essence of the person, "the actual innermost germ of life," which is intensified in death (Schelling 1810: 36).

Schelling's qualified Neoplatonic anthropology allows him to make a case for the necessity of death. Since each of the powers (spirit, soul and body) is equally necessary to the whole person, and all three cannot dominate at the same time, for their relations are oppositional (spirit being the opposite of body, while soul is in a way the opposite of both spirit and body, for it includes while the others exclude), a temporal sequence is necessary; they must each have their moment in the light, so to speak. The point here is that a whole can be composed of opposed parts so long as no part is permitted to dominate the others absolutely. One way to resolve the contradiction between parts is to make the whole temporal, a whole that changes over time, compensating for the inevitable one-sidedness of any one of its states with a new state in which the underdeveloped part assumes dominance. Whereas in this life, body "bewitches" soul, in the next life, spirit rules over body. Moreover, we experience spiritual-soul even in this life each night when we dream and our soul, no longer bound by the body, is entirely subservient to spirit (Schelling, 18010: 39). What Schelling has in mind here becomes clearer when we recall that by spirit, Schelling does not mean passionless intellect or thinking in abstraction from feeling; on the contrary, the essence of spirit is feeling, desire and will.[32] Thus Schelling's offhand remark about dreaming betrays a sophisticated psychology of sleep: in sleep, the soul is not without consciousness; rather, sleeping consciousness is set free from the limitations of the body and delivered wholly over to its desires and wants.

Schelling takes another tack on this complex anthropology by introducing the binary of internal/external (Schelling, 1810b: 40 ff.). What is internal in this life is externalized in the next and what is external here is internalized there. Spirit is internal in this life; body is external. It follows that in the next life, spirit will be externalized, i.e., it will contain and express the body, rather than being contained and limited by the body. Since spirit is separated from the body in death, Schelling requires a new kind of body to sustain the immortal soul after death: the body which is contained and expressed by spirit in the next life is a "subtle body" (ein feinere Leib) which is already present "in germ" in this life (Schelling, 1810b: 40). With the notion of a subtle body, Schelling is on firmly Western esoteric terrain—the notion is central to Paracelsian medical alchemy.[33] The subtle body in us does not separate and divide us from other bodies, as does our coarse body; rather it unites us with other bodies. After a vague reference to "the electrical interplay of forces or to chemical transformations" which seem to indicate a deeper connection and exchange among bodies (i.e., alchemy), Schelling offers a definition of death: "Death . . . is the release of the inner form of life from the external one that keeps it suppressed. . . . And death is necessary because those two forms of life that couldn't exist together at the same time had to exist one after the other instead, once nature had sunk down into the purely external (Schelling, 1810b: 41).

*Clara* is marked by Schelling's exploration of the notion of a fall from the absolute which he first postulated in *Philosophy and Religion*. Ideally "the external" should be a perfect expression of the internal: the body should express and reveal the soul rather than hold it back and conceal it. But something has happened to the human being, indeed to nature itself, such that the ideal relation of the internal to the external is disturbed: in this life, the external suppresses and obstructs the internal; matter does not mediate spirit but obstructs and distorts it. In death a *transmutio* occurs and the internal is released from its oppressive and obfuscating external shell (Schelling, 1810b: 41). Death is not dissolution of the self into the absolute but a reduction of the individual to its essence, an "essentification" (Horn, 1954/1997: 58).[34] When death frees the individual's essence from the material shell that is maladapted to it, the person does not become less of what he was, but more.[35] Death is not the extinction but the intensification of the individual identity constructed in time, for even the drop of water submerged in the sea still remains the drop it was. Far from being dissolved, individual existence is "raised to its greatest profundity" when it is united with the divine (Schelling, 1810b: 52).[36] Schelling's ontology of ground/existence provides for an essential distinction between the finite self and God which is notably missing from the identity-philosophy. "Even when this dark and obscure speck of our existence . . . is completely liberated and transfigured, it nevertheless always leaves something behind in us *that was not from God*" (Schelling, 1810b: 53). The irreducible remainder in the transfigured soul images the dark ground in God which is not identical with God himself, "nature" – not that which *is* actively in God, but that in God which always strives to be without ever attaining actuality (Schelling, 1810b: 54). In this life the struggle with the dark ground is thus inevitable. Without this recalcitrant quasi-material core, the soul would have no individuality and no possibility of blessedness. But this same dark ground is responsible for all the evil in the world. The greatest challenge for the human being is to tend self-will, with its primordial roots in the dark ground of spirit, neither extinguishing primitive ipseity nor letting it consume the world, but caring for it so that it can serve the soul's higher purpose. The subordinating of the dark ground to love, the ordering of ipseity and alterity – the core of Schellingian psychology – comes to its sharpest expression in *Clara*:

> Don't you feel that something lies at the very basis of your conscious-ness that no concept can unravel, something dark and obscure, some-thing that acts as it were as a support for your personality?
>
> I certainly feel the dark obscurity, Clara said, but it is just this obscurity that I wish would go – it disturbs the purity of the essence [of the soul].
>
> My dear, once aroused it cannot be made to go away, I said, and nor should it go, either, for with it personality, too, would disappear. But it can become transformed, it can itself become clear and light, that is, as the mute vessel for the higher light, keeping individuality for this alone rather than for itself, and to let the light have a root and a base.
>
> (Schelling, 1810b: 49–50)

The transmutation of what Boehme describes as the dark fire is in this life never finally accomplished. But repressive moralism is as deadly to the soul as unbridled egoism. To counteract the former, one must occasionally descend, awaken the ground, the madness beneath consciousness, and ensure that our "virtues" do not become a thin disguise for our vices. Becoming a person for Schelling is a continual transmutation not only of the base into the sublime but of the sublime into the base.[37]

At one point in the dialogue, Schelling has Clara exposit on the clair-voyant state into which the soul enters in the first moments of sleep before dreaming begins. "Its clarity surpasses even the most vivid waking thoughts, and any normal mode of existing seems to be only a dream, a slumbering, or a death by comparison" (Schelling, 1810b: 47).[38] The vision is only a fore-taste, and fallen nature extinguishes the aroused "internal light" with "mere sleep" (Schelling, 1810b: 47). Schelling then relates this higher consciousness to the psychic alterations produced through the medical practice of inducing "magnetic sleep," artificial somnambulism, what we now know as hypnot-ism, which he describes as "a wakeful sleep or a sleeping wakefulness" (Schelling, 1810b: 48). As if recovering from an illness, the magnetized enter into an improved physical as well as psychical condition in which they are "released from the sensible world."

> They have an indescribable sense of well being. All the strains of illness fade from their features, they look happier, more spiritual, often younger. All traces of pain fade away from the gladdened face; at the same time everything becomes more spiritual, especially the voice.
>
> (Schelling, 1810b: 48)

They retain a connection to the external only through the influence of the magnetizer, whose psychic rapport holds them captive. The release from the tyranny of the present frees up the past and the future, which now become wonderfully available to them, as if "their whole essence were pressed into one focal point that unites past, present, and future within itself" (Schelling, 1810b: 49). Schelling connects the magnetized condition to death: in artificial somnambulism we get a glimpse of the seed of life, buried in the unconscious, which only fully blossoms after death.

The idea is further developed in the second draft of the unfinished *Ages of the World*, written three years later, in which Schelling endeavours to explain magnetic sleep and clairvoyance in terms of the triadic ontology of ground/existence/personality. Ground individuates the person; it is the universal hunger for being (*Seyn*) at the foundation of the personality. Existence lends consciousness the power to unify the "inner forces." It is determinate being (*das Seyende*) or the form of the self. In sleep an alteration of the ground–existence relationship occurs such that the external unity of the conscious personality is suspended and a second, unconscious personality becomes manifest. "A freely willed sympathy takes the place of an externally determined unity" (Schelling, 1813: 158). Sleep is a relaxation of the determinate being of the self and the release of the dark ground. The alteration does not bring about the death of the individual, for the life of the mind is not identified with the activity of the conscious personality. Rather, sleep awakens what Schelling's disciple Schubert describes as a second self.[39] Consciousness is external to the life of the individual; when it is weakened, as in hypnosis and sleep, "the free inner relations of life" are set loose, and another dark centre of selfhood emerges into prominence (Schelling, 1813: 158).[40]

Following Schubert's 1808 *Ansichten von der Nachtseite der Naturwissenschaften*, Schelling distinguishes grades of sleep, from partial unconsciousness, which is still sentient, to a state that is "completely cut off from the sensuous world and entirely removed to a spiritual realm" (Schelling 1813: 159).[41] Most interesting here is Schelling's sketch of a psychology of dreams. Referencing the ancient distinction between divine or clairvoyant dreams and mundane dreams, Schelling elaborates ascending stages of clairvoyant dreaming. In the lowest grade, "the life-spirit [*Lebensgeist*], that intermediating essence between body and spirit," attracts "the objective of the soul [*das Objektive der Seele*]," which results in the soul's momentary freedom from the body and a simultaneous awakening of healing powers (as reported by animal magnetists, for example Puységur's famous patient Victor Race, who could heal others when magnetized).[42] In the next grade, the life-spirit illuminates the soul "in order to show it what lies within its own self, as if in a counterpoint, and to bring it to knowledge of what is still wrapped up in itself and awaiting the future" (Schelling, 1813: 159). At this level of dreaming the soul becomes "a slate" on which the life-spirit "is able to read what lies concealed within itself" (Schelling, 1813: 159). At the highest level, "the process of freedom spreads up to what is eternal in the soul itself, within which alone free communication takes place between what is eternally objective and what is eternally subjective of the soul" (Schelling, 1813: 159). Dreaming on this scale is nothing short of a momentary reversal of the effects of the fall, a restoration in the microcosm of functional relations between the soul and God.[43] Schelling describes a new level of personality, self-knowledge raised to a higher power, consciousness become cognizant of higher levels of spiritual reality: the spirit-world, the angelic, and the archetypal. The highest grade of the clairvoyant dream is buried so deeply in the unconscious that it is rarely remembered, but some residue of it appears in the lower grades of dream that are more easily remembered.[44]

Somnambulists are not hallucinating; they are travelling between worlds.[45] A cosmic catastrophe, the fall of man, has resulted in a disruption of the community of souls (living and dead): after the fall we have only sporadic contact with the other world through visionaries and in somnambulistic states. Magnetism is an "escape" from sleep "from within sleep," a penetration in sleep to a waking state (Schelling, 1810b: 47). On the assumption that the essence of the soul's life lies hidden in our present state of existence, like a germ of the future life, sleep is held to be the foreshadowing of a higher state of being. It is for this reason that falling into sleep is such "an indescribable joy" (Schelling, 1810b: 47). The reverse is also true: waking up is an indescribable pain.

In such a tumultuous and transitory state of existence, melancholy is not a passing mood or a pathology, but a sign of man's "sympathetic relation to nature" (Schelling, 1810a: 230). Nature is itself essentially melancholic, "for it, too mourns a lost good" (Shelling, 1810a: 230). The self is a microcosm and feels in its inner life what all of nature suffers. "Because all life is *founded* upon something independent of itself [ground]," "an indestructible melancholy" inheres in it (Schelling, 1810a: 230). At the core of human nature is the longing of the heart, which is desire in its purest form, as Wirth puts it, "non-object oriented desire, desire that moves beyond itself" (Schelling, 1815: 146, n. 94). Tragic longing is a familiar enough motif of romanticism, but Schelling gives the feeling an ontological explanation. Longing (*Sehnsucht*) is nothing other than an expression of the need (*Sucht*) for being, as such the symptomatic effect of the dark ground longing for that the existence of which it simultaneously refuses to recognize. *Sucht* is impossible desire, desire that cannot be satisfied insofar as it is constitutive of the desirer. "Since there is consequently an unremitting urge to be and since it cannot be, it [ground] comes to a standstill in desire, as an unremitting striving, an eternally insatiable obsession [*Sucht*] with being" (Schelling, 1815: 21).

The restlessness of the dark ground, the obsession and need of the heart, permeates all levels of the personality and animates the whole psyche. "The deepest essence of spirit is therefore need [*Sucht*], desire [*Begierde*], want [*Lust*]" (Schelling, 1810a: 230). Lacanians would make this impossible desire the lack constitutive of subjectivity, the barred subject, but Schelling stresses the positive contribution of the dark ground to the health of the personality. The desire that can never be satisfied gives the ground consistency, makes it possible for it to *ground*. Persistent and incurable melancholy, longing and need make the human being human, a being that in everything reaches itself.[46]

In *Clara* Schelling mediates two extreme positions on the relationship of spirit to nature. One view is tragic, holding that nature is essentially out of balance: isolation, disconnectedness, and melancholy are inescapable and meaningless conditions of human life. The other view is optimistic: that nature and spirit are two sides of a cosmic whole that is eternally balanced: we need only readjust our attitude to connect with the "other-side" and dissipate the clouds of depression. Schelling rejects both the extreme pessimism of the first view and the naïvete of the second. Nature and spirit might have originally been in cosmological balance, but they are no longer, something has happened to disrupt the unity. Momentary ecstatic foretastes of restoration, like sporadic communication from the other side, are not impossible, but are not the rule. In this life we must reckon with "the horror of nature" and the dark implications of correspondence. If "everything is related to man," then it follows that the sins of man affect the whole. The "eternal night and retreat of light," the desperate struggle of being to achieve actuality, are signs that things are out of joint.

Schelling's ambivalence about nature is not uncharacteristic of the early romantic attitude to nature. On the one hand, the romantics affirm the autonomy, dignity, and spiritual power and beauty of nature. Over and against the secular humanism of the Enlightenment, romantic nature is once again a theophany, a revelation of the divine that surpasses human comprehension. On the other hand, there is nothing naïvely pagan in the romantic attitude. "Visible" nature is not in itself divine; it is only the "appearance" of the divine (Schelling, 1810b: 27). More disturbingly, something is basically wrong with objective nature, inclining the romantic to look for a resolution of the basic problems of life in subjective experience, which is not limited by external realities. The romantic penchant for fantasy is often derided as romanticism's inability or unwillingness to face the grim "facts of life." The exact opposite is the case. The romantic fantasizes not because she is out of touch with reality, but because the grim facts are all too real for her. Romantic melancholy, the morbid fascination with the tragic, with illness, death, and transience, stands in marked tension with the romantic affirmation of the subject's deep feeling for life and experience of meaning. Novalis famously writes,

> The world must be romanticized. Only thereby will one re-discover primordial meaning. To romanticize is nothing other than a qualitative potentization. In this way the lower self is identified with a higher self. Insofar as I give the common a higher meaning, the familiar, a

mysterious importance, the friend, the respect of a stranger, the finite, an infinite aura, I romanticize it.

(Novalis, 1969: 384, n. 37)

Notice that the prescribed romanticization is not meant to be a departure from reality but a "potentization" through a transformation of attitude (not cancelling the real but raising it to a higher power). The implication is that reality appears "common," "familiar," and uninteresting because the self has lost touch with its higher organs of perception; it has become trapped in what Heidegger calls "everydayness," and needs to practise "romantic" thinking in order to be liberated from the veils of superficial and accustomed categories. The liberation is not a flight into the unreal that frees us from melancholy but an ever-more resolute turning to the real that intensifies the longing for being. Melancholy is therefore the break-through feeling: as the ontological mood that most keenly feels the longing of the ground, it puts us in touch with the depths of the personality, the night-side of nature.

The nub of romantic ambivalence is a wavering between pantheism and pessimism, immanentism and transcendentalism: the romantic desires to be dissolved into nature and released from it into a better world at one and the same time. This conflicted romantic attitude is plainly illustrated in the exchange among the three interlocutors in *Clara* about the "secret, consuming poison" within nature, which momentarily appears, only to be suppressed again by "normal life" (Schelling, 1810b: 22), the chaos that is older than order referred to in Schelling's *Freedom* essay. The same force that poisons life also heals; the same power that destroys also creates.[47] The melancholic cannot hide from the real; the everyday strategies of self-distraction and superficial pleasure do not work for him. He too keenly feels the cosmological effects of freedom's fall: chaos, natural disasters, disease, death, evil – all of which disrupt the beauty and joy of life and foreclose any kind of Enlightenment optimism. "The whole Earth is one great ruin" (Schelling, 1810b: 25). But the chaos is not original, nor is it necessarily final; as caused by freedom, it can only be undone by freedom, a "spell that only another magic charm can undo" (Schelling, 1810b: 25).

## Notes

1 Beiser has shown that the early Schelling's realism (largely overlooked by commentators, who tend to identify romanticism with subjectivism) was typical of early romanticism. Schelling was still collaborating with Fichte on the work of transcendental philosophy when both Hölderlin and Novalis were writing realist critiques of Fichte.

2 "In one move Schelling had both objectified the subjective and subjectified the objective: ego became nature as nature became the ego" (Beiser, 2002: 530). The roots of Schelling's theory are ostensibly Spinoza's concept of *natura naturans* and Kant's theory of the natural polarity of attraction–repulsion, first developed as an alternative to mechanism in Kant's 1786 *Metaphysical Foundations of*

*Natural Science* (Kant, 1922). But we cannot rule out a theosophical influence through Oetinger, who had developed a similar theory of natural polarity (centrifugal–centripetal psychic drives) in his 1765 *Theologia ex idea vitae deducta* (Oetinger, 1765). It is an open question how well Schelling knew Oetinger's theory at this stage of his career. See Schneider (1938), Benz (1955), Matthews (2011).

3   On the romantic taste for self-transcendence, see Korff (1954: 16ff.).

4   "As long as I am *identical* to nature I understand what a living nature is as well as I understand my own life" (Schelling, 1797: 196). Schelling's argument at this stage anticipates Schopenhauer's later argument that the thing-in-itself, the will, hides itself from the empiricist gaze but reveals itself to introspection – because in one case alone, the human being, both sides are given.

5   "The empirically infinite is only the external intuition of an absolute (intellectual) infinity whose intuition is originally in us, but which could never come to consciousness without external, empirical exhibition" (Schelling, 1799a: 15).

6   See Beiser (2002: 488).

7   Heidegger makes a similar argument in the Daseinanalytic: Dasein is the being that understands being; therefore access to the meaning of being is via Dasein's understanding of being, but this should not be mistaken as grounds for assuming an idealist reduction of being to understanding.

8   Schelling repeats Kant's analysis of the organism from the third *Critique*, but adds a decisive question about the regulative status of Kant's notion of *telos*: "Every organic product bears the ground of its existence within *itself*, for it is its own cause and effect. No single part could *arise* except *in* this whole, and this whole exists only in the *interaction* of the parts. In every other object the parts are *arbitrary*, they exist only insofar as I *divide*. Only in an organized being are they *real*; they are there with no effort on my part, because there is an *objective* relationship between them and the whole. Thus every organization is based on a *concept*. But this concept dwells within *the organization itself* and cannot be separated from it. It *organizes itself*, and is not simply a work of art whose concept is present *outside* itself in the understanding of the artist. Not its form alone, but its *existence* is purposive" (Schelling, 1797: 190).

9   "The point of absolute indifference exists nowhere, but is distributed equally over many individuals. The universe, which constitutes itself from the centre against the periphery, seeks the point, where the most external oppositions of nature resolve themselves; the impossibility of this resolution guarantees the infinity of the universe" (Schelling, 1799a: 66).

10   "Life is common to all individuals, what distinguishes one from another is merely the form of its life. The positive principle of life cannot be unique to any individual, it is distributed through the whole creation, and penetrates every individual being as the common breath of nature. What is common to all spirits – if the analogy holds – lies outside the sphere of individuality (it lies in the immeasurable, the absolute); what distinguishes one spirit from another is the negative individuating principle in each. So does the universal principle of life individuate itself in every singular being (as in a particular world), according to the degree of its receptivity. The whole multiplicity of life in the entire creation consists in the unity of the positive principle in all beings and the diversity of the negative principle in individuals" (Schelling, 1798: 192).

11   The editors of the *historish-kritische* edition of *Weltseele* add this cross-reference from one S. Maimon, *Philosophisches Wörterbuch* (Stück 1, Berlin, 1791, Stichworte: "Weltseele," p. 188): "Der Verfasser erinnert auch den Leser, daß bei ihm das Wort Bildungstrieb, so wie die Worte Attraktion, Schwere etc. zu nichts mehr und nicht weniger dienen soll, als dadurch eine Kraft zu bezeichnen,

deren konstante Wirkung aus der Erfahrung anerkannt worden, deren Ursache aber so gut wie die Ursache der genannten noch so allgemein anerkannten Naturekräfte für uns *Qualitas occulta* ist, in dem es von allen Kräften gilt" (cited in Schelling, 1798: 404–405, n.).

12 "Nature leads the product in both directions only for the sake of letting it sink (back) into indifference, as soon as it reaches the apex of development. For Nature was not concerned with either the one or the other of those directions, its concern was for the sake of the common product that was divided into them. Therefore, as soon as the product has reached the highest point in both directions, it fosters the universal striving of Nature toward indifference" (Schelling, 1799a: 40).

13 "From this moment forward, since the *joint product* is secured, Nature will abandon the *individual*, will cease to be active in it, or rather it will then begin to exercise an antithetical effect upon it; from now on the individual will be a *limit* to its activity, which Nature labours to destroy" (Schelling, 1799a: 41).

14 The resonance between Schelling's nature-philosophy and Freud's economic model of the psyche has been noted before. "Freudian psychoanalysis is to a significant degree the disenchanted form of Schelling's philosophy of nature" (Marquard, cited in Norman, 2004: 6).

15 See Freud (1922).

16 "The aim of the first of these basic instincts [*eros*] is to establish ever greater unities and to preserve them thus – in short to bind together; the aim of the second is, on the contrary, to undo connections and so to destroy things" (Freud, 1926: 6).

17 "Throughout life, the ego remains the great reservoir from which libidinal cathexes are sent out on to objects and into which they are once more withdrawn, like the pseudopodia of a body of protoplasm" (Freud, 1926: 8). From an early Schellingian perspective Freud's position is too subjective: the universe itself, the infinite source of *eros*, draws the ego out of itself into erotic relations.

18 We must not place much stock on throwaway phrases such as the following from *Beyond the Pleasure Principle*: "Thus the Libido of our sexual instincts would coincide with the Eros of poets and philosophers, which holds together all things living" (Freud, 1922: 64).

19 See Freud (1922: 64): "And we cannot disguise another fact from ourselves, that we have steered unawares into the haven of Schopenhauer's philosophy for whom death is the 'real result' of life and therefore in so far its aim, while the sexual instinct is the incarnation of the will to live."

20 Identity-philosophy occupies Schelling from 1801 to 1806 and takes up over 1,200 pages of his collected works.

21 Intellectual intuition is "the capacity to see the universal in the particular, the infinite in the finite, and indeed to unite both in a living unity" (SSW 4: 362).

22 This is the central insight of Schelling's identity-philosophy, but the thought was with him from his earliest work on nature-philosophy. See Schelling (1797: 169): "Mere reflection is a mental disorder in man, and when it takes control of the whole person it kills the seed of his higher existence and the root of his spiritual life, which proceeds only from identity. Reflection is an evil that accompanies man throughout his life and destroys all his intuition." Schellingian philosophy works to demote reflection, to show it to be merely a means and not an end; it is "a corrective of reason gone astray, it works in this sense towards its own annihilation" (Schelling, 1797: 169–170). See Vater (1978: xxvii): "Finitude means that intellectual intuition is not unitary, immediate and fully self-reflected, that self-consciousness is not pure self-awareness. The philosopher in his

imitation of intellectual intuition discovers a fragmented consciousness which can be gathered back into itself only through mediation – through experience, reflection, and finally systematic philosophy or its surrogate, aesthetic intuition."

23  See *Khândogya Upanishad*, 6.8.7: "Now that which is that subtle essence (the root of all), in it all that exists has its self. It is the True. It is the Self, and thou, O *S*vetaketu, art it." Translation: Müller (1879).

24  For what follows, see Galland-Szymkoviak (2010).

25  See Schelling (SSW 4: 114–126).

26  This argument is worked out in detail in Schelling (1804a).

27  As Beiser has argued, the logical outcome of the identity-philosophy is apophaticism. To know the absolute one would have to be the absolute, which means that, strictly speaking, it cannot be known at all (Beiser, 2002: 545).

28  The dating of Clara is disputed. I follow Steinkamp in dating it to 1810. Its similarity to the language of both the *Freedom* essay and the *Stuttgart Seminars* supports this dating. See Steinkamp (2002: xiii). Some related reflections on the subject of life after death appear in the *Stuttgart Seminars* and the second draft of *Ages* (Schelling, 1813: 158–161).

29  Zovko (1996) offers a detailed account of this period of Schelling's career.

30  See Swedenborg (1758).

31  Cf. Baader (BSW 13: 221–222).

32  See appendix B, The anthropology of Schelling's *Stuttgart Seminars*.

33  See Paraclesus (1979: 18).

34  See Schelling (1810a: 237): "Death is therefore not an absolute separation of the spirit from the body, but only a separation from that element of the body that is in opposition to the spirit . . . of the good from the evil, then, of the evil from the good. This means that it is not just part of the person that is immortal, but rather the whole person in regard to the true essence – death is a reduction to the essential [*reductio ad essentiam*]."

35  This happens for good or ill. Whereas the evil that men do in this life often goes unpunished, "the damned" in the next life are those whose outer life finally matches their inner corruption. See Schelling (1810b: 58).

36  The fear of death in those who cling to their individuality without any sense of the divine is propagated by believers who speak of the afterlife as a disappearance into God. "Don't many people generally fear that once they have become completely transfigured their self-will will be completely overcome and they might disintegrate entirely? Don't they fear that they will no longer actually be anywhere, but will become indistinct within God?" (Schelling, 1810b: 52).

37  "It seems, Clara said, that man is in this way like a work of art. Here, too, what is delicate or spiritual receives its highest worth only by asserting its nature through mixing with a conflicting, even barbaric element. The greatest beauty comes about only when gentleness masters strength" (Schelling, 1810b: 76–77).

38  Schelling references Johann Caspar Lavater's 1778 *Aussichten in die Ewigkeit* (written, Schelling says, by "a famous minister, whom we all know" (Schelling, 1810b: 47)). According to Lavater the higher consciousness momentarily enjoyed by the sleeper is a foretaste of the heavenly life. "This . . . condition seldom lasts more than a second, although countless moral and metaphysical ideas radiate through me with clarity one after the other . . . . I am placed into new points of view from which I can see everything quite differently from usual and yet so incontrovertibly clear, so true and with such conviction and with such a view and feeling of truth and harmony. It is as if I were capable of thinking without pictures or signs . . . everything can be cognized immediately and in their true similarities and relationships . . . every usual way of existing seems to be only a

dream, a slumber, a death in comparison" (Lavater, cited by Steinkamp in Schelling, 1810b: 92, n. 5).

39  "Man [for Schubert] is a 'double star'; he is endowed with a second centre, his *Selbstbewusstsein,* which gradually emerges in his soul" (Ellenberger, 1970: 205). It is clear from the context that *Selbstbewusstsein* is not "self-consciousness" in the ordinary sense but the dawning of awareness in the unconscious centre of the personality. Ellenberger connects Schubert's notion of the self with Jung's "archetype of the self," thus identifying an important link between Schellingian psychology and analytical psychology. See Ellenberger (1970: 729).

40  "He [the magnetized] appears dead externally, while internally, a steady and free connection of all forces emerges from the lowest up to the higher" (Schelling, 1813: 158).

41  Another possible source is Carl Alexander Ferdinand Kluge's 1811 *Darstellung des animalischen Magnetismus als Heilmittel.* Kluge distinguishes six degrees of magnetic sleep: (1) waking state; (2) half-sleep; (3) "inner darkness" or insensitivity; (4) "inner clarity," consciousness within one's body, extrasensory perception, vision through the epigastrium; (5) "self-contemplation," perception of the interior of bodies, one's own and that of others; (6) "universal clarity," the removal of veils of space and time (Ellenberger, 1970: 78).

42  On Race, see Ellenberger (1970: 72).

43  "Here, what-is of the soul [*das Seyende der Seele*] would become free even from its own eternal being [*von seinem eigenen ewegen Seyn*], and would be put in a relation to this being such that it could, so to speak, distinguish and read its deepest thought in this latter" (Schelling, 1813: 159–160).

44  Schelling suggests a process of dream interpretation that would unravel what Freud will later call the condensations and displacements that occur in dreaming. "We entirely fail to recall many dreams in the waking state. This fact can be accepted as certain, since we are certain through experience that many dreams have only the general memory of having-been-there, and that others vanish just after waking (and sometimes even then not permanently). It is just possible that the more external dreams often mirror the more internal dreams, and that in this manner internal dreams can come immediately to consciousness, although confusedly and not in their pure and complete condition" (Schelling, 1813: 160). Schelling's son adds this interesting note to the manuscript: "In mesmeric sleep we have the example of a state in which there is, externally, no subject at all, and yet there is an inner subject who judges, concludes, thinks and comprehends, often considerably exceeding his normal capacity, and is fully alive and operational" (Schelling, 1813: 160, n. 1).

45  See Schelling (1810b: 47–48). In a footnote to this passage Steinkamp suggests that the influence here is Schubert's 1808 *Ansichten von der Nachtseite der Naturwissenschaft.* Schubert explores the heightened states of consciousness exhibited by magnetized somnambulists and suggests that "above all it is this relationship between animal magnetism and death which deserves the very best attention" (Schubert, cited by Steinkamp in Schelling, 1810b: 93).

46  Wirth notes: "*Sucht* is the constant and insatiable striving for what one cannot have" (Schelling, 1815: 138, n. 23).

47  This is the Paracelsian principle of the coincidence of healing and destroying power in natural medicines. "It seems that the very force that creates is also that which destroys" (Schelling, 1810b: 23). Cf. Paracelsus (1979: 78): "There where diseases arise, there also can one find the roots of health. For health must grow from the same root as disease, and whither health goes, thither also disease must go."

# Chapter 4

# The speculative psychology of dissociation

## The later Schellingian unconscious

> The man who cannot separate himself from himself, who cannot break loose of everything that happens to him and actively oppose it – such a man has no past, or more likely he never emerges from it, but lives in it continually.
>
> (Schelling 1813: 120)

At some indeterminable point between 1804 and 1809, Schelling breaks with the assumption, so foundational for all of his early work, that the absolute must exclude all real difference. For the sake of the production of self-consciousness and self-revelation, Schelling argues in his middle period, the divine must divide itself into ground and existence, a dialogical pair, like the Father and the Son of the Holy Trinity, abnegating and also thereby delimiting their respective selves by deferring to the other. "We have articulated the first theory of personality," Schelling writes, somewhat grandiosely, in the *Freedom* essay (Schelling, 1809: 73). Self-consciousness is inherently relational and personal. A non-dual ground remains at the origin of personality – Schelling speaks of the deep grounding of the triune divinity in "the unground" (as he expresses it in *Freedom* (Schelling, 1809: 68)) or the "godhead" (so expressed in *Ages* (Schelling, 1815: 24)), the inexpressible, absolutely one, and essentially hidden infinity of the divine. But the indifferent absolute now withdraws into inaccessible negativity as the play of potencies takes centre stage.

The middle Schelling is at the hub of a philosophical tradition of thinking about the self as dissociative, a tradition that spans much of the nineteenth century, from animal magnetism through the now forgotten romantic psychologists Schubert, Carus, Troxler, and Fechner, to Freud's contemporary and ultimately vanquished rival Pierre Janet. Something of the dissociative tradition survives in Freud's triadic topology (id, ego, superego), and, more markedly, in Jung's theory of complexes. Dissociationists regard personality as constitutively split, but the split is not necessarily repressive or pathological. Personality is not monolithic but plural, a network of relations among alternative centres of cognition and desire. Successfully negotiating functional relations among these centres is the basis of mental health. Schelling's identity-philosophy proves that from a strictly rational a priori perspective the absolute in itself must be undivided. But if the absolute were only one, nothing else could exist – individuality, multiplicity, and time itself would be illusory. If multiplicity and relationality are real, if personality exists, the absolute must have divided itself from itself. In the *Freedom* essay Schelling describes this primordial division within the absolute in Boehmian terms: the absolute splits itself into opposite poles of desire for the sake of self-revelation. In the *Ages of the World* the division is described as the emergence of potencies, each with its distinctive properties and equally legitimate claims to existence. Schelling takes from Boehme the notion of will as "primal being" (Schelling, 1809: 21). There is no will without tension, no willing without resistance and counter-will. While the late Schelling abandons the historical immanentism of his middle period, the psycho-logic of dissociation remains nonetheless essential to his philosophy of mythology and revelation. The late Schelling interprets the Trinity as constitutively dissociated; the history of the world becomes an exteriorization of multiple personalities in God, which God undertakes for the sake of cultivating personality in the human being.

## Dissociative ontology

Schelling's dissociative logic is grounded in a neo-Fichtian theory of predication, which harks back to his earliest works.[1] If a predicate is to be identified with a subject, it must first be disjoined. The copula not only conjoins, it also disjoins (a point familiar to readers of the late Heidegger): identity is not sameness. "A is B" presupposes its opposite, that "A is not B." It is only because there are two distinct terms (A and B), only because the subject (A) is not the *same* as the predicate (B), that predication itself is possible. Applied transcendentally, to the theory of subjectivity, the logic yields the following result: any act of becoming conscious of myself, any act of self-identification (and all self-consciousness is self-identification, for example, "I am a man," "I am a woman," "I am young," "I am old," et cetera), is founded upon a dissociation of myself from that with which I identify. It is only because the I is not the *same* as "man," "woman," "young," or "old" that it can be identified with it. Predication is only possible because a third unnamed term in which the subject and the predicate participate withdraws into the pre-predicative background. A can be identified with B because some unknown X is in one respect A and in another respect B. It follows that in all acts of self-consciousness or self-identification, some aspect of the self goes unnamed, an anonymous indifferent ground withdraws from the identification and is never denominated by either the subject (the I) or the predicate (whatever the I happens to identify itself with).

The notion that the identity expressed in A=A is not sameness is a Fichtian point pursued in different ways by Schelling and the early romantics. In his *Fichte Studies* (1796), Novalis writes: "The essence of identity can only be established in an apparent proposition [*Scheinsatz*]. We leave the identical in order to represent it" (cited in Bowie, 1993: 49). Wolfgang Hogrebe has famously argued that the theory of predication is the essence of Schelling's *Ages*. "In my view, Schelling's metaphysical project in the *Weltalter*, according to his internal method, is nothing other than what one could call a hermeneutic of predication, that is: explication of the schema of predication as a schema of the world" (Hogrebe, 1989: 11). Hogrebe admits that this interpretation must suspend or ignore Schelling's overtly theological intentions. But for Hogrebe's secularist reading, such theological intentions can only be accidental to Schelling's contribution. When formalized the three potencies of *Ages* become "pronominal being" (A), the being of the subject (in the logical sense of bearer of the predicate), which can only be indexically pointed to; "predicative being" ($A^2$), the being of whatever attributes are predicated of the subject; and "propositional being" ($A^3$), the being of the conjoined subject and predicate. Pronominal being (A) is distinct from any of its predicates, grasped in a pre-predicative experience of sheer givenness and disappearing behind any predicate applied to it. The thing contracts into itself as its objective properties expand into predicative being.

Markus Gabriel has carried Hogrebe's formalization of Schelling's ontology further into a re-reading of Schelling's *Freedom* essay.[2] The unground (non-predicative being), so often ignored by commentators such as Heidegger or Žižek, who see in it nothing more than a recursion to onto-theology, becomes in Gabriel's reading as essential to the logic of predication as pronominal being (ground) and predicative being (existence). Gabriel's departure point is Schelling's anti-Hegelian argument that any effort to conceive or map the whole of reality always excludes that upon which the whole depends for its existence. If the map is a map of the whole, then it leaves nothing out. The map either belongs to the whole or it does not. If it does not, then the map leaves something out and is not a map of the whole. But if the map belongs to the whole, then we need another map that would include it and the whole of which it is a map. If an infinite regress of maps is to be avoided, an elusive "other of reflection" must be allowed for, something which is never objectified but always remains behind the act of reflection, making it possible and grounding it in an unreflective non-predicative space. According to Gabriel, Schelling's introduction of the unground at the end of the *Freedom* essay serves exactly this purpose. Since ground and existence, pronominal and predicative being, have effectively been mapped in the ontology, ground has been brought forward out of hiddenness. Something must therefore withdraw from the reflection upon ground and existence, just as ground itself withdraws from predication, only this something must be irretrievably withdrawn, entirely without predicates. The unground, therefore, is Schelling's answer to how it is possible to refer to ground and existence, pronominal and predicative being, or as Gabriel prefers, "substance" and "structure," as a whole.

Notwithstanding the accuracy of Hogrebe's and Gabriel's analysis of Schellingian logic, the formalistic reading of the middle Schelling is an all too common imposition of late twentieth-century presuppositions (atheism, eliminative materialism, dysteleology) onto a figure who would have opposed them in every way. These presuppositions act as a filter, sifting through exactly that in Schelling which we find most difficult to understand, and extracting from his multi-dimensional work a modicum of philosophy which agrees with our own convictions. Lost in the formalization is not only the theology but also the specifically volitional aspect of the potencies. What Hogrebe and Gabriel flatten into pronominal and predicative being are, according to Schelling, specific directions of *will*, vectors of volition or desire; the potencies are not merely structural features of language but basic elements of nature. Hogrebe recognizes the volitional dimension of the Schellingian triad but tends to dismiss it (along with its theological overtones) as "metaphor." Gabriel, concerned to absolve Schelling of onto-theology, goes so far as to say that the metaphysics of will is *not* essential to Schelling's thought for the unground has no predicates and therefore "will," "drive," and "desire" cannot be attributed to it. This is only half-true: the predicateless unground gives rise to the will to revelation, and therefore the one thing that we can accurately say of it is that it wills to reveal itself even if some essential aspect of it always retreats from self-revelation. The will to revelation is nothing less than the *telos* of being for Schelling. The continuity of the nature-philosophy with the philosophy of freedom, and thus the materialist significance of the latter, depends upon a recognition of this *telos* and a non-formal reading of ground and existence. The latter are not only semantic structures; they are also teleologically ordered natural forces. Although he is certainly also talking about language, Schelling is primarily speaking of nature in the works of his middle period, an extra-linguistic material order of conflictual force and desire.

Nevertheless, Gabriel has given us a solid argument for the necessity of positing the unconscious, for the unground presupposed in every act of predication is the unconscious in itself, the unconscious that can never be made conscious and upon which all acts of consciousness depend. No doubt, the transcendental logic of predication is an essential feature of Schelling's psychology of dissociation (he returns to it in all the major treatises), but logic itself is too static to express the point Schelling wishes to make and he finds himself driven by the necessity of the subject matter itself into mytho-theological language, sketching the law of self-revelation through dissociation by modelling its highest instance, the becoming-personal of God. Hogrebe and Gabriel question how essential God is to the story Schelling is telling. Can the speculative psychology be reconstructed without God? Is a purely immanent reading of Schelling coherent? Or is God for Schelling more than a mere scaffold, more than a thought experiment or screen upon which ontological principles are enlarged for the sake of being understood? Hogrebe's and Gabriel's formalization of Schelling leads to a trivialization of Schelling's speculative metaphysics (the three potencies reduced to grammatical forms). Schellingian philosophy is essentially theological and cannot be reduced to a theory of language – there is something rather than nothing for Schelling because God wills it so and the voluntarist structure of creation/revelation is inscribed into everything that is.

Dissociation constitutes the difference between ground and existence, the basic duality of desires which founds all other differences, both in the material and immaterial world. The division between the logical subject and its predicates – like the division between the psychological subject and its desires – is an effect of this original splitting of the divine being. The dissociated self is distributed among a plurality of different desires, which is not to say that some unification of this plurality is not possible or even necessary. But the unity of personality will not be a unity imposed at the expense of the distinctions among its constitutive members. The unity of the dissociative self is a federation of freedoms, a spontaneous collaboration of independent wills.

The Freudian notion of repression is typically read back into Schelling (Hogrebe, 1989: 102; Bowie, 1993: 96–97; Žižek, 1996: 27–32), but dissociation is not necessarily repression. Every repression is a dissociation but not every dissociation is a repression. Freud's innovation on romantic psychology lies in his dysteleological interpretation of the dynamic relations between the split parts of the psyche: Freudian repression does not require a metaphysics of individuation, an unconscious *telos* or final cause to explain the splitting of the psyche: the splitting can be understood as entirely an effect of the past, a reaction, not in essence different from the mechanical effect of one external force upon another (plugging a spring of water with a rock). It is enough to assume that reality is intolerable to the psyche and must be strategically forgotten for the sake of functionality to explain the splitting. The teleological theory of dissociation holds that psyche requires duality *in order* to become personal: the cosmological duality of ideal and real, the interior duality of consciousness and unconsciousness, and the social duality of I and Thou, are ultimately all for the sake of the achievement of personality. One could put the repressionist/dissociationist difference as follows: where for the repressionist, the split does not produce a higher state of consciousness but rather a fractured being constituted by loss and the absence of wholeness, for the dissociationist, the structures that emerge out of the split are, in their functional relations to each other, always richer than what precedes the division: wholeness is not past, but future, not something lost by the splitting but rather the promised state of being that drives the psyche forward and which can only be achieved by dissociation and unification of the semi-autonomous parts.

Primordially God himself divides being, contracts infinity into an ineffable point so that personality, and its most personal act, love, might exist. Boehme's paradigm of personality comes to its full expression in Schelling: a person is a being which is inherently doubled, one who is authentically related to others only insofar as he or she has achieved a difficult self-relation. Personality can never be made totally transparent and rational; it is a complex self-mediation, "founded . . . on the connection between a self-determining being and a basis independent of it" (Schelling, 1809: 59), on the one side reaching out to other persons, and on the other retreating into hidden depths that descend into primordial and unconscious self-assertion.

## The difference between ground and existence

We have established through our historical contextualization of Schelling that the distinction between God's ground and God's existence (the real beginning of the *Freedom* essay, after the prologue on pantheism) is a metaphysical variation on Boehme's dialectic of principles, "dark fire" and "light fire." Schelling's originality, then, does not consist in drawing a distinction in God between that which is God and that which grounds God; his innovation is to give a philosophical argument for this theosophical distinction already well developed theologically in Boehme and Oetinger. The principle of sufficient reason stipulates that nothing is without a ground, including God; therefore, the ground of a being must be distinct from the existence of the being it grounds, otherwise being would be without a ground. Schelling adds to this metaphysical argument the psychological insight that ground and existence are basically opposed directions of will. Ground is not a foundation in the traditional metaphysical sense because, strictly speaking, it *is* not. Existence is grounded in that which is not, that which desires to be: this is the radicality of Schelling's voluntarist ontology which so interested Heidegger: "Higher than actuality stands possibility" (Heidegger, 1927: 63, 1971: 177–183). Schelling, however, would not say that ground, desire, or possibility is *higher* than actuality, but only that it is *older*, more basic, the presupposition and condition of being (which is no less a reversal of traditional metaphysics).

God as infinite has nothing outside himself; hence the distinction between ground and existence must fall within God himself, God must have *something* in him that is not the same as himself. As a volitional vector, ground is the opposite of existence: where existence expands and communicates as form, light, and structure, ground contracts and withdraws from self-communication into a formless interior infinity. Because existence depends on communication (participation in a shared structure), ground is dark and unstructured, the material substratum of being. Ground becomes ontologically stable in supporting existence: if it is to exist in any way, ground must exist for the sake of something other than itself. Ground is both attracted to and repulsed by existence – in the late Schelling, the first potency, *das Sein könnende*, is equally the possibility of being and of non-being (Schelling, 1831: 25–32). Ground is attracted to existence insofar as it longs for actuality. But ground can only have actuality insofar as it lets itself be the ground of that to which it is subordinated; its actuality is always only a borrowed actuality. Hence ground is equally repelled by existence, for the being that it initially yearns for is not differentiated from itself, that is, in an unconscious way, ground yearns for its own existence, an infinite and undifferentiated fullness of being. It is therefore repelled by any intimation of otherness, it withdraws from the possibility of beings, the existence of which threatens and delimits its own unlimited possibility for being. Ground must humble itself and become nothing more than the condition of the possibility of the existence of something other than itself if it is to exist at all. But at its dark centre ground can desire to be for itself, to be without existence, however futile and self-destructive the desire may be. Ground is thus in potential contradiction with itself, it can become a will striving against itself.

It is essential to the interpretation of Schelling at this point to avoid imposing the later psychodynamic notion of repression onto the relation of ground to existence. Ground does not need to be repressed. It does not need to be coerced from outside into subordination. Ground has a "dark presentiment," an intuition that its life is only possible in subordination to another. It is free to resist this presentiment. But if it does not resist, if it allows another to be, it follows its own inner necessity. The difference between Schelling's ground and Freud's Id is that the Id possesses no inherent intelligence guiding it to serve the ego and the reality principle. The Id must be restrained by the ego and the superego if its energy is to be used in the service of civilization. The Id is tragic and directionless; ground is inwardly directed toward life and love.

The ground–existence duality in God is mirrored in all creatures in the natural tension between a centripetal drive toward self-assertion and individuality (the "dark principle"), and a centrifugal drive in the opposite direction, toward participated existence, universality or shared being (the "light principle"). Without the dark principle the creature could have no centre of existence distinguishing it from others (and thus no possibility of sharing its being); without the light principle the creature would have no essence, no intelligibility, no category by which it could communicate or share being with other beings.

A perfect balance of ground and existence reigns in God; everything less than God is defective in this respect. In God ground never wills to be "on its own"; it is always with its other, existence, which releases it from the torment of its narcissism. This stability of the ground–existence relationship is curiously mirrored in the life of non-rational beings, the plants and animals, who stand in a certain way above the human being. Here the relationship of ground to existence is stable because it is externally determined, never having suffered the crisis of self-determination. The stability of existence is purchased at the price of the fullness of personality; while they image one aspect of God, the harmony of interior order, the non-rational animals are wholly lacking the primordial freedom which undergirds God's existence. Insofar as the unity of ground and existence in non-rational life is fixed, non-human organisms are not given the opportunity to freely determine their existence. Spirit, on the other hand, possesses freedom, which means it is grounded in the possibility of a definitive disruption of ground and existence. The relationship between these two countervailing wills in personality is always the product of free self-determination; spirit chooses whether it will turn in on itself in self-destructive narcissism, or out toward others in participation in a wider world.

Because personality gives birth to itself freely, it can freely abort itself. Ground can detach itself from existence and assert itself as something independent, but this act of will remains a mere assertion because it is impossible for ground to exist independently from the being which it grounds. When this negation of existence happens, evil "comes to be." The principle of darkness, animated by a demonic and stolen life, separates itself from the will of love and declares a pseudo-independence, setting itself up as a counter-absolute and bringing about its own dissolution (Schelling, 1809: 34). But there are two forms of evil in the *Freedom* essay: every bit as destructive of the life of the self as the swamping of the understanding by the selfishness of the ground is the suppression of ground by the categories of the understanding. Such a bourgeois over-management of passion eviscerates the self and brings about the rule of the merely reasonable, *die Herrschaft des Verstandesmenchen*.[3] The self needs a lively understanding if it is to thrive, which is nothing other than a coordinated madness:

> What, then, is the foundation [*die Basis*] of the human spirit in the proper sense of the word foundation? Answer: the irrational [*das Verstandlose*] . . . . The most profound essence of the human spirit – *nota bene*: only when considered in separation from the soul and thus from God – is madness [*der Wahnsinn*]. Hence madness does not originate but merely surfaces when what is properly non-being (i.e., the irrational) becomes an actuality and seeks to attain an essence and existence. In short, it is the irrational itself that constitutes the very foundation of our understanding. Consequently, madness is a necessary

element, albeit one that is not supposed to manifest itself or become an actuality. What we call the understanding, if it is to be an actual, living, and active understanding, is therefore properly nothing other than a coordinated madness [*geregelter Wahnsinn*]. The understanding can manifest itself and can become visible only in its opposite, that is, in the irrational. Human beings devoid of all madness have but an empty and barren understanding. Here we find the source for the inverted proverb: *nullum magnum ingenium sine quadam dementia* [attributed by Seneca to Aristotle: "no great genius has ever existed without some touch of madness"], as well as for the divine madness alluded to by Plato and the poets. That is, when madness is dominated by the influence of the soul [*durch Einfluss der Seele beherrscht ist*], it is a truly divine madness, and it proves the foundation of enthusiasm and efficacy in general. More generally, the understanding, if only it is a vigorous, living one, is properly speaking but a controlled, restrained, and coordinated madness [*beherrschter, gehaltener, geordneter Wahnsinn*]. To be sure, there are instances when the understanding is no longer capable of controlling the madness that slumbers in the depth of our being. Thus the understanding proves unable to console us when we feel intense pain. In that case, when spirit and temperament exist without the gentle influence of the soul, this primordial, dark force [*das anfängliche dunkle Wesen*] surfaces and seizes the understanding (i.e., a non-being relative to the soul), and madness emerges as a terrifying sign of the will when separated from God.[4]

(1810a: 233)

In this passage Schelling strikes the characteristic notes of early romanticism: the feeling for nature, the non-rational, as something infinitely above and beyond the human being; the intuition of a hidden foundation of nature and humanity in the unconscious; the displacement of Cartesian reason in the face of something sublime, which reveals itself as much in the non-human as in the human. But this is also the beginning of Schelling's turn toward the personalist realism characteristic of his later work: the conflict at the heart of being is now understood to be a crisis in the subject's experience of the real, a crisis out of which personality is born. Two ways of going wrong are possible: the ground dissociates from the understanding and selfishness without boundary mangles the self, or the understanding suppresses the ground and the soul dies from depletion.

Most of the *Freedom* essay is concerned with the first form of evil, which Schelling carefully distinguishes from the *privatio* tradition, the Neoplatonic notion that evil is parasitical on the good and has no being in itself. The tradition is right, he acknowledges, in holding that evil "never is, yet always wants to be" (Schelling, 1809: 54). Nonetheless, the language of *privatio boni* is, for Schelling, too caught up in the Neoplatonic error of identifying evil with matter, imperfection, and ignorance. *Privatio*, at least in its conventional formulations, overlooks the spiritual nature of evil. Schelling reads the Jewish-Christian scriptures as asserting that the ground of evil is not something base or material, but rather spiritual. Sin does not appear as unintelligent and low, a mere absence of goodness. On the contrary, it appears in the uppermost tier of the angelic hierarchy, seething with dark inspiration and intelligence.[5] Lucifer is the highest of all creatures. Good and evil are formally different configurations of the same basic "material" or "elements". To some degree, understand each other, for each contains what the other has, albeit ordered differently.

The positive dimension of evil is the will of ground, eternally contained in God, run amok in nature, and become a constitutive part of every entity. Ground is the potential for evil; it is not evil as such. When it is quasi-actualized as evil (quasi because evil is never fully actual; its moment of full actualization is the moment of its extinction), ground asserts itself over and against being and sets itself in opposition to the good. But there is no ultimate opposition: the good is entirely out of proportion to evil. Ground must be mediated by being if it is to become a principle of life rather than a principle of death. In evil, a borrowed and derivative existence becomes an instrument of the rebellious ground, and a state of madness ensues that can only end in the individual's self-destruction. The individual in the grip of evil is possessed by a natural longing to *be*. Because of her self-willed isolation, however, she cannot find herself, for the self can only be fully actualized in relation. Consequently evil plunges the possessed into depression and madness.

There is no Hegelian equivocation between finitude and evil in the middle Schelling: evil originates as a free and absurd choice on the part of finite spirit to abort participation in being.[6] Unlike Hegel, who must ultimately argue for the necessity of evil even while recognizing contingency and irrationality as essential moments in its unfolding – for only thus is the real rational and the rational real – the middle Schelling holds evil to be contingent and unfathomable. Where Hegel sees the "No" of evil as continuous with the negation of finitude, necessary if God is to be revealed, Schelling distinguishes evil from finitude.[7] While finitude is, for Schelling, necessary to the revelation of God, evil is not. *De facto*, finitude has become evil in the rebellion of spirit, but the result of this defection is disease and absurdity, not higher harmony. God in fact reveals himself in this situation, and we cannot but stand amazed at what beauty and glory he has achieved through what appears to be a deeply flawed creation. The question is, does God need a flawed creation in order to reveal himself as love? This is the core of Žižek's "perverse" reading of Christianity.[8] According to Žižek, the Christian God abandons the creature to self-denigration only so that he can forgive and heal him, like a five-year-old who hits a younger child to make him cry so that he can then play Mommy and soothe him. To be sure,

Schelling is far from clear on the issue in the *Freedom* essay. While the historical revelation of God as love is bound up with the degradation of the creature and the actualization of evil, God does not need actual evil as the other that mediates his self-revelation; the finite as such others God. Evil is finitude fixated on itself and refusing to be God's other; at root, it is a denial of finitude. Finite being at the highest echelon of development (spirit, nature become conscious of itself) must freely be itself, which means it can also refuse to be itself and reject its position in the whole. For Schelling, this anarchic quality of finite spirit remains integral to the structure of freedom. Insofar as evil must remain a free act, there can be no necessity to the actualization of evil. Finitude, made possible by ground, reaches its highest point of development in this possibility of self-negation (Schelling, 1809: 33).

The upshot of the underwriting of necessity by contingency is not only a more robust notion of freedom but also a turn to a more Christian notion of God than is found in Kant or Hegel: Schelling's God makes himself vulnerable to the creature, he implicates himself in the free choice of a finite being who is, if not destined to fail, as likely to fail as to succeed. The creature cannot impede God's self-revelation, but it can modify it. God wills to be revealed in the free decision of his creature. The history that results from this decision is a product of two freedoms: the freedom of God in willing to be so revealed, and the freedom of the creature to collaborate or attempt to confound the revelation. Historically the creature decided on the latter course. The result is a God who is revealed in the history of sin and redemption, a history which, as the product of unfathomable freedom, can only be known a posteriori through the history of mythology, ancient Judaism, and, above all, the events recorded in the New Testament, which the later Schelling will raise into a "philosophical religion."

The middle Schelling is however more involved with theosophy than he is with the New Testament. In an uncharacteristic acknowledgement of debt (likely because the one to whom the debt was owed was carefully reading the text as it developed), Schelling argues that Baader's view of evil as an inversion of the principles of being is the only correct one (Schelling, 1809: 35). Other explanations of evil – as privation, finitude, imperfection, weakness, or ignorance – are inadequate because they fail to recognize the positivity of evil, both as a necessary possibility of freedom and a contingent fact of human history. As coextensive with the moral and physical suffering of human beings, evil could never be described merely as an absence of goodness; it is above all an inversion of goodness, an abuse of freedom, with tragic material and spiritual consequences. On the other hand, gnostic dualism, which posits evil as a counterstriving force equal to the good, explains nothing, for the duality of the two forces remains a mere side-by-sidedness of two opposites without any higher principle of unity to explain them. As personality striving to be without relation, evil is an impossibility and a contradiction, thus wholly out of proportion to the good; it always fails to achieve unity and is pulled apart by warring appetites (Schelling, 1809: 34). Schelling speaks of evil as a kind of spiritual disease: although it feels real, it is in fact "nothing essential," "a phantasm of life, a mere meteoric appearance of it – a hovering between being and non-being."[9]

Ground is the reason for the gaps in reality, what Schelling calls the "irreducible remainder" (*der nie aufgehende Rest*), that which is left over after every calculation and cannot be reduced to any lower term: on an epistemological level, the excessive positivity and singularity of things, on an anthropological level, the contingency of freedom, and last but not least, on a psychological level, the unconscious motives, complexes, and inspirations that hinder and guide human action. Schelling's genius here is to have gathered together these surds of the history of philosophy under a single indexical and so referenced them to one recalcitrant ontological principle. The clue to the real is not however the tension between universal and individual or even the tension between unconscious and conscious activity, but the tension between freedom and reason: a free act has no sufficient reason; it is not reducible to concept or ideality. In *Philosophy and Religion* Schelling argues that multiplicity, finitude and time itself could only be the result of a break with the undifferentiated identity of the absolute, a fall which does not happen necessarily or arbitrarily but as the result of a free act of the absolute's image of itself, which is granted the autonomy and dignity of the absolute itself.[10] The thought is further developed in the *Freedom* essay, in which creation is described as God activating the ground, letting it loose, apparently going mad (the madness of the artist, not the psychotic) and acting in a way that strictly speaking defines evil itself (Schelling, 1809: 45). For the activation of the ground independent of being – the elevation of ground above being – is Schelling's formal definition of evil. God "let ground be active in its independence; or expressed in another way, he set himself in motion only in accordance with his nature [ground] and not in accordance with his heart or with love" (Schelling, 1809: 45). In *Ages* we read how, in the act of creation, God "decided simply to be the No . . . [and] emerged into His blind, dark nature, which was concealed within Him and which could only become manifest through the cision" (Schelling, 1815: 84). God makes himself into nature, "that negating potency," "spirit that has become substance," "a blind, unconscious, necessary, and, so to speak, instinctual intellect" (Schelling, 1815: 88). The late Schelling will return to a more traditional notion of god as *actus purus* but will still insist on this heterodox view of creation as *ex Deo*: creation in the late Schelling is the dissociation and materialization of first potency (*das Sein könnende*).

This decision produces the material order with its intrinsic flaws, "the poison of life that needs to be overcome, yet without which life would pass away" (Schelling, 1815: 89). That which should have remained below – ground (in *Ages*, first potency) – is elevated above the higher. The temporal order comes into being as an inversion of eternity, where ground and being remain functionally related to each other, precluding any discontinuities, events or temporal succession. In the language of the potencies first potency, A, becomes B (instead of remaining within the order of eternity and becoming $A^2$), and the many, like a thousand newborn demons, are unleashed into actuality. "Matter, as if posited in a self-lacerating rage, shatters into individual and independent centres that, because they are also still held and driven by averse forces, likewise move about their own axes" (Schelling, 1815: 91). This cataclysmic event is the beginning of time – "the whole B, because it is one with being, lacerates itself as one in discontent says, 'I would like to tear myself to pieces'" (Schelling, 1815: 91, fn. viii) – the beginning of the war of all against all, and the source of the "discontent" and "anxiety" that Schelling describes as "the fundamental sensation of every living creature" (Schelling, 1815: 91).

But Schelling is not as gnostic as he sounds here: creation is not the botched project of an idiot demiurge, something that ultimately ought not to be. A teleological movement cannot be judged statically, a-historically: purpose and value of the movement can only be discerned in its end or *telos*. The volitional trajectory of ground is away from the universal toward singularity, that which is never idealized and has no category above it. God brings an order of singulars (material creation) into existence by tapping into this will to singularity in his unconscious depths and letting beings emerge from the will of ground. Being as such (the light principle) can only give rise to form, universality, or ideality. Material creation cannot arise directly from the essence of God as God – this is the crux of Schelling's objection to Spinozism. If it is to enjoy autonomous existence, the material world must be grounded in something other than God. God's free decision to create, his letting the ground loose, generates the surd of singular being, which in turn makes possible the free decision for evil at the pinnacle of creation. But a teleology of love drives the whole process: only if the negative has the possibility of going all the way, so to speak, only if the formal possibility of a complete negation of ideality is granted to it, only then is the autonomy (*Selbständigkeit*) of creation itself possible, and only in a genuinely autonomous creation are love and revelation possible.[11]

> The unground divides itself into the two exactly equal beginnings, only so that the two, which could not exist simultaneously or be one in it as the unground, become one through love, that is, it divides itself only that there might be life and love and personal existence. For love is neither in indifference nor where opposites are linked which require linkage for Being [Hegel's notion of love] but rather . . . this is the

secret of love, that it links such things of which each could exist for
itself, yet does not and cannot exist without the other.

(Schelling, 1809: 70)

In both the middle and the later works, Schelling attributes multiplicity,
contingency, materiality, and time to God activating the ground (the first
potency), or, more accurately, letting it self-activate; in the middle works,
the *telos* of this seemingly arbitrary act is God's becoming conscious: still
working within the German Idealist model that he helped to found (even if
Hegel had perfected it), Schelling for the moment endorses a realist
historical immanentism, the idealist version of which is most associated
with Hegel; that the absolute begins unconscious and incomplete, in a state
of empty universality or being-in-itself, and creates his other, his negation,
the world, for the sake of returning to himself through it; that is, God needs
the world in order to become self-conscious and fully actual, being-in-and-
for-itself, and the history of the world is nothing other than the history of
God's becoming conscious.[12] In the late Schelling's polemic with Hegel,
which involves a reappraisal of his own early work as "negative philosophy," a priori conceptualism that never touches real history, Schelling
comes to see that a world upon which God depends for his becoming
conscious is not historically real, not an order constituted by contingent
events, but necessary, and a God who so depends on the world is not
originally free or personal: only a world that is created by freedom for
freedom is a genuinely historical world.[13] Despite this rather crucial change
of view, the point remains as true for the later Schelling as for the middle
Schelling, that there is no consciousness without dissociation, a dissociation
that is not an end in itself but for the sake of revelation or self-knowledge.
In the middle Schelling, the dissociation of God from himself is identified
with the creation of the world; in the later Schelling the dissociation
happens prior to the existence of the world, i.e., within the Trinity. The
negative moment that initiates creation in both accounts is inconceivable
without the subsequent two moments, the checking of the rage of the
activated ground (first potency become B) by the self-donation of existence
(second potency), and the self-appropriation of both ground and existence
in the full self-revelation of God (third potency). There is no birth without a
contraction and negation of the all, a singularization of being. It is as
though every finite being must initially arrogate to itself the act of existence
that is common to all, selfishly identifying it with itself by dis-identifying it
with everything else. This cutting off or dissociation then makes possible a
new kind of association, which ultimately culminates in self-awareness.

Once we notice these two principles in ourselves, that is, when an
internal division occurs within us whereby we oppose our own selves,

and when the better part in us elevates us above our inferior parts, at that moment consciousness begins.

(Schelling, 1810a: 207)

The act of God by which the duality of ground and existence is made a law of life and consciousness is not the random act of a madman but the stroke of genius, the crucial difference being that the madman produces only pain and suffering; the divine genius produces love.[14]

The consciousness achieved through dissociation does not abolish the unconscious; on the contrary, it is precisely the "residual obscurity," the irreducible unconsciousness in the self, that constitutes the content, the object, of self-consciousness (Schelling, 1810a: 207). To be a person is to know that one has come to be out of a dark ground that remains a foundation of one's identity.

All birth is birth from darkness into light; the seed kernel must be sunk into the earth and die in darkness so that the more beautiful shape of light may lift and unfold itself in the radiance of the sun.

(Schelling, 1809: 29)

The unconscious, which in the early Schelling denotes the collective, impersonal identity of subject and object in the absolute, undergoes massive revision in the *Freedom* essay: not only does it become the expelled underside of being, it is personalized, becoming the foundation of the individual's psychological identity. The ordering of ground is the key to "ego-formation"; ground dissociates from existence so that spirit might have an autonomous foundation, and personality, self-consciousness and moral life might exist.[15] This is not Freud, it is esoteric Christology: God allows sin to be so that he might raise divinity out of it; the base note is introduced into the music of creation so that it might serve as support for the melody of life. It is also Renaissance alchemy (another esoteric interest of the middle Schelling), the essence of which is not gold-making but harnessing the power to transmute the worthless into the precious, showing that the lowest is essential to the production of the highest (*in stercore invenitore*[16]). This, and not, as Hogrebe would have it, the all too familiar atheist-existentialist equation of being with the absurd, is Schelling's *Weltgeheimnis*.

## The unconscious decision

The dissociation of ground from existence is only the beginning of a series of dissociations necessary to the life of the personality; the decision for good or evil must also be dissociated from consciousness if it is to serve as a moral foundation for personality. The decision, which Schelling, invoking Kant, calls "the intelligible deed" (*der intelligible Tat*), is "an act of freedom, which in accordance with its origin, is utterly unconscious."[17] In the decision, a life-generating option to subordinate ground to existence is taken – or refused, with fatal consequences. The decision is pre-reflective, spontaneous, akin to the unconscious design that guides the hand of the artist. Schelling's unnamed departure point here is an observation made in Kant's *Religion within the Limits of Reason Alone*. We judge the morally corrupt person to be someone who is corrupt to the core of their being; corrupt acts are understood to be expressive of corrupt character, or as Kant calls it, a corrupt "disposition" (*Gesinnung*), "the subjective ground of maxims" (Kant, 1799/1960: 20). And yet we hold the morally corrupt culpable. Because freedom is spontaneity, Kant argues that it cannot appear; it has no phenomenality, no presence in the order governed by causal relations. Our decisions and choices of maxims appear as causally conditioned in the web of nature; their ultimate condition, the disposition of the agent, does not and cannot appear in time. Hence the paradoxical experience of guilt as both necessary and morally culpable.[18] Because of the dependency of our choice of maxim on disposition, Kant pushes the burden of responsibility further back than he had left it in the *Critique of Practical Reason*: it is not in my choice of maxim that I am free but in the authoring of my disposition, which determines my choice of maxim. According to Kant, disposition is the product of a free act occurring outside the phenomenal order, "an intelligible deed" that "precedes all experience" and cannot in itself be known even though its effects are everywhere visible in the moral choices of the individual. The intelligible deed is the "ground of the exercise of freedom" (Kant, 1799/1960: 34, 35).[19] Kant does not explain how this self-authoring is possible, only that it must be possible and can only be noumenal (trans-temporal) if we are to concede both the causal dependency of maxim on character *and* the fact of freedom.

Schelling follows Kant quite closely on this point:

> Idealism actually first raised the doctrine of freedom to that very region where it is alone comprehensible. According to idealism, the intelligible being of everything and especially of man is outside all causal connectedness as it is outside or above all time.
>
> (Schelling, 1809: 49)

Determinism and libertarianism are equally one-sided perspectives on a structure that can only be understood dialectically. The determinist is right insofar as he recognizes that the web of causality has no gaps in it to allow for spontaneous agency; the libertarian is right insofar as he holds that the good will authors itself; both are wrong insofar as they imagine that freedom can be accounted for in temporal-causal terms. Schelling speaks of a beginning outside of time, but we should not cling too tightly to the image of a pre-Lapsarian state of being "prior to" the creation of the world:

rather we should understand that the inside of every moment is a timeless ground that can only appear as always past, otherwise put, that every act of consciousness has a hidden, unconscious ground. The unconscious is not behind the person but accompanies him or her at every moment: it touches consciousness at every point of the line that stretches between the person's origin and end. The free will acts out of the necessity of its nature, a necessity that is not mechanical but teleological: individual acts unfold out of the ground of the being of the will just as the properties of a being express the essence of the being.[20]

What is demolished by this account is *libertas indifferentiae*: personality only exists as determined, for good or evil; the notion of a finite undetermined will is a construct of the already determined will imagining itself otherwise. Prior to its determination personality is not in a state of vacillation between equally un-compelling alternatives (the false dilemma of Buridan's ass); rather, it does not exist at all. With Fichte, Schelling insists that the subject *is* its own activity: the act by which consciousness constitutes itself, therefore, cannot itself be conscious.[21] The act happens outside the causal context; it is extra-phenomenal, or paradoxically "prior" to time. The decision that either unleashes evil or transforms personality into love cannot be fixed at any biographical point. Hence we feel ourselves destined to play out a certain role in life; we feel a necessity that binds our actions to our character, and yet our character itself is our own timeless creation. The decision cannot be observed from without; it is a purely unconscious event, something hidden in our origin.

We have arrived at the most mysterious point of the *Freedom* essay, one to which Schelling is driven in order to make sense of freedom: we must be entirely the author of our good or evil character, otherwise we cannot be held imputable. If we are not free, the sense of imputation, the feeling of moral responsibility (Kant's "fact of freedom"), is an illusion. The possibility of conversion, of turning from good to evil, is not denied: but even this turn must be understood to be foreordained in the decision by which we are constituted. Hence for Schelling the conscious self finds itself beholden to an unconscious decision that predestines its character, a foundational moment of self-making at which the ego was not present and of which it bears no conscious trace. And yet, Schelling insists, the intelligible deed is absolutely free, entirely the self's own act. As Heidegger puts it, freedom for Schelling is no longer a property of the human being; rather, the human being is a property of freedom (Heidegger, 1971/1985: 11).

The primordial decision at the ground of the Schellingian self is much deeper, older and more elusive than the fleeting feeling of spontaneity disclosed in the experience of Cartesian introspection; it does not coincide with the I that grasps itself in the act of thinking but rather with the being that always withdraws from view in any self-reflective act and which reflection itself presupposes, the *sum* unthought in Descartes' *cogito ergo sum*. The decision by means of which I choose myself cannot be self-reflexive, for it is my beginning and my beginning is never available to me. I did not experience it consciously, for there was no I to experience it, nor can I revisit it in consciousness. The beginning is the past that was never present. The person can only experience a free decision as something irretrievably past, that is, as necessity. The intelligible deed is a contraction of possibility to a single actuality. Only the being that descends into actuality is conscious, for it alone exists for itself: it alone has a history, a character, and a destiny. As Schelling repeats like a mantra throughout the works of his middle period, whoever reserves the right to reverse a decision never decides. To decide is to cut (*de-cision*, like the German *Ent-schiedung*, is literally a cutting off), to draw a line between oneself and one's past; only on the basis of such a decision does one have a past for the first time.[22] But notice that this decision is not repression, it is not the deliberate forgetting of an act or an experience that is unbearable to consciousness, incompatible with an "ego-ideal," and destined to return as an irremovable obstruction to life; it is the production of the new, not the cancellation and preservation of the old (*eine Erzeugung* rather than *eine Aufhebung*). The only way to get anything started is by choosing, in an irreversible way and without full consciousness of what is beginning in one's choice. An order of possibility opens up in the decision that was not implicit prior to the decision; prior to the decision, the possibility did not exist at all. Only by letting the new disrupt the present – by letting personality be pluralized – is anything started. "The beginning does not know itself as such" (Schelling, 1815: 86).

However paradoxical, Schellingian responsibility is close to our everyday moral experience. When I take responsibility for a course of events (say, the influence I have on my child's development), I am not saying that all that I do in this regard I do deliberately, with full knowledge of what I am doing and why I am doing it. Rather I am owning what I do, even though much of what I do I do not understand. I can neither fully understand my motives, nor can I foresee the consequences of what I do, but the more I grow in self-knowledge, the more I realize that in some fundamental sense I could not have done otherwise. Schellingian responsibility is not self-mastery but self-appropriation: to appropriate myself means to take over the ground of my being as *mine* and to assume the burden of my willing. This "taking over the ground" is the act of one who is first of all divided: I can only actively own that which is initially not me, I am called to appropriate the ground because it is other than I am, at first glance alien and foreign. To paraphrase Heidegger, it is not *through* myself but released *to* myself that I am called to take responsibility *for* myself.[23]

A simple example from the psychology of addiction brings Schelling's point closer to home. The first of the "Twelve Steps" in AA is for the alcoholic to admit his powerlessness over alcohol; the fifth is for the alcoholic to take responsibility for his alcohol abuse. On one reading of responsibility this is a plain contradiction: the alcoholic makes amends for actions that he did not intend to perform, actions that in a strict sense he did not consciously will. On a Schellingian reading, it makes perfect sense: personality must be dissociated from its ground, but this dissociation happens for the sake of self-appropriation, that is, so that there might be a self to appropriate. Just as the disjunction of the subject and the predicate makes their conjunction possible, the dissociation of personality from its ground (the unconscious) happens for the sake of their conscious identification.

## The personalization of God

In the *Ages of the World* drafts, Schelling struggles to make clear what is left at the level of suggestion in the *Freedom* essay, that the intelligible deed is a repetition of what has happened in the absolute itself. Working out the full consequences of the idealist thesis of historical immanentism (with which he will later break), the *Ages* drafts wrestle with the thought that, insofar as the universe of finite being exists, the absolute must have individuated, dissociated itself from eternity (the "will that wills nothing") and become a creator (a "will that wills something"). In language that directly repeats the Kabbalistic *zimzum* and Boehme's theogony, Schelling's absolute contracts, withdrawing into inaccessible unconsciousness and thereby making possible revelation, theophany, and consciousness. The intelligible deed re-enacts the drama of *Ein-Sof* negating itself so that it can be a self, setting limits to its boundlessness in order to have something to give away. When God creates, he breaks the circle of his infinity and inaugurates the drama of time with a violent, interruptive event. The decision to create is as much a self-limitation, that is, a negation, as it is a self-donation or affirmation. Like personality, which is the ultimate product of God's creative act (God's own personality and the possibility of other personalities), creation is both contractive and expansive, selfish and altruistic, negating and affirming – but not in the same respect. The principle of contradiction remains the inviolable moving force that propels eternity into time. Schelling's assumption here, though clearly a development of the drive theory of the nature-philosophy, is entirely Boehmian: as absolute indifference, the unground has no relation to itself, that is, it is not conscious. If consciousness is to be, the unground must establish a relation to itself, which means that it must self-divide internally.

The beginning of the personalization of the absolute is the disruption of the peace of the predicateless unground by the will to revelation. This disruption is simultaneously the positing of the indifference of the unground as past and the introduction of contradictory desires, which generate the movement of life and self-revelation. The will that wills nothing transforms into a negative will, a contradictory non-being, a will that actively negates revelation and being, a will that *wills* nothing. Such a will cannot exist apart from its opposite. Simultaneous with its appearance is the appearance of the opposite will, the affirmative, altruistic will that actively wills *something*. These two cannot both be active in the same way, since they are opposites. If it is to exist at all, the will that actively wills nothing must become subordinated to the will that wills something, must will to serve as its ground. Schelling describes this as occurring naturally in God – the unconscious tendency of the ground is to subordinate itself. We could call this the law of productive humility: the two wills can only be actual if the contradictory relation becomes a grounding relation and one will assumes a subsidiary grounding role for the other. What is always already achieved in God is a struggle and drama in time, indeed the original source of all drama, all events, history itself. The Luciferian option, to resist transformation into the new by withdrawing into narcissistic self-isolation, must remain open if spirit is to be free.[24] That finite spirit is free to negate itself, to resist self-revelation, does not mean that there is no natural teleology in it urging it in the opposite direction. When the collaboration of ground and existence occurs in God, it occurs indeliberately, "in a flash," for the wisdom of the ground is only expressed in non-reflective action.[25] The unconscious knows what to do, without knowing that it knows. The collaboration is "an action that can be conceived only on the assumption that [the members have] incomprehensible mutual knowledge and understanding in the inexpressible" (Schelling, 1813: 175). Schelling remains a naturalist on this point: if ground lets be, follows its natural inclination to support its other, all will be well. On the other hand, if ground resists and denies the other, being sinks into a self-destructive vortex. The unconscious is not the enemy of personality in Schelling. The antinomy of the unconscious to the life of the individual, a thought that is profoundly Freudian, is Schopenhauer's contribution to the history of the unconscious, not Schelling's.

The third draft of *Ages* describes the divine being "before" creation as an eternity constituted by an endless rotation of three mutually exclusive possibilities of willing: a will that contracts into itself and desires only itself (A); a second will that expands outwardly and affirms otherness ($A^2$); and a third will that unites both the negation of the first and the affirmation of the second ($A^3$). Each potency is qualitatively (in essence) identical and quantitatively (in existence) distinct: the dissociation of one potency from another occurs through an intensification of the essence, a potentization, that raises the common essence to a higher power and brings forth an existent.[26] One might ask, with Hegel, who saw the doctrine of potencies as arbitrary and lacking any logical necessity: why three potencies and not four or five? The only logical possibilities for the determination of will (the essence of being) are self-withdrawal (negation of the object of will, negation of determination, or pure possibility), self-donation (affirmation of the other, determination, actuality), or a mean between the two, a self that withholds itself by giving something of itself away, or a self that receives itself by giving itself – that is, a No and a Yes at the same time (self-limitation). The three can be parsed out in various ways: pronominal, predicative, and propositional being; negation, affirmation, and qualification; contraction, expansion, and rotation; ipseity, alterity, and community; selfism, altruism, and personality, et cetera. Since the absolute is indifferent to all distinction, each of these potencies or wills has equal claim to being God; no one of them can assume primacy over any other. In eternity, each one "emerges into presence" only to invite succession by the next, *ad infinitum*.[27] Schelling describes the three potencies of the absolute endlessly giving way to each other, no one able to maintain itself against the other. If something had not happened to break this cycle, nothing would have happened subsequently: there would be no events, no history, no happening whatsoever. The condition of the possibility of history is an initial decision that breaks the cycle of eternity, a first act in which God decides, one-sidedly, non-rationally (without sufficient reason, that is, freely), to assert *something* over and against all other possibilities. Whereas in eternity, all is ordered to the universal (A is "succeeded" by $A^2$, which is succeeded by $A^3$, which is in turn succeeded by A), in creation God elevates the singular above the universal.

Much has been made of the aimlessness of the rotation of potencies in eternity by Hogrebe and Žižek, who describe it as a kind of madness, an unsustainable senseless back and forth movement.[28] But for Schelling, the eternal rotation is neither senseless nor unsustainable. On the contrary, because eternity is eventless, the beginning of history must be spoken of as a violent interruption of a timeless order of endless movement that preceded it, a break with the unity of a perfect form of eternal succession: "Eternity opens up into time in this decision" (Schelling, 1815: 76). The point of the rotation is that, although the archetypes of all possible movements must be found in God, there is no beginning in eternity, and therefore no after, no real movement at all; in order for something to begin, the play of possibilities must cease; a contraction of universal being to a singular actuality, inevitably arbitrary, must occur. We could also describe the rotation of the three potencies as perpetual motion, like a juggler keeping three balls in the air by refusing to hold on to any one of them.[29] For the middle Schelling, the rupture is in essence God's decision to become a person, God's decision to be revealed to himself; the means of his self-revelation is (factually) a created universe in which love triumphs over evil. "It was precisely at the same time thereby determined that God as the eternal negation of external Being should be surmountable by love" (Schelling, 1815: 77). God hides himself to reveal himself, he begins something, opens up time, by becoming unconscious – not in an act of repression but of dissociation, for there is no censoring of conflicting interests, no tragic accommodation to a reality that is incompatible with desire. God becomes active as the No for the sake of the revelation of love.

Schelling returns to the triadic doctrine of potencies in all of his major lectures and unpublished writings after 1809: the *Stuttgart Seminars*, the *Ages of the World*, the Erlangen lectures (1821–1826), the Munich lectures (1827–1839), and the Berlin lectures (1840–1846) – a period spanning over thirty-five years. The doctrine is without doubt the centrepiece of his later philosophy. The triadic model of potencies includes a volitional element missing from the first formulation of the concept of potency, the 1801 *Presentation of my System*. Nevertheless in 1833 Schelling uses the later triadic model to explain the structure of his early philosophy (Schelling, 1833: 114–133). The whole of his early contribution is characterized as nature-philosophy and summed up with an account of the triad of potencies. This tells us three things:

1   The doctrine of potencies pre-eminently describes the ultimate principles of divine being, a metaphysics of God which is indissolubly linked to a metaphysics of nature. Nature is therefore theophany, and only through the metaphysics of God can nature be fully understood. The converse is also true: only through reflection on nature can the metaphysics of God be worked out.

2   Schelling understood all of his work prior to the positive philosophy (and possibly also the positive philosophy itself) as nature-philosophy: the identity-philosophy is nature-philosophy, the philosophy of freedom is nature-philosophy, the theogony and metapsychology of *Ages* are nature-philosophy. The typical periodization of Schelling's career, which situates nature-philosophy in the years 1797 to 1800 (the period immediately following his first Fichte studies), is misleading. That Schelling continues to talk about nature as "the real" that is not reducible to "the ideal" – not only in the *System* but in the work most often associated with the identity-philosophy, the 1804 Würzburg lectures (Schelling, 1804a), as well as in the *Freedom* essay (where ground is called "nature" (Schelling, 1809: 27)) and in *Ages* (which Grant rightly describes as nature-philosophy (Grant, 2006: 17)) – should serve to remind us that Schelling thought about nature in much broader terms than the canonical history of philosophy does. Grant is correct: "Schellingianism *is* naturephilosophy throughout" (Grant, 2006: 5).

3   The algebraic formulae by which Schelling illustrates the doctrine of the potencies – the sense of which has proven elusive to most English commentators (major recent studies such as Bowie (1993), as well as classic German treatments such as Furhmans (1954), do not mention it[30]) – remain consistent throughout these thirty-five years of his later philosophy. The most mysterious of the equations is the *Weltformel* of

the third draft of *Ages*, which can be read as a complete expression of Schelling's nature-philosophy. An explanation of what Schelling means by the *Weltformel* (should one be possible) will unlock the "system" not only of the nature-philosophy, but (since it is on Schelling's own account the core of his thinking) also of Schelling's logic, ontology and speculative psychology.

$$\left(\frac{A^3}{A^2 = (A = B)}\right)B$$

Schelling's "Formula of the World" (*Weltformel*) (Schelling, 1815: 84)

Before we venture a reading of the *Weltformel*, some preliminary remarks are needed. The triad of potencies is first explicitly introduced in Schelling's middle period as a translation of theosophy into dialectical philosophy – a point that contemporary commentators continually shy away from. This is not only demonstrable on the basis of the clear parallels between the later doctrine of the potencies and Boehme's theogony (with a related but more distant resonance with the Lurianic Kabbalah); we also have Schelling's own word for it. At the time of the composition of the *Ages* drafts (Schelling's Boehme period), Schelling believed that theosophy exceeded philosophy "in depth, fullness, and vitality of content," but that it needed to pass through "the dialectic" – needed to be mediated by discursive concepts – if it was to count as "knowledge."[31] Schelling's close personal and public association with Baader (popularly known as "Boehme redivivus" at the time), together with the general popularity of Boehme among the German romantics, meant that no one among Schelling's literate contemporaries would have missed the theosophic origins of the 1809 turn. Schopenhauer was certainly not alone in believing Schelling's philosophy of freedom to be a plagiarism of Boehme (given the influence of Boehme on Schopenhauer this is the pot calling the kettle black). Zovko's suspicion that the *Ages* project was stillborn not because Schelling could not master the material, but because he did not want to be seen as a follower of Baader, who was lecturing extensively on Boehme at the time, is, in my view, well-founded (Zovko, 1996: 121). Later on, Schelling qualifies his mid-career enthusiasm for theosophy and makes clear that his own philosophy should not be understood (either positively or negatively) as theosophy, which he now describes as a kind of incommunicable empiricism. But even under this censure, theosophy might still serve as a source of data for speculative philosophy.[32]

Remembering the theosophical origin of the later Schelling's triad of potencies will help us to keep the theological dimension at the forefront of the interpretation. This is not to underplay the philosophical significance of the doctrine – quite the contrary: the *Weltformel* receives decisive illumination when it is read against Kabbalistico-Boehmian theogony as

a rigorously philosophical expression of ideas that receive only mytho-
poetic expression in theosophy and Kabbalah. We are not suggesting that
Schelling's *Ages* is a theosophical treatise; Schelling provides logical, cosmological and theological *reasons* for the theogony, which he regards as
logically necessary if we are to avoid the Hegelian identification of being
and nothingness (the denial of non-contradiction), cosmologically necessary
if we are to account for the transition from the one to the many, and
theologically necessary if full justice is to be given to the biblical revelation
of God as personality, that is, as self-determining freedom.

It is also vital to remember from the outset that Schelling's dialectic is not
Hegel's dialectic. As Beach has made clear, Schelling's is an *Erzeugungs-
dialektik*, not an *Aufhebungsdialektik* (Beach, 1994: 85–91). This means that
the potencies are not derived from one another by logical necessity, nor do
they "cancel and preserve" (*aufheben*) one another. "Once and for all, it is
impossible for anything to be sublated [*aufgehoben*]" (Schelling, 1813: 168).
Although sharing a common essence, each potency emerges into existence
as the addition of something new to what the other offers, just as each
moment in time represents the eruption into being of something that is not
entirely prefigured by or causally reducible to the preceding moment, while
time itself remains one, identical in itself.

### First potency (A=B)[33]

The first act of creation, production of difference, is negative. Paradoxically, the new begins in a refusal of newness.[34] First potency refuses the very
newness that it initiates; it is a movement that negates movement. "Prior"
to creation the absolute neither renounces nor affirms the possibility of
creation; it is indifferent to both options. In first potency God withdraws
from the possibility of otherness; this "retreat" into himself clears a space
for the coming to be of things other than God. Why must the transition
from the infinite to the finite begin with negation? Considered in itself, the
absolute lacks nothing, it has no need of creation, and therefore there is no
necessary reason for creation to be.[35] Even considered in light of its lack of
distinction, its freedom from the subject–object, self–other distinction, the
absolute cannot ultimately be said to *lack* anything. Difference is not
"something"; it is privation of identity. Lack must first be introduced into
being. "Precisely that which negates all revelation must be made ground of
revelation" (Schelling, 1815: 16).

The beginning is an eternally withdrawing principle and an eternal
concealment of the ground of being.

> What is first in God after the decision or, because we must assume that
> as having *happened* since all eternity (and as still always happening),
> what is altogether first in God, in the living God, the eternal beginning

of itself in itself, is that God restricts itself, denies itself, withdraws its essence from the outside and retreats into itself.

(Schelling, 1815: 17)

The Lurianic Kabbalah speaks of a necessity for *Ein-Sof* to "make room" for something other than itself, hence the necessity of a contraction or withdrawal of the infinite, God absenting himself so that the finite might have the freedom to be. If God did not absent himself, the sheer excess of his actuality would preclude any diversity, just as irresistible goodness forecloses the possibility of finite freedom. The contraction of infinity is the production of desire; as Boehme puts it, God awakens a hunger in himself that can be nothing other than a hunger for himself (Boehme, 1622: 2.7). "A being cannot negate itself without thereby making itself turn inward and thereby making itself the object of its own wanting and desire" (Schelling, 1815: 16). By excising ground from existence and dissociating from his own eternity, God creates the theatre of desire, i.e., nature, an endlessly productive finite order.

Schelling argues that, because every movement is an effort to redress a contradiction, the beginning of movement can only be a contradiction. Movement is being's effort to avoid the negative – not by annulling it or transforming it into identity, as in Hegelian dialectics, but by moving out of the space divided by the contradiction and evacuating the contradicted being. If being were not initially diminished in its intensity – if the excessive actuality of being were not broken up by the introduction of lack – nothing would move, there would be no change, no time, no plurality. Since change, time, and plurality are real, we must posit an initial contraction or negation of the infinite. For this reason, the rationality of the world that comes to be in time rests on something that finite reason can only see as "irrational," something unfathomable, "unprethinkable."[36] By the third draft of *Ages*, Schelling is beginning to disentangle himself from historical immanentism, arguing that to maintain, with Hegel, that the absolute begins as imperfect, in contradiction with itself, and then necessarily develops through a negation of its original state, is to annul the principle of the divine aseity. "A transition from unity to contradiction is incomprehensible. For how should what is in itself one, whole and perfect be tempted, charmed and enticed to emerge out of its peace?" (Schelling, 1815: 12). Contradiction cannot be implicit or natural to the absolute; it can only be posited by it for the sake of setting being into motion. The one does not "naturally" disintegrate into the many, collapsing because it is inherently empty or "abstract," rather, the perfectly complete absolute introduces contradiction into being; it says No, freely limits itself, so that desire, movement, and the unity of love (the unity of two that could be apart) might be.

First potency is the introverted moment in the life of God, "the personal I hood (that rejects the outside)" (Schelling 1813: 171). Schelling describes it as "a force of selfhood," expressed in the Bible as divine "wrath" (Schelling, 1815: 9).

> This force is the white heat of purity, intensified to a fiery glare by the pull of nature. It is unapproachable, unbearable to all created things, and would rage against every creature like ruinous fire, an eternal wrath that tolerates nothing, fatally contracting but for the resistance of love.
>
> (Schelling, 1813: 171)

First potency appears in creation as "the self-will of creatures," "pure craving or desire" (Schelling, 1809: 32). This is not the egoism of self-affirmation; first potency affirms nothing. It only "asserts" itself negatively by refusing to recognize its other. As negativity itself, first potency is not only the condition of the possibility of revelation, it is the condition of the possibility of evil. Herein lies the core of the "solution" to the problem of evil that Schelling advances in the *Freedom* essay: things could only have come to be on the condition that ground *could* operate independently of grounded. Such an inversion of the hierarchy of being defines evil. In *Ages* we read how God introduces lack and negativity into being for the sake of creation/revelation. But the condition of the possibility of there being anything at all is also the condition of the possibility of evil itself.

The internal division of the absolute from itself begins with A negating itself by positing itself. A posits A, but that which is posited is different from that which posits, otherwise there is no positing. Thus the positing of A by A is the negating of A, a negation expressed by the introduction of another term to distinguish the *posited* A from the *positing* A. The posited A is signified by B. Thus A=A (A posits A) means A=B (A posits not-A or B).[37] The positing of A is the absenting of A from itself, the substitution of B for A – the first (temporal) potency. Difference is older than identity: "The affirmative principle, the authentic being or that which has being (A) as not active, that is, as not having being, is posited in the originary negation" (Schelling, 1815: 13).[38] A as such never appears: it can only be retroactively posited as that which is usurped by B in first potency, exponentially doubled in second potency, and exponentially tripled in third potency.

## Second potency ($A^2$)

First potency's introversion and renunciation of otherness calls forth the correction of second potency, the extraverted affirmation of otherness, the expansive moment or "the ideal," $A^2$. The tension between these two opposites of negation and affirmation, contraction and expansion, requires (logically) a third potency that both negates and affirms, contracts and expands, $A^3$.

Before looking in detail at the structure of $A^2$, it is worth circumventing a likely misinterpretation. Because of the hegemony of Hegelianism, we tend to read Schelling through Hegel: we think of second potency as the concealed truth of first potency made explicit, the truth that first potency has no truth, and that second potency is the "synthesis" implicit in the "antithesis" of the first two potencies. We think of the potencies succeeding each other temporally, as though first potency cannot maintain its one-sided stance and "sets itself aside," *becomes* second potency, and so on. We think of the transition between these "moments" as strictly logical. None of this is faithful to Schelling, who denies that anything can become the opposite of itself.[39] The doctrine of potencies is crafted as an alternative to Hegelian dialectics, which Schelling believed violated the freedom of the absolute, the principle of contradiction, and the contingency of the real. Moreover, the order of the potencies differs significantly from the order of the moments in Hegel's logic. First potency is not a negation masquerading as an affirmation, nor is it "abstract," "universal," or "immediate." It is a volitional negation of the possibility of being. It is not just "nothing" in some abstract sense (the absence of distinction); it is the will "that *wills* nothing" (Schelling, 1815: 24). Second potency, which redresses the renunciation of first potency, is not implicit (in the Hegelian sense) in the first; rather, it differs from it in every way. Second potency is the will that wills *something*. We could say that the will that wills nothing "implies" second potency inasmuch as it posits it as negated, but this is not to say that affirmation is "the truth" of negation.

Equally important to remember is that contingency (not necessity, reason, or "the notion") grounds the Schellingian dialectic. Although the movement from one potency to the other is logical, the whole sequence itself is not. God freely introduces lack into being and sets the sequence of potencies into self-actualization. The contingency, anarchy, and spontaneity of the actualization of first potency undergirds the logical necessity of each of the successive potencies. This is the heart of Schelling's thinking, what Markus Gabriel calls "the contingency of necessity" (Gabriel, 2009: 81). The unground's "lack of difference" is not a deficiency; it is a perfection. The unground in itself lacks nothing (since difference is a modality of nothingness). It is pure excess of being, infinite identity. There is no "insufficiency" or "inadequacy" driving the unground into differentiation, as is the case in Hegel's first moment, and it is here that the analogy with the Lacanian subject breaks down. Žižek speaks of God driven out of unity by the unbearable "vortex of drives," the mad rotation of potencies in eternity, which God finally brings to an end by converting freedom into a predicate, giving birth to the subject (Žižek, 1996: 70). But Schelling's eternity is not a madhouse; God does not "personalize" himself because he finds undifferentiated eternity unbearable. On the contrary, the indifference of the unground is the freedom from desire (*Gelassenheit*) that all beings long for, the peace that passes understanding. If it were otherwise, the break with eternity would not be a spontaneous act, but a necessary resolution of an unbearable situation.[40] For Schelling, the emergence of the many from the one could only be the product of a contingent act – not an accident, but a free decision, a spontaneous act of self-determination. Schelling's insistence on this point in *Ages* echoes remarks made in the *Freedom* essay that align him with what might be called the German Neoplatonic tradition (Eckhart, Silesius, Boehme): the unground is not one of the potencies, it is not involved in the movements determining the transitions from A=B to $A^2$ to $A^3$. Citing Silesius ("The Gentle Godhead is nothing and beyond nothing"[41]), Schelling writes:

> It [the unground] certainly is nothing, but in the way that pure freedom is nothing. It is like the will that wills nothing, that desires no object, for which all things are equal and is therefore moved by none of them. Such a will is nothing and everything.
>
> (Schelling, 1815: 24)

To be distinguished here is the will that wills *nothing*, the indifference and desirelessness of the unground, and the will that *wills* nothing, the active negation of otherness of first potency. The transition from the former to the latter is precisely the contraction of being that marks the emergence of first potency from the unground.[42]

The "contingent necessity" driving second potency is the need to reassert the A that is lost in first potency. Second potency is not self-affirmative, but self-diremptive; it does not assert itself, but asserts its other. Second potency also fails to simply posit A, for the product of its assertion of A is not A, but $A^2$. Using a word he coined in his nature-philosophy, but with a new sense, Schelling calls this finitization or reduction to actuality of A "potentization."[43] Second potency fills the gap created by first potency; it is the potency that counters the No of the first with an unequivocal (and equally one-sided) Yes. As the mirror of A, second potency is "the ideal," "the outpouring, outstretching, self-giving being" that counterbalances the narcissism of A=B (Schelling, 1815: 6). $A^2$ is A doubled in several senses. It is first potency reflected back to itself – the successful positing of first potency achieved by virtue of the positor's deliberate renunciation of itself. Thus what A=B *means* (but does not intend), $A^2$ *intends*. That is, first potency intends itself (A determined) but means the other (B). It asserts itself (A=A) and in the assertion loses itself, and in effect posits the other (B). Second potency asserts the other and achieves itself. Hence in the *Weltformel* Schelling will write $A^2$=(A=B). But what $A^2$ *means* is still other than A. It is A exponentially intensified. Second potency is also a doubling of A because it mirrors first potency back to itself, a mirroring discussed in the *Freedom* essay, where second potency is described as "the understanding" or "the word" that reflects the "yearning" of ground back to itself.[44] What is manifest in the one potency is latent in the other (Schelling, 1815: 18). Second potency decommissions the negativity of first potency (renders it "non-active" and "dark"), but only for the sake of focusing the concealed affirmative and productive power of first potency. Ground *is* only itself insofar as it defers to that which it grounds, allows itself to "stand under" the grounded. Its deferral, contraction, and withdrawal opens the space for existence, which Schelling also describes as "understanding," the ecstatic act of being outside oneself and in another. Consider an architectural metaphor: a foundation is not identical to the building that it founds; it pulls away from the sky and "wills" to sink into the earth. Because it does so it can serve as the stable support for the building that reaches upward toward the sky. The foundation and the building are two countervailing wills that, when synchronized, constitute the whole structure. Fichte's moments, which stood statically facing each other as thesis and antithesis, become in Schelling volitional vectors, drives counterbalancing each other.

But $A^2$ is every bit as determined as A=B, for it stands in essential opposition to it. As such, $A^2$ depends upon A=B. "That potency, which in accordance with its nature, is spiritual and outstretching, could not persist as such were it not to have, at least in a hidden manner, a force of selfhood" (Schelling, 1815: 9). The point is not merely logical; it is also ethical and psychological. There is no goodness without a seed of evil overcome, no self-diremption without a self that is given away. Here Schelling channels Boehme's proto-Nietzschean Christianity: "If there were not the No, then the Yes would be without force. No 'I' without the 'not-I'" (Schelling, 1815: 18). The negative potency that would "save its life," posit itself, loses itself (A=B); the affirmative potency that "loses itself" posits its other and gains itself ($A^2$). First potency's self-assertion by negation (Lucifer's "nothing else shall be but me") results in the destruction and loss of that which it would above all possess. The point is an algebraic summary of the philosophy of evil explored in the *Freedom* essay. Evil would elevate its particular will over the universal will, but only succeeds in destroying itself, for it can only *be* insofar as it is subordinate to the universal. Second potency "redeems" first potency by achieving what it sought but in a reverse fashion: rather than egoism, altruism; rather than contraction, expansion; rather than self-assertion, self-donation.

### Third potency ($A^3$)

Only together do first and second potency constitute a whole, just as only as an existing being do ground and being function properly. A=B in conjunction with $A^2$ equals $A^3$, the figure for what in the *Freedom* essay Schelling calls personality. Here at last is sustainable self-affirmation achieved. $A^3$ can genuinely affirm itself because it can also deliberately deny itself. Personality is neither entirely self-centred nor other-centred, but "the whole composed of dual forces" (Schelling, 1809: 33). $A^3$ is the unity of the No and the Yes, not as a *coincidentia oppositorum*, but rather as a third that is in one respect negative, in another respect affirmative.[45] Third potency regains something of the indifference characteristic of the unground (Schelling, 1815: 19). But $A^3$ is not merely a return to the absolute. The antithesis of the first two potencies, which was only a possibility in the absolute, is now actual, generating singularities and individuating. $A^3$ is realized personality, freedom, is the capacity for good and evil.

### The formula of the world

The *Weltformel* is not an equation but a diagram. Remembering that in Schelling's theory of predication the copula is both conjunctive and disjunctive (= is also ≠), the "formula,"

$$\left(\frac{A^3}{A^2 = (A = B)}\right) B$$

could also be diagrammed, less elegantly, but perhaps more clearly, as follows:

$$(A^3 = [A^2 = \{A = B\}])B$$

The line dividing the upper field from the lower field in Schelling's diagram does not indicate division, but rather symbolizes the finality of $A^3$. The formula of the world illustrates the containment of the lower potencies in the higher: in my rewriting of it each of the sets of brackets – (), [], {} – indicates a distinct level of containment. Each container transcends what it contains (= is ≠). $A^3$ is the container of containers. Beginning in the middle of our version of the diagram above, $A^2$ is the becoming conscious (or containing) of the antithesis between A and B. A=B does not mean that A qua A is equal to not-A, which would violate the principle of non-contradiction. It means that what is in one respect A is in another respect B. $A^2=(A=B)$ means that what is in one respect $A^2$ is in another respect A, where A is in one respect A and in another respect B. In the same way, $A^3$ is the becoming conscious or containing of the antithesis of $A^2$ and (A=B). It is both identical and different from $A^2$. It "equals" $A^2$ in that it potentizes or intensifies that which is coming forward in $A^2$, namely the counterbalancing of negativity by positivity, of ipseity by alterity. $A^3$ redoubles the other-centredness and ipseity affirmation of $A^2$ to the point where it transcends and includes that which $A^2$ excludes, namely the negativity of (A=B).

B is in one sense the product of the negation of first potency, the irreducible remainder and the moving principle of the whole formula. It is the self-activated ground, the cleft of difference at the non-tautological core of every judgement, and the duality concealed in every identity. But it is also, or rather it stands in the place of, the unground, the ground which has no ground and can never be represented, rendering every system non-total, excluding one thing upon which everything else depends. B makes all predication, all movement, and all self-consciousness possible. Each of the potencies depends upon B; hence the whole formula is qualified by it. Without the negative, the exclusion, no separation of A from itself would occur, thus no consciousness of A would be possible. The bracketing out of B indicates that everything up to one (the unground) is idealized, rationalized, and ordered. This is Schelling's great insight, the core of his dispute with Hegel, and the secret to why he refused to build a final system (in the idealist sense of deriving all elements from a self-evident principle): the condition of the possibility of structure, intelligibility, and consciousness is the exclusion of something (B) that the whole structure depends upon. We are not far from Gödel: every system rests upon an axiom that is not explicable in terms of the system. Or in Hogrebe's words, "The true is the whole with the exception of one."[46] B gives the lie to every idealist system: the rational is not coextensive with the real; the rational depends upon an exclusion, the absence of precisely that which makes it rational. B is the symbol of unground, of irreducible remainder, of the eternal past, the deep unconscious, etc. But nothing Schelling says justifies Žižek in describing the exclusion of B as a Freudian "repression" (*Verdrängung*)[47] – unless we are already with Nietzsche and Freud, for whom every dissociation is a way of managing a reality that is in essence horrible and senseless. B is the split in the self necessary for consciousness, yes. B is the incomprehensible presupposition of every system of comprehension, yes. B indicates that personality is constitutively dissociated, yes. But why does personality dissociate? Nietzsche and Freud say personality dissociates in order to manage. Schelling says personality dissociates for the sake of self-knowledge and love. The Nietzschean-Freudian answer can be fused with the Schellingian answer only if we have already decided that self-knowledge and love are fundamentally illusions, that reality is absurd and tragic and that the subject constructs myths of self-knowledge and love as a means of coping.

After inserting the formula into the third draft of *Ages*, Schelling adds the following:

> Hence from this point forward, we step into the path of time. The contradiction is decided by the exuberant deed similar to the one in which a person decides to be utterly one thing or another. From this point forward, God is exclusively singular. God is only negation with respect to Being. As this negating force, God is fire that draws Being into itself.

(Schelling, 1815: 83–84)

The principle of sufficient reason requires that we posit a ground of God. The principle of identity requires that we identify God with his ground, for every dependency is an identification of the dependent with that upon which it depends. The principle of non-contradiction requires that we separate the time of the divine ground from the time of the divine God, for two opposites cannot be predicated of the same thing at the same time. The ground, B, is God's unconscious.[48] B, then, is not just a figure for the excluded negative; it is a place-holder for the absent God. B is a trace of the *Deus absconditus*, the sign of the unsignifiable, the absenting of which makes the world possible. We are back at the *zimzum* of the Lurianic Kabbalah: the absence of the infinite, the contraction of *Ein-Sof* into an unconscious abyss is the condition of the possibility of there being anything at all. The dynamic that structures the inner life of God also structures God's relation to creation. God stands to the world as its excluded ground, the hidden ground that must remain inexplicable in intra-worldly terms. God is the unconscious of the world. Viewed from the perspective of the world, from the perspective of finite things (from which we can say this or that *is*), God *is not*.[49] This is not to say that God does not exist. Indeed the existence of God is the presupposition of the world. But what existence means in application to God is something quite different from what existence means in application to inner-worldly beings.

The negative-theological language applied to the finite person could be translated as follows. The person is intrinsically temporal, enjoying self-consciousness by virtue of the dissociations essential to life in time. In its innermost core, the person is an ineffable singularity, "negation with respect to Being." As such the person stands in an erotic relationship to the universal or the whole, is drawn to it and draws it to herself, even as she necessarily dissociates from it. The person's singularity is for the sake of the achievement of a union of love with all that is, a union that does not abolish the distinctions among beings (for love unites that which is really distinct) but fulfils them on a higher plane. The unconscious is the past, dissociated from the person's present identity for the sake of the growth of consciousness, that is, for the sake of the future.

## The God outside God

At the same time that he distanced himself from idealism with its more or less explicit divinization of human reason and became increasingly interested in a real that is not simply experienced as the other side of the absolute but as that which reason can never mediate, Schelling moved closer to orthodox Christianity. Schelling first makes references to Christ in the *Freedom* essay (Schelling, 1809: 46), more directly in the *Stuttgart Seminars* (Schelling, 1810a: 228), and crowns his career with the speculative Christology of the *Philosophy of Revelation*. The foundation of the latter is the *Philosophy of Mythology*, a lengthy recapitulation of the essential moments in the history of world-mythology (to the extent of Schelling's knowledge of it) as concrete expressions of the ontological determinants of historical consciousness, the three potencies, now reconceived as possibility (*das Sein könnende*), existence (*das Sein müssende*), and self-ordering being (*das Sein sollende*). The history of mythology is for Schelling crypto-Christology, for the unifying principle of pre-Christian paganism, the true subject of all myth, is nothing other than the pre-existing Christ, the logos, or the second potency prior to its incarnation in Jesus, which Schelling calls, literally, "the extra-divine of the divine" (*das außergöttliche des Göttlichen*), or more figuratively, the God outside God. Noting how the significance of Christology for Schelling ascends as the significance of identity-philosophy decreases, we discern a conceptual association of ideas: the extra-conceptual reality of the world, the contingency of history, the finitude of reason, the personal nature of being, and Christianity. The late Schelling argues that we cannot think any one of these all the way through without the others; they are all mutually implicating. A philosophy such as Hegel's, which presumes to have sublated nature, history, and religion into a system, remains as un-historical as it is un-Christian. When in the lectures on *The Philosophy of Revelation*, Schelling declares baldly, "Christianity is an eminently historical religion, where there is no Christianity, there is no history" (Schelling, 1831: 5), he is not unveiling yet another front of eclectic philosophical interest but rather expressing a hard-won insight into the essential poverty of human reason. Idealism remains as out of touch with the really existing God as it is out of touch with the real for it presumes to know a priori that which can never be conceptually known: contingent reality, existence, event. Only a philosophy that recognizes this essential poverty of reason – and the only way to know it, the late Schelling says, is by going the full distance with idealism ("negative philosophy") – only an experientially humiliated philosophy can also recognize the rationality of Christianity, not the Christianity of Kant and Fichte, which serves as a mere concrete exemplification of concepts that are the inalienable possession of reason, but the Christianity of the New Testament, the truth about man, the world, and God, which could never have been known had it not been revealed. But now that it has been revealed and has become part of history (indeed for German Idealism, history *is* revelation), Christianity can and must be thought by reason, a thinking which will be speculative, autonomous and fully independent of external (i.e., ecclesiastical) norms. This is what the late Schelling means by "philosophical religion," religion without religion, the successor of church-mediated Christianity, and to its inauguration he dedicates the last two decades of his career.

In order to philosophically thematize the brute contingency of the world the late Schelling deems it necessary to renounce the historical immanentism which was once central to his metaphysics and return to a more traditional notion of God, the Aristotelian-Scholastic concept of God, the *actus purus*. God is complete prior to creation, eternally free, always already a person; therefore the creation of the world is pure contingency, not something God needs in order to become conscious but an unfathomable event, and the history of the world is a real history or a history of the real, not to be explicated from a logical idea. However theologically conservative this view, the late Schelling retains key elements of his earlier psychology of dissociation that he worked out in his middle period, which he applies to the construction of an original theory of the Trinity. The dissociations necessary to personal identity and interpersonal relation happen eternally within God through the emergence of the three divine potencies that are now understood to be three distinct personalities in God, each with their own distinctive attitudes and roles to play in the history of the world (in the history of Trinitarian theology Schelling tends towards the tri-theism of Joachim of Fiore). The birth of consciousness through unconscious decision, the intelligible act by which the self breaks with a prior state of undifferentiated unity with its unconscious in order to become self-conscious, is no longer applicable to God, who is now held to be never without consciousness. Schelling does not abandon the essential core of his earlier theogony; rather he transfers it to the history of the human race. In the history of mythology and revelation, humanity gives birth to itself as free, self-conscious, and personal by breaking with its primitive immediate consciousness of the divine, a merely natural presence of God to the human, which Schelling describes as spontaneous, unfree, and only relatively monotheistic. Humanity descends into history, the history of peoples diversified by their polytheistic religious devotions. Prior to Christianity, a people is defined over and against other peoples by its unique mythology, its history of gods and goddesses, which Schelling describes as neither objective entities nor subjective representations but as genuine experiences of the divine in however fragmented and limited a form. The descent into diversity is necessary so that free religion, genuine monotheism, can arise out of history and unite the human race once again under God, but now freely and self-consciously, in a third phase of religious history in which ecclesiastical religion is succeeded by philosophical religion: the epoch of the spirit. The personality that comes to birth out of the splitting of the unconscious is now the human race itself, summoned forth from nature by the personal God who seeks to give himself to one like himself.

The prolegomena to Schelling's late Christology is his progressive discovery of the ontological impotence of reason, its inability to fulfil its natural teleology and think the absolute in the only way that it can be fully thought, as a system that excludes nothing and derives everything from a single self-evident principle. The latter is often described as *the* programme of German Idealism, a programme which Schelling announced in various ways in the major works of his early period as the only task worthy of philosophy only to have Hegel actually attempt to accomplish it, with no more success, in Schelling's view, than he himself had achieved as a young man. The failure of German Idealism leads Schelling to the foot of the cross. In the historical revelation of the absolute as the crucified, reason encounters, not only an image of itself as fallen and incapable of redeeming itself but, more importantly, the historical reality of the immense distance that opens up between the first and second potency in God's redemption of nature. In the crucified, God becomes the other to himself in every way: God becomes man, and through man (the microcosm), God becomes fallen nature; the infinite becomes finite; absolute goodness becomes sin; eternal life becomes death. This, according to Schelling, is the true *coincidentia oppositorum*, a forgery of which Hegel forces onto logic, and so divests of blood and reality, not only distorting logic in the process, but insulating thought from a vital encounter with the real. The genuine *coincidentia oppositorum* is not a dialectic of concepts but a series of unforeseeable historical events in which that which thought hitherto regarded as impossible actually happens. In the light of these events, the prior history of human culture as recorded in mythology becomes understandable as a dramatization in time of the ontological relationship of the three divine potencies.

The full account of Schelling's late philosophy cannot occupy us here.[50] We conclude this chapter on Schelling's psychology of dissociation with a brief look at the late Schelling's Christology because for Schelling Christ is the dissociation of God from himself that redeems fallen nature. As a second personality in God, Christ is dissociated from the Father at the creation of the world, which is also its fall, and re-united in love in the crucifixion/resurrection. But this second dissociation presupposes a first, the contraction of first potency into the real or the creation of the material world, which after the fall floats freely of God like a lost child. The historical union of the first and second personalities in God is also the beginning of the historical career of God's third personality, third potency, the Holy Spirit, who has a special relationship to philosophy and its mission, to found a philosophical religion, a universal religion without religion, a religion of freedom and reason.

The poverty of reason, its inability to think the absolute and so fulfil itself, does not lead to a deduction of the necessity of revelation, for that would leave philosophy in its negative moment, dialoguing with the concepts that it produces out of itself. Rather, the impotence of idealism leads to philosophy's recognition of the need for "positive philosophy," which takes its point of departure not from concepts, but from existence, and above all from the truth mediated by certain extraordinary historical facts. Schelling first speaks of the "ecstasy of reason" in 1821 (SSW 9: 230), a phrase that stands in uneasy tension with intellectual intuition: whereas the earliest sketches of intellectual intuition presented it as the subject's own grasp of itself as absolute, an entirely immanent act of reason catching itself in the act of reasoning and experiencing its interior infinity, the ecstasy of reason is exactly the opposite gesture: it is the turning outward of the subject, its self-abnegation and confession of interior poverty, the lowering of reason before absolute reality, which makes it ecstatic, open to the truth that comes to meet it from outside.[51]

Schelling first suggests that reason cannot complete its mission and think the absolute in the *Stuttgart Seminars*. While Schelling has still not broken with historical immanentism in 1810 – the *Stuttgart Seminars* is in some ways its apogee – the need for a historical revelation of the absolute, and therefore a history of the real, is first mentioned here. Because we cannot achieve the absolute in our fallen state, Schelling argues in 1810, we need a historical revelation, the culmination of which would be the incarnation of the absolute in time and space as a mediator that could restore our sundered relation to being. Man was intended to be the link between God and nature; he was called to mediate the two by raising nature to God, but instead he identified himself with the lower and damaged his spiritual faculties to such a degree as to have lost consciousness of God altogether. The situation can only be remedied if God not only comes to meet man on his own terrain, in history, but also somehow becomes the mediator between nature and himself (Schelling, 1810a: 228).

How did Schelling the neo-Spinozistic philosopher of immanence become a philosopher of transcendence in both the realistic and theistic senses of the term? The question is enormous and would require a careful reading of many pages of Schelling's identity-philosophy as well as a careful consideration of Schelling's own spiritual history. In his *Jugendschriften* Schelling was miles away from Christian philosophy even if he had been well educated in it. We cannot rule out a religious conversion in the tumultuous years that brought Schelling's astonishing publication record to an end, 1809–1815, the dark years in which Schelling lost his beloved muse, Caroline Schlegel, to a tragic death, and formed arguably the most important friendship of his life (even if it did not last), with the Christian theosophist Franz von Baader. The steady stream of publications which began when Schelling was 18 years old came to a sudden halt with the short 1815 tract, *The Deities of Samothrace* (SSW 8: 345–369). Schelling's biography, however, cannot concern us here. What cannot be denied is that prior to 1809, Christianity is of no particular philosophical importance to Schelling, while after 1809, Christianity appears in Schelling's writings and lectures as the key to the history of being, until in his last lectures, Schelling dedicates himself, not to the construction of a system that would rival Hegel's (what everyone expected of him), but to the textual and hermeneutical explication of the philosophy implicit in the New Testament (which few were interested in hearing).

The gap between Schelling's early non-Christian philosophy of immanence and his later Christian philosophy is bridged by the historical immanentism of his middle period. Although he will later abandon it, historical imman-entism provisionally unites the teleological unconscious of the nature-philosophy (man is nature become conscious of itself) with the Christian doctrine of the atonement. In this regard the middle Schelling is not so far from Hegel who does something similar in his *Encyclopedia*. Nevertheless Schelling's historically immanentist approach to Christianity, at least as presented in the *Stuttgart Seminars,* is markedly different from Hegel's: where for Hegel Christianity is an imagistic, historically dependent first sketch of a rational truth that must be reconceived on a priori grounds, for the middle Schelling, Christianity is the historical, entirely a posteriori, culmination of the becoming conscious of God in nature. The Schellingian absolute is the identity of subject and object, the real and the ideal, but such a concept, however correct, remains merely a concept; the decisive question for a reason that now experiences the depths of its impotence is: can the absolute be affirmed to really exist?

> Primordial being [*das Urwesen*] as the absolute identity of the real and the ideal is itself only subjectively posited, however we must grasp it objectively: it must not remain merely in itself but must also be the absolute identity of the real and the ideal outside itself, that is, it must reveal itself as such, actualize itself – it must show itself as such also in existence.
>
> (Schelling, 1810a: 200, translation mine)

In contradiction to claims he made in the identity-philosophy, Schelling argues in the *Stuttgart Seminars* that reason does not innately possess a genuine knowledge of the absolute; the philosophical idea of the absolute is "subjective," a merely conceptual understanding of the identity of the real and the ideal. Needed is a *real* experience of the absolute, not a concept or a proof, but a historical experience, a positive, radically empirical, revelation of God. Clearly Schelling is not talking about traditional philosophical theology and the industry of proving God's existence. The existence of God is no doubt logically necessary, for God's essence is to exist, God's ideality is always also reality – thus far does Schelling follow Anselm. But logical necessity is not real necessity; all that Anselm proves is that if God exists, he exists necessarily, not contingently. For the later Schelling, there is no transition from the conceptual necessity of the identity of the ideal and the real in God to the objective existence of the absolute; if the latter is to be known, it can only be known a posteriori, that is, it can only be known to the degree that it reveals itself.[52] Something can reveal itself only in its opposite, Schelling argues: love is only revealed in its overcoming of hate, light is only revealed in its abolition of darkness. But outside God there is nothing, no opposite, no place where God is absent and in which he could be revealed. However, there *is* opposition *within* God, the duality of ground/existence, which Schelling now refers to as the duality of being and being (*Sein*/*Seiende*) where *being* is the opposite of *a being* inasmuch as it grounds it without itself being grounded while *a being* is always grounded. The question the middle Schelling asks is this: how can this internal opposition in God become an external opposition that would allow God to be revealed to man? The answer to this question leads into his historical immanentist revision of the Christian atonement. In short, God freely creates the world and allows it to fall so as to come to consciousness of himself through the incarnate Christ.

The early Schelling had already identified consciousness as the *telos* of natural history; what the middle Schelling adds is a theogony: the emergence of consciousness out of nature is not a natural evolution or an immanent movement of the lower to the higher, it is rather an unfathomable act of a free God, who seeks to become conscious of himself through the creation of his other. In God first potency (ground/*Sein*) logically precedes and grounds second potency (existence/*Seiende*); so long as this harmonious dialectic is undisturbed nothing besides God exists and God remains unrevealed even to himself, i.e., God stays unconscious. If something is to exist and God is to be revealed, the relationship of first and second potency must be disrupted, first potency must dissociate from second potency and its logical priority must become a historical priority, that is, first potency must somehow come to exist in itself. But since first potency cannot stand fully on its own, the existence to which it would give rise in its dissociation from second potency could only be a half-existence, a derivative existence, an order of being that could be just as truly characterized as a modification of nothingness. The absolute must contract its being so that first potency is expelled from the eternal balance, so to speak, excreted from eternity:

> If the primal being [*das Urwesen*] wills the dissociation [*die Entzweiung*] of the potencies, it must posit the priority of first potency as real [*wirkliche*] (the merely ideal or logical priority must be changed into a real priority), that is, it must freely contract itself into the first and negate the simultaneity of the principles as they are primordially in God.
>
> (Schelling, 1810a: 203, translation mine)

As expressed in the *Freedom* essay, God lets the ground loose, allows it to try to satisfy its selfish, chaotic, and impossible desire, to exist in itself, so that the "simultaneity" of the potencies will be disrupted and something other than God come to exist. The contraction does not disrupt the eternal simultaneity of the principles in God, Schelling is careful to point out, for the eternal balance of potencies must remain as that against which the now really existent (first) potency contrasts.[53] Because eternal being can only be revealed in its opposite, God allows his opposite to be, he creates finite being, which is in fact existent nothingness, matter, the spacio-temporal order, history, so that he might be revealed in it. The contraction of first potency is at once the creation of matter and the beginning of time, for what pre-exists simultaneously in the absolute now unfolds dramatically in the three ages of the world, the past, the present, and the future.[54]

"Creation is above all a lowering of God [*eine Herablassung Gottes*]" (Schelling, 1810a: 204, translation mine) – the middle Schelling, in an apparent departure from his earlier immanentism, recognizes that to lower oneself, to empty oneself, is not a base act but the highest and most divine of all acts.

> He [God] lowers himself into the real, contracts himself entirely into it. But there is nothing unworthy of God here. In Christianity the lowering of God is the greatest. A metaphysically immobile God [*ein metaphysisch hinaufgeschraubter Gott*] who cannot lower himself satisfies neither our head nor our heart.
>
> (Schelling, 1810a: 204, translation mine)

In the version of the *Stuttgart Seminars* corrected by Schelling himself, the lowering of God in creation is even more clearly aligned with the Christian doctrine of incarnation through the explicit use of the term, as well as the use of the German "self-emptying" (*Entäusserung*), which translates Paul's word *kenosis* (Philippians 2:7): "Inasmuch as God contracts himself in the real, so is the beginning of creation a lowering of God: it is an effect of the divine self-emptying [*eine Wirkung der göttlichen Entäusserung*], the becoming man [*Menschwerdung*], the first incarnation of God."[55] The question guiding Schelling's research in the *Stuttgart Seminars* is no longer: "How do we raise the finite to the infinite?" The question is: "How does the infinite become finite?" (Rosenau, 1985: 88). The highest act of being is its self-emptying (*Entäusserung*) into the finite; God incarnates himself as world, contracts his eternity ($A^1$ become B) so as to progressively become conscious of himself as God in the history of the world and the evolutionary increase in human consciousness. The end result of this incarnation could not simply be a return to the eternal: what begins as unconscious ends as conscious; what begins as impersonal (the absolute) ends as personal (the Christ).

Man's role in history has changed from what God originally intended it to be: called to become himself the Christ, that is, to freely complete the revelation of God by mediating all that was below him, matter, merely animal existence, the will of the ground, and raising it above him into spirit, man failed to rise to the occasion; he resisted the transformation of the lower into the higher and actualized the selfish drive of the first potency (Boehme's Lucifer pattern).[56] Ancient evil lies buried in first potency, unsustainable self-centredness, the negation of life and existence; if it remains buried, it supports the evolution of consciousness – indeed it is the essential condition of the development of personality. But if it is awakened instead, it destroys itself and aborts personality. This is the essential core of the proto-Freudian Schelling and the cue for Žižek's Lacanian reading of *The Ages of the World*: for Freud repression of drive is the necessary prerequisite for the development of ego. For Schelling, the point is primarily theological: by awakening the ancient evil in the ground, the gap between God and nature, which man was called to bridge, widened instead and could no longer be bridged by an act of man alone, for in falling from his place in the divine economy, man lost his natural spiritual capacities. Only God could redeem the situation, through a second revelation, which would correct the first that man aborted, the revelation of a God who descends into fallen nature and does what man ought to have done (Schelling, 1810a: 228).

The decisive difference between the late Schelling and the middle Schelling is that the late Schelling denies process in God: in the *Philosophy of Revelation* the dialectical development of consciousness from the unconscious applies primarily to man and only to God insofar as he is identified with man, that is, to Christ. The ontology that founds the whole late Schellingian enterprise remains the doctrine of potencies revised into a theory of the three co-inherent modes of being.[57] The first mode (first potency now designated -A) is pure possibility (*das Sein könnende*); the second mode (+A) is pure existence, that which stands outside of its essence and exists as such or the being that must be (*das Sein müssende*); the third mode is the synthesis of the two (±A), the being that can and must be or the being that should be (*das Sein sollende* – moral rather than logical necessity). As pure possibility, being is "subject," that which could be in and for itself; as pure existence, being is "object," that which stands outside of its possibilities and exists for another, i.e., for a subject; as subject-object, being possesses itself, it has come to be through a reduction of potentiality to act. The first mode, possibility, is sometimes referred to as being-in-itself (*das in-sich-Sein*), the second mode, existence, is referred to as being-outside-itself (*das ausser-sich-Sein*), and the third mode is referred to as being-with-itself (*das bei-sich-Seinde*). The first mode is unlimited, the second, limited, and the third, self-ordering. The first corresponds to Aristotle's material cause, the *dynamis* of being, and the Platonic unbounded, the second to efficient cause, the *energeia* of being, the ecstatic and self-emptying moment – "it is pure cause since it wants and expects nothing for itself" (Hayes, 1995: 173) – and the third to final cause, the *entelecheia* of being, which brings about order. The three together constitute a unity, which is not a fourth mode, but the whole itself, corresponding to Aristotle's formal cause.[58]

What does the late version of the potencies add to the ground/existence/ personality triad of the middle Schelling? With the retrieval of *actus purus* as the divine nature and the elevation of the Godhead above all processes, the primordial possibility associated with Boehme's unground is absorbed into first potency (*das Sein könnende*). *Actus purus* refers to the complete realization of perfection or goodness understood as *kenosis* or absolute self-surrender. The triune God resolves and realizes his own nature as perfect love. Why the shift from the Boehmian abyss of possibility (unground) to this apparently more traditional theology? Because if God is personal – and after 1809 Schelling understands personality to be the highest ontological determination   then he must be the active origin of his own identity, not the effect of a natural process of becoming (as is Hegel's God). The move from the unground to pure act is not so much a regression to Scholastic metaphysics as a progression from pantheism to personalism. The late Schelling's rethinking of the divine nature (suggestions of which were already present in the *Ages* drafts, particularly in those passages where Schelling substitutes the Eckhartian term *Gottheit* for the Boehmian term *Ungrund*) leads to a significant alteration in the notion of ground/first potency. Where the middle Schelling's concept of ground refers to negation, negatively self-assertive drive, *das Sein könnende* is both negation and affirmation, but always only as possibilities, never actualities. First potency, which under the figure of ground was associated with self-centred drive, is now a site of the indifference previously reserved for the unground/ Godhead. *Das Sein könnende* can be self-centred or it can be other-centred because it is actually neither.

The Sartrian overtones in Schelling's reference to first potency as "subject" (a term he previously associated with second potency, with logos, understanding, etc.) have been commented upon before.[59] To be a subject (in both the logical sense of a possible bearer of predicates and the onto-logical sense of a being-for-itself) is not to be anything at all. The subject is never fully defined, never to be entirely identified with any particular actuality; subjecthood is the possibility of being an object, the possibility of being objectified, the possibility of bearing predicates or of being something or other for someone, but not actually being anything at all (hence Sartre identifies being a subject with nothingness, and being an object with being fixed by the gaze of another). Subjecthood never fully coincides with objecthood – except in God. Thus does a new emphasis on the unconscious as pure possibility emerge in the ontology of the late Schelling. Where the middle Schellingian ground, the eternal past, the decision for being that has always already been made, can be read as the Freudian unconscious which determines the psychological subject from behind, *das Sein könnende* is and must remain forever open: it is the unconscious, not as determining but as determinable, the unconscious as infinite source of possibilities, the unconscious as forever forward looking.

While all three modes of being are essential moments of the divinity, the third alone represents the logically complete idea of God, the absolute subject-object, being-in-itself that is no less outside itself and being-outside-itself that remains in itself.[60] The complete idea of the divine then is triadic: a synthesis of possibility (essence), existence (difference), and the ordered relations between them (essence-existence synthesis).

The late Schelling's narrative of the creation of the world by the Trinity no longer presumes historical immanentism, for the Trinity does not need creation in order to become personal and free; rather the Trinity creates out of its infinite self-mediation, its eternally achieved freedom. Creation is now described as a series of incarnations of the three distinct personalities in God, still beginning with a contraction of infinity, for something can come to be outside of God only if the potencies are dissociated from each other. In order for time to begin, eternity must cease to be. This happens when the first potency is "set free" by God: -A, no longer subordinated to +A, becomes B and "incarnates" itself as matter, as that which is in itself and *wills* to be but cannot be for itself. At the moment of the contraction, second potency descends and initially concretizes itself as a demiurge, "the lord of being." But in its first moment of existence, creation falls as a result of the human being's resistance to its mediating role in the cosmogonic drama. Thus the first incarnation of second potency is as the spirit of an order of being that is doubly alienated from God, not only creation in its natural dissociation from the Trinity, but fallen being, creation become something that God does not intend. Second potency therefore becomes the God outside of God, "the divine personality outside the divinity" (*das außergöttlich-göttliche Persönlichkeit*) (Schelling, SSW 14: 163). This extreme alienation of God from himself (God at three removes from himself, separated from his eternity, first, by the contraction of first potency into matter, second, by the fall of creation, and third, through the first incarnation of second potency), this theology of dissociation, is for Schelling the essential core of Christianity.

> It is absolutely necessary for the understanding of Christianity – the *conditio sine qua non* of perceiving its true meaning – that we comprehend this cutting-off [*Abgeschittenheit*] of the Son from the Father, this being in his own form and hence in complete freedom and independence of the Father.
>
> (Schelling, SSW 14: 39)

The dissociated second potency begins a historical career that culminates in his full incarnation and crucifixion as Jesus, the nadir of his descent and the explicit revelation of his divinity. The pre-existent Christ is the subject behind all ancient myths, God wandering homeless and in exile from eternity, but retaining his own divine status, "the light of the pagans," defending them against the ancient evil aroused by the fall and working everywhere towards the reconciliation of creation with God. The tension between these two incarnate potencies, the fallen first potency (-A become B) and the dissociated second potency (+A), is resolved when Christ becomes man in history, incarnating himself in the figure of Jesus. Because Jesus is fully human, second potency thereby assumes fallen first potency (matter) as a property of itself, overcoming its rebelliousness and negating its negativity by becoming obedient unto death. Thus does Christ do what man was intended to do, mediate time and eternity by reconciling first and second potency. The moment of the reconciliation, the crucifixion and resurrection, is also the moment of the descent of third potency (±A), the Holy Spirit, who inaugurates the third era of revelation.

Schelling's cosmogony elevates ancient mythology well above the place allotted to it by his contemporaries, who were equally divided among those who regarded mythology as bad science, i.e., an effort to explain natural phenomena through personifying natural forces, those who regarded mythology as idealizations of historical figures, and those who regarded mythology as poetry, of literary significance only, without reference to physical or historical fact. All three schools refused to regard mythology as the ancients did, as true stories of gods and goddesses whose activities determine human life for good or ill. Schelling's Christological interpretation of mythology allows the ancients the dignity of their religious experience: mythology expresses a "real relation of God to human consciousness" (Schelling, SSW 11: 81; Hayes, 1995: 84). Mythology is nothing less than the hidden history of the Christ before his historical birth, the peregrinations of the God outside God. Polytheism is not atheism, Schelling argues, on the contrary, it presumes a unity in which the gods and goddesses participate, a common and shared divinity, in short, it presumes theism. "The gods, properly speaking, must *somehow* have God as their ground" (Schellling, SSW 11: 74; Hayes, 1995: 81). But God is doubled by the creation, fall, and first descent of second potency; what lies at the ground of mythology is therefore not the eternal and unbegotten God (the Father) but the pre-existent Christ, the logos of John's Gospel, who "was" "in the beginning," the divine existing outside the divine as the inspiration and guide of the fallen human race.

The primordial revelation of God to human consciousness was a primitive form of monotheism belonging to a period before the formation of peoples and the sundering of the primordial community by the differences of race and language. The loss of this primitive presence of God and the advent of polytheism was due to a spiritual crisis that occurred while mankind still existed in its original homogeneous, undivided state. By becoming "variable and inwardly dissimilar" (Schelling, SSW 11: 105; Hayes, 1995: 91), the logos brought about the dispersion of the human race and its fragmentation into the diversity of peoples and gods. The same power which caused the dispersion into polytheism raised one elect group toward true religion, a people, the ancient Jews, whose distinction was entirely their homelessness and lack of national identity (Schelling, SSW 11: 166; Hayes, 1995: 103).

That the religious consciousness of mankind expresses itself in polytheistic mythologies which display recurring motifs and themes confirms for Schelling his earliest view of the unconscious as an abiding stratum of primitive, common, pre-reflective mental life. Mythology is not an individual invention but the "instinctive invention" of a whole people (Hayes, 1995: 74). Just as certain kinds of insects and animals instinctively collaborate and display a unity of purpose, so do a people constitute a naturally united communal mind that expresses itself in collaboratively produced cultural forms. Myths and legends are expressions of this collective consciousness, as are folk-poetry, songs of forgotten origin, proverbs, riddles, jokes and parables. The cultural forms indigenous to a group have striking parallels with the cultural forms of other peoples, parallels which cannot be explained by direct transmission or through a theory of historical influence; rather they are evidence of the authentically religious nature of mythology, indirect proof that mythology is animated by a single world-historical spirit.[61] Throughout the philosophy of mythology Schelling produces anticipations of the Jungian collective unconscious: "the primordial unity and community of consciousness" (*die urspüngliche Einheit und Gemeinschaft des Bewußtseyns* (Schelling, SSW 11: 64)); "the universal human consciousness" (*der allgemein Bewußtseyn der Menschheit* (Schelling, SSW 11: 65)); "We have to consider the mythologies of the various peoples as in fact only so many moments of a single and identical process which passes through and affects the whole of mankind" (Schelling, SSW 11: 211; Hayes, 1995: 117). The logos is refracted through the consciousness of a particular people, the mythological world-view of a historical community that defines a people's identity, first by granting them a language, for the first forms of language are tales of the gods, then an ethics and a religion. The collective mind of man does not produce a common mythology; it rather produces a plurality of mythologies revolving around certain recurring motifs (i.e., archetypes[62]).

Crucial to the psychology of the late Schelling is the claim that the unconscious is religious, possessed by a primordial monotheism (*Monotheismus des Urbewußtseyns*) (Schelling, SSW 11: 187). The primitive state of human consciousness consists in an all-absorbing, grounding, non-reflective grasp of the reality of God. Man is in essence the God-positing-being. Before he is conscious of himself, before he has a self to be conscious of, he is conscious of God. "He does not possess this consciousness, he is it, and it is precisely in his non-act [*im Nichtactus*], his immobility [*in der Nichtbewegung*], that he is the one who posits the true God [*das den wahren Gott Setztende*]" (Schelling, SSW 11: 187; Hayes, 1995: 109). Self-consciousness only comes through dissociation from God-consciousness, as in the Genesis account of the expulsion from Eden: man cannot both possess God in immediate and impersonal consciousness and have consciousness of himself; the one excludes the other. The primitive presence of God to the unconscious is not a personal relationship to God; for such a relationship, man must first be dissociated from God. Consciousness in its primitive unitive state is pre-personal and un-historical – time literally does not exist for it – because primitive man has not yet separated himself from God or from himself and so constituted himself as one with a past. If he is to exist not only in himself but also for himself, man must defect from the primordial bliss of undifferentiated unity with the absolute: the first movement toward self-consciousness is exile from God, departure from "blind monotheism" (Schelling, SSW 11: 187) into polytheism and the diverse myths of those who possess consciousness of themselves as distinct historical peoples. The movement is not itself a conscious one, the act by which consciousness is born cannot itself be conscious, it is something that happens to man, the product of a necessary process, which the late Schelling describes in the language of "the intelligible act" of his middle period.[63] Primitive man does not *have* an unconscious, he *is* unconscious; only with the advent of history, the beginning of mythology, which divides the human race into nations, does man "contract" his being into an unconscious. Henceforth man is not unconscious, he has an unconscious, a religiously saturated unconscious, a vague memory of the fullness of the immediate presence of God, which drives his philosophical and religious search.

With the dawn of consciousness, the gods appear, not as things outside of man, but neither as mere fictions or fantasies; consciousness is surrounded by gods; they are as undeniable as consciousness itself.[64]

> Both peoples and individuals are mere instruments in this process; they cannot transcend it. . . . The representations do not come to them from outside; they are in them without them knowing how or why, for they come out of the depths of consciousness itself, and present themselves to consciousness with a necessity which leaves no doubt as to their truth.
>
> (Schelling, SSW 11: 194; Hayes, 1995: 112)

Allegorical interpretation of mythology – any interpretation of myth which makes the mythic into a sign – is to be rejected as unfaithful to the historical experience of myth. The interpretation of myth must be "tautegorical," for myths mean what they say.[65] This leads Schelling into his elaborate reconstruction of mythology as "a real theogony, a real history of the gods" (Schelling, SSW 11:198), a story which cannot concern us here in any detail.[66] The point is not to naïvely imagine a time when gods roamed the earth but to understand that consciousness once genuinely experienced the universe as peopled by gods; as always, Schelling refuses to choose between either naïve realism or subjective idealism: the real is always already partially idealized and the ideal is composed of real elements. "In the mythological process, man is not dealing with things at all, but with powers that rise up in the depths of consciousness – powers by which consciousness is moved" (Schelling, SSW 11: 207; Hayes, 1995: 115). The gods are, on the one hand, beings of the psyche, "the theogonic process which gives birth to mythology is a subjective process in as much as it unfolds in consciousness and manifests itself in the formation of representations" (Schelling, SSW 11: 207; Hayes, 1995: 115). On the other hand, the gods are expressions of metaphysical forces.[67] Schelling's psychology of gods is founded upon a metaphysics of the psyche – here the analogy with archetypal psychology ends – the mythological representations of divinities, which arise spontaneously in the psyche, are rooted in ontological potencies that create and continue to determine consciousness.

Mythology is not revelation in the special sense that the late Schelling reserves for Christianity alone, and the Christ who is the essential content of the Christian revelation is not a mythic or archetypal figure. Revelation is the real history of the second potency, the hidden architect of mythology, myth become fact, as C.S. Lewis was fond of saying.[68] The mythological process is the estrangement of man from the divine self necessary for the birth of free self-consciousness, which makes man capable of an encounter with God. Prior to the revelation, Christ exists as a demiurgic personality who wanders anonymously through human history; "the same natural potency that was to die in Christ was the one by which they [the pagans] were illuminated and which alone took care of them" (Schelling, SSW 14: 75; Hayes, 1995: 237–238). Christ therefore is not the possession of the Jews or a revelation exclusive to those with the proper ecclesiastical faith; he is "the proper potency of Paganism," or better, "the Pagan light" (Schelling, SSW 14: 75; Hayes, 1995: 237–238). In the revelation of the crucified and risen Jesus, he becomes visible as such.

For Schelling no less than for Kierkegaard, whom he unquestionably influenced in this regard, the essence of Christianity is the revelation of Christ crucified and resurrected. The apogee of the revelation is not the teaching of Christ, as secular humanists and Enlightened "Christian" philosophers would prefer; rather the Christ himself, the crucified and resurrected Jesus, proclaimed as such by the evangelists, and especially by Paul, is the full revelation of the personal God. "Christ is not the teacher, as the saying goes, he is not the founder (of Christianity), he is the content of Christianity" (Schelling, SSW 14: 35). The Christology of the late Schelling focuses on two New Testament texts, which Schelling takes to be the heart of the Christian revelation: the kenosis hymn in Paul's Letter to the Philippians[69] and the prologue to the Gospel of John. Through a detailed analysis of both texts, Schelling produces a quasi-monophysitic Christology, the essence of which is the extreme dissociation of the Son from the Father which makes possible the reconciliation of God and fallen nature. The pre-existent Christ possesses an ontological independence from the Father that he received when he became implicitly existent in pagan consciousness. He renounces this independence in his historical incarnation as the human being Jesus. Christ is not simply God become man, for if the Christ is God in an unqualified sense before the incarnation, then the latter cannot be regarded as a surrender of sovereignty, a self-emptying or *kenosis* (*Entäussurung*). Christ is the God outside God become man, and, through man, re-united with the Father.

Schelling's heterodox theory of atonement needs some explaining. If the incarnation is a genuine self-abasement of the Christ and a real change in being, a surrender of Christ's divinity, a supreme sacrifice in which he "Who, being in the form of God, thought it not robbery to be equal with God, but made himself of no reputation, and took upon him the form of a servant, and was made in the likeness of men" (Philippians 2:6–7), then Christ must possess an independent ground of divinity, an extra-divine divinity, a claim to sovereignty which he renounces. Paul, in Schelling's reading of him, is not describing the eternal God emptying himself of his divinity, for that makes no sense. If the subject who abases himself in Christ is God *sensus strictus*, for whom is the self-abasement performed? What condition does the sacrifice satisfy? What law outside of the Christ could make this death necessary? Rather, as the God outside of God, Christ has his own proper claim to being the God of the fallen world, a claim which he renounces. Paul describes the divinity of Christ as "in the form" of God, which Schelling understands to mean, Christ's divinity is something other than the divinity of the Father; Christ is a distinct mode of God and can therefore become even further ontologically dissociated from the eternally divine in the crucified.[70] By entering into the being of the fallen world to the point of becoming himself a fallen being – and only such a self-abasement of the divine could atone nature and God – Christ negates the wrath of the Father.

> It [second potency] is a divine personality as lord over the being which the Father has *not* given it, the being which it possesses independently of the Father. In this way it is itself *independent* of the Father and hence, in this moment, it is to be defined, as far as its being is concerned, as an extra-divine divine personality (*außergöttlich-göttliche Persönlichkeit*) – as "divine," since it is lord of being; as "extra-divine," since it possesses this being as something *not* given it by God. Since it possesses it independently of the Father, it can do with it what it will, and could possess it permanently as something independent of the Father. *Therein* lies its freedom. *That* is what one must know if one is

to understand the obedience of Christ of which so much is said and on which, at the same time, so much store is set. The Son could exist in his own sovereignty independently of the Father. To be sure, he could not be the true God outside the Father, but he could be God, i.e., lord of being outside of and without the Father. In other words, he could be God not essentially but actually (not *dem Wesen nach*, but *actu*). The Son, however, rejected this sovereignty which he could have had independently of the Father, and *therein* is he Christ. *That* is the fundamental theme of Christianity.

(Schelling, SSW 14: 36–37; Hayes, 1995: 228)

This is the speculative psychology of dissociation become a soteriology: just as the Father can only become a creator by dissociating from his infinity, so can the Son only become a saviour by dissociating from the Father. In creation, the nothingness, lack, and need for being of first potency (subject-hood) is potentized to the point of introducing a real difference in being, the production of something other than God; in redemption the divinity of second potency, its actuality, self-externality, and being for another (objecthood), is potentized to the point of particularization in the anti-divine order, culminating in the granting of autonomous being to Christ as lord of creation. The pre-existent Christ is in one sense what the Father is, true God, but with a crucial difference: the divinity of the Father is proper to the Father; the divinity of the Son is granted to the Son by the Father. The original dissociation of second potency in the production of the logos is compounded by the fall of creation, which unleashes a form of being that should not be, a material order in convulsive rebellion against the Father, a monstrosity in which Christ nonetheless becomes originally existent. Christ first enters history as lord of a fallen creation, God materially grounded in something which is counter to God, God become "un-holy" (Schelling, SSW 14: 181). Schelling's Christ is a double agent: inwardly united with the Father, outwardly he is wholly alienated from him. As such he works within material and cultural history as a force for reconciliation of nature with God. If Christ did not enjoy real autonomy from the Father, his own independent ontological basis, his own freedom grounded, as all freedom must be, in something that is *not* God, his sacrifice would have been a simple necessity. As it is, it is a genuine sacrifice, a free and absolute renunciation of power. In the crucified and risen Jesus, the pre-history of Christ comes to an end and the Son's mission of atonement is fulfilled: Christ incarnates himself as a condemned human being, thus renouncing his rightful claim to be God in the place of the Father and breaking the pattern of usurpation, presumption and self-will in the grips of which all of creation lies. "And being found in fashion as a man, he humbled himself, and became obedient unto death, even the death of the cross" (Philippians 2:8).

## Notes

1  See also Schelling (1809: 343–345, 1815: 15; 1833: 117).
2  See Gabriel (2006b). The summary given here is based on a paper Gabriel gave at the University of Wuppertal, 14 May 2011, entitled, "The Non-Ground as the Elusive Other of Reflection: Schelling's Departure from Idealism."
3  In a letter of 1807, responding to a lecture by Jacobi in which the latter attributed the political problems of the day to the reign of rationalism, Schelling distinguishes true rationality from the petty rule of the understanding. See Gulyga (1989: 223–224): "In my view, humanity is not served by a separation of forces, a repression of particular powers, but only by their highest and most perfect unification – divine peace." Schelling goes on in the letter to distinguish two types of people: one group are sunk into sensuality (*in den Schlamm der Sinnlichkeit versunken*); the others are men of mere understanding (*reine Verstandesmenschen*). Sadly the men of reason and supra-rationality (*Vernunft und Übervernunftmenschen*) are few and far between.
4  See also Schelling (1815: 104): "One could say that there is a kind of person in which there is no madness whatsoever. These would be uncreative people incapable of procreation, the ones that call themselves sober spirits. . . . The other kind of person is governed by madness and is someone who really is mad. One cannot say, strictly speaking, that madness originates in them. It only comes forth as something that is always there (for without continuous solicitation of it, there would be no consciousness) and that is not now suppressed and governed by a higher force."
5  See Schelling (1809: 36): "The ground of evil could not in any way lie in lack or deprivation. The devil, according to the Christian point of view, was not the most limited creature, but rather the least limited one. Imperfection in the general metaphysical sense is not the common character of evil, since evil often shows itself united with an excellence of individual forces, which far more rarely accompanies the good. Thus ground of evil must lie, therefore, not only in something generally positive but rather in that which is most positive in what nature contains."
6  Schelling (1809: 55): "In evil there is the self-consuming and always annihilating contradiction that it strives to become creaturely just by annihilating the bond of creaturely existence and, out of overweening pride to be all things, falls into non-Being."
7  I have explored this difference between Schelling and Hegel in more detail in McGrath (2006).
8  See Žižek (2001, 2003).
9  Schelling (1809: 34). The full passage reads: "But since there can indeed be no true life like that which could exist only in the original relation, a life emerges which, though individual, is, however, false, a life of mendacity, a growth of restlessness and decay. The most fitting comparison here is offered by disease which, as the disorder having arisen in nature through the misuse of freedom, is the true counterpart of evil or sin. Universal disease never exists without the hidden forces of the ground having broken out; it emerges when the irritable principle, which is supposed to rule as the innermost bond of forces in the quiet of the depths, activates itself."
10  See Schelling (1804b: 26): "In a word, there is no continuous transition from the absolute to the real; the origin of the sensible world is conceivable only as a complete falling-away from absoluteness, by means of a leap." On the next page, Schelling attributes the break to the actualization of finite freedom, the freedom of the absolute's image of itself (*der Gegenbild*), which can only be free

by dissociating itself from the absolute. But the dissociation results in its sinking into necessity. See Schelling (1804b: 27–28): "The exclusive peculiarity of absoluteness lies in the fact that when it bestows its essentiality upon its counter-image, it also bestows upon it its self-dependence. This being-in-and-for-itself, this particular and true reality of the first intuited, is freedom, and from that first self-dependence outflows what in the sensible world appears as freedom, which represents the last trace and the seal, as it were, of divinity in the fallen-away world. The counter-image, as an absolute entity and having all its attributes in common with the originary image, would not truly be in itself and absolute if it could not grasp itself in its selfhood, in order to have true being as the other absolute. But it cannot be as the other absolute unless it separates itself or falls away from the true absolute. For it is truly in itself and absolute only in the self-objectification of the absolute, i.e., only insofar as it is simultaneously in the latter; this very relationship to the absolute is one of necessity. It is free of the absolute only in its absolute necessity. Therefore, by being its own, as a free entity, separate from necessity, it ceases to be free and becomes entangled in that necessity, which is the negation of absolute necessity, ergo purely finite."

11 Schelling is not saying that evil is necessary, for such a claim would violate the whole anarchic structure of his system; he is saying, rather, that the possibility of evil is necessary to the existence of love. God has allowed evil to actualize itself (the fall) for the sake of creation/revelation. Nothing is said about the possibility or impossibility of God having achieved his purposes otherwise. It is not impossible that God could have achieved creation/revelation without a fall. But this is not what happened. Evil actualized itself, and God made that self-actualization of evil the means of his revelation. Schelling's thought here is, contrary to appearances, perfectly orthodox. Cf. Aquinas, *Summa Theologica*, 1a, q. 2, a. 3, ad. 1.

12 See Schelling (1810a: 206): "The entire process of the creation of the world – which still lives on in the life process of nature and history – is in effect nothing but the process of the complete coming to consciousness, of the complete personalization of God."

13 Horst Furhmans clearly recounts the stages in the late Schelling's transition from pantheistic idealism to speculative theism. See Furhmans (1940: 17–95).

14 See Schelling (SSW 14: 24) "One could answer the good-natured folk who simply must have a rational God in their sense, by asking if they have never yet noticed that God is an extraordinary creative-genius who cares little for what they call rational or non-rational. They are unable to grasp the profound irony of all divine behavior." Translated Hayes (1995: 215).

15 See Schelling (1810a: 207): "Yet just as the progressive self-formation and development of self-consciousness involves man's exclusion of the dark and unconscious within himself, which he opposes to himself – though not for the purpose of leaving it in this exclusion and darkness, but to progressively elevate this excluded and dark to clarity and to transfigure it *in the direction of* his own consciousness – so God, too, excludes the inferior of His essence from the superior one and expels it as it were from Himself; yet not for the purpose of leaving it in this state of Nonbeing but to raise what He excluded from Himself as non-divine – that which *He Himself* is not and which therefore He separated from Himself – to educate, transfigure, and create from it what will be similar and cognate to Him."

16 The phrase might be translated as "found in shit." It indicates the inestimable value of the discarded for the alchemical act of transmuting metals and other

substances, for in the matrix of nature, the highest and the lowest are different potentizations of the same primal substance. See entry for "prima materia" in Abraham (1998: 153–156).

17  Schelling (1809: 52). The unconsciousness of the deed does not mean that the consequences are not felt by consciousness. See Schelling (1810b: 16): "People whom I see living normal lives always appear to me to be essentially fluctuating and uncertain. Who knows whether the person, whom I now see acting with greatness and truth, will not subsequently be bowed down by the force of circumstances and will later act timidly and against his heart. Who knows whether the person who today appears clear, free, and pure will not sooner or later become eclipsed, shackled, and torn apart by a violent passion. The person who makes a resolution about his whole life and who makes it in such a way that he calls God and the world as his witness, who makes this resolution under conditions which stamp it with the seal of indissolubility, and if I understand him as acting levelheadedly and through his own free will, it is *this* person who will always waken my respect."

18  Schelling (1809: 51–52): "That Judas became a betrayer of Christ, neither he nor any other creature could change, and nevertheless he betrayed Christ not under compulsion but willingly and with complete freedom. It is exactly the same with a good individual; namely he is not good arbitrarily or by accident and yet is so little compelled that, rather, no compulsion, not even the gates of hell themselves, would be capable of overpowering his basic disposition (*Gesinnung*). The free act, which becomes necessary, admittedly cannot appear in consciousness to the degree that the latter is merely self-awareness and only ideal, since it precedes consciousness just as it precedes essence, indeed first *produces* it; but, for that reason, this is no act of which no consciousness at all remains in man since anyone, for instance, who in order to excuse a wrong action, says 'that's just the way I am' is surely aware that he is like he is through his guilt, as much as he is right that it was impossible for him to act otherwise."

19  See Kant (1799/1960: 20): "To have a good or an evil disposition as an inborn natural constitution does not mean that it has not been acquired by the man who harbours it, that he is not the author of it, but rather, that it has not been acquired in time (that he has *always* been good, or evil, *from his youth up*). The disposition, i.e., the ultimate subjective ground of the adoption of maxims, can be one only and applies universally to the whole use of freedom. Yet this disposition itself must have been adopted by free choice, for otherwise it could not be imputed. But the subjective ground or cause of this adoption cannot further be known."

20  See Schelling (1809: 50): "But precisely this inner necessity is itself freedom; the essence of man is fundamentally *his own act*; necessity and freedom are in one another as one being that appears as one or the other only when considered from different sides, in itself freedom, formally necessity."

21  Schelling (1809: 52–53): "We too assert a predestination but in a completely different sense, namely in this: as man acts here so has he acted from eternity and already in the beginning of creation. His action does not *become*, just as he himself does not *become* as a moral being, but rather it is eternal by nature. This oft-heard and tormenting question also falls by the wayside: Why is exactly this individual destined to act in an evil and base manner while, in contrast, another is destined to act piously and justly? For the question presupposes that man is not initially action and act and that he as a spiritual being has a Being which is prior to, and independent of, his will, which as has been shown, is impossible."

22 Schelling (1815: 85): "So that there would be a true beginning, this higher life had to sink back down into unconsciousness of itself. There is a law in humanity: there is an incessant primordial deed that precedes each and every single action and through which one is actually Oneself. Yet this primordial deed sinks down into unfathomable depths with respect to consciousness that elevates itself above it. Thereby, this primordial deed becomes a beginning that can never be sublimated, a root of reality that cannot be reached through anything. In the same way, in the decision, that primordial deed of divine life also eradicates consciousness of itself, so that what was posited as ground in divine life can only be disclosed again in the succession through a higher revelation. Only in this way is there a true beginning, a beginning that never ceases to be a beginning. The decision that would make any kind of act into a true beginning may not be brought before consciousness. It may not be *recalled*, which rightly means as much as taking it back. Whoever reserves it to themselves again and again to bring a decision to light never makes a beginning. Hence, character is the fundamental condition for all morality." See also Schelling (1815: 44): "There is no dawning of consciousness (and precisely for this reason no consciousness) without positing something past. There is no consciousness without something that is at the same time excluded and contracted. That which is conscious excludes that of which it is conscious as not itself. Yet it must again attract it precisely as that of which it is conscious as itself, only in a different form. That which in consciousness is simultaneously the excluded and the attracted can only be the unconscious [*das Bewußtlose*]. Hence, all consciousness is grounded on the unconscious and precisely in the dawning of consciousness the unconscious is posited as the past of consciousness. Now it is certainly not thinkable that God was unconscious for awhile and then became conscious. But it is certainly thinkable that in the same inseparable act of the dawning of consciousness the unconscious and the conscious of God were grasped at the same time. The conscious was grasped as the eternally present but the unconscious was grasped with the ascertainment of what is eternally past."

23 Heidegger is never more a Schellingian than when he writes, "Being ground, that is, existing as thrown, Dasein constantly lags behind its possibilities. It is never existent *before* its ground, but only *from it* and *as it*. Thus being ground means *never* to gain power over one's ownmost being from ground up. This *not* belongs to the existential meaning of thrownness. Being ground, it itself is a nullity of itself. . . . *Not through* itself, but *released to* itself from ground in order to be *as this ground*. Dasein is not itself ground of its being, because ground first arises from its own project, but as a self, it is the *being* of its ground. Ground is always ground only for a being whose being has to take over being-the-ground" (1927/1962: paragraph 58).

24 "For the negating will can simply deny itself, give up the expressible [the will to revelation] altogether, and remain by itself in concealment. And precisely this is the only sense in which it can be thought of as a negating will, a will that wills a determinate nothing. For only when it does not posit itself does it not posit the other. On the other hand, if it posits itself first, it can (by virtue of the equipollence of both wills) only posit itself as the ground of the other" (Schelling, 1813/1997: 174).

25 "It is an action that is not decided upon by anyone (for how can something decide when it cannot be?); and yet the will of all is there, because no one can be forced" (Schelling, 1813/1997: 175).

26 Schelling retains the Spinozistic notion of quantitative difference throughout his career. The concept is first defined in the 1801 *Presentation of my System of*

*Philosophy*. See Schelling (SSW 4: 123): "Between subject and object only quantitative differences are possible." "The one and the same identity" is posited with "a surplus of subjectivity or objectivity." Cf. Schelling (1831: 13, fn.): "Any determinate quantitative difference of subjectivity and objectivity through which a particular is posited as finite in opposition to the totality of the universe, that is, as this determinate form of being over and against universal being [*das Sein*] in general, is a potency. Each particular finite potency consists in a positive and a negative factor, both of which are infinite in themselves. Since A=B is the general expression of finitude, A, the subject, is the grounding or negative factor, B, the object, is, in contrast, the primordial existent [*das Seiende*], or that which is in itself unlimited but limitable and the positive factor. Insofar as the one and the same thing are identical in both, both factors are in themselves infinite, although the one is determined by a preponderance of subjectivity or objectivity. . . . so neither A nor B in any particular part of the all, that is in any particular individual, can be posited as absolute subjectivity or absolute objectivity but only the identity of both [is absolute], with an opposed preponderance of subjectivity or objectivity in both poles and, in the centre, a quantitative indifference."

27 See Schelling (1815: 11): "God, in accordance with the necessity of its nature, is an eternal No, the highest Being-in-itself [*in-sich Seyn*], an eternal withdrawal of its being into itself, a withdrawal within which no creature would be capable of living. But the same God, with equal necessity of its nature, although not in accord with the same principle, but in accord with a principle that is completely different from the first principle, is the eternal Yes, an eternal outstretching, giving, and communicating of its being. Each of these principles, in an entirely equal fashion, is the being [*das Wesen*], that is, each has the same claim to be God or that which has being [*das Seyende*]. Yet they reciprocally exclude each other. If one is that which has being [*das Seyende*] then the opposed can only be that which does not have being [*das nicht Seyende*]. But, in an equally eternal manner, God is the third term of the unity of the Yes and the No. Just as opposites exclude each other from being what has being, so again the unity excludes the antithesis and thereby each of the opposites, and, in turn, the antithesis or each of the opposites excludes the unity from being what has being." There are two things worth noting in this passage. Schelling distinguishes "being" [*Seyn*] from determinate being [*das Seyende*, translated somewhat clumsily as "that which has being"] such that that which *is* may not always *determinately exist*, that is, may not always have being. Secondly, Schelling, unlike Hegel, maintains the principle of non-contradiction in his dialectic. Without the principle of non-contradiction there would be no tension in the divine and no need for a decision.

28 Hogrebe calls it "the primordial rotary madness" (*der ursprüngliche rotatorische Wahsinn*) (Hogrebe, 1989: 103). Cf. Žižek (1996: 35).

29 The motion of three juggled balls describes a figure eight, an emblem of eternity. My thanks to Peter Duchemin for this insight.

30 Hogrebe (1989: 111–118) is a notable exception.

31 See Schelling (1815: xxxviii–xxxix): "The human being can let run through themselves and, so to speak, immediately experience that succession of processes through which the infinite manifold is, in the end, produced out of the highest simplicity of being; nay, to speak more accurately, the human being must experience this in themselves. But all experience, feeling, and vision is, in and for itself, mute and needs a mediating organ . . . . Here runs the boundary between theosophy and philosophy, which the lover of knowledge will chastely seek to

protect. Theosophy is much ahead of philosophy in depth, fullness, and vitality of content in the way that the actual object is ahead of its image and nature is ahead of its presentation . . . [but] all knowledge must pass through the dialectic."

32 See Schelling (1833: 181–182): "The greater part of the speeches of the theoretical mystics, of the real theosophers, are to a large extent incomprehensible . . . . Theosophy is in complete conflict with the vocation of contemporary life . . . . It is not our vocation to live in visions, but rather in belief, i.e., in mediated knowledge. Our knowledge is incomplete, i.e., it has to be created bit by bit, successively, according to gradations and classifications . . . . There is no understanding in vision in and for itself . . . . A person *might* also experience in himself that transcendent process through which everything has developed, as the theosopher boasts he can, but this would not lead to real science. For all experience, feeling, vision is itself mute, and needs a mediating organ to be expressed." But then Schelling adds his highest praise for theosophy: "The theosopher, however, to the extent to which he is speculative, is also essentially and primarily a natural philosopher" (Schelling, 1833: 183).

33 We remember that A=B is the formula for finitude in Schelling's identity-philosophy. We also note that the formula for infinity, A=A, does not as such appear in the formula of the world. See Schelling (SSW 4: 131).

34 See Schelling (1815: 16): "The beginning really only lies in the negation. All beginning is, in accordance with its nature, only a desire for the end or for what leads to the end and hence, negates itself as the end . . . . Negation is therefore the necessary precedent (*prius*) of every movement. The beginning of the line is the geometrical point – but not because it extended itself but rather because it is the negation of all extension. One is the beginning of all number, not so much because it itself is a number but because it is the negation of all number, of all multiplicity. That which would intensify itself must first gather itself together and transpose itself into the condition of being a root. What wants to grow must foreshorten itself and hence, negation is the first transition whatsoever from nothing into something."

35 Schelling is ambivalent on this point in the *Ages* drafts, suggesting at times that he is still a historical immanentist, i.e., God becomes self-conscious through creating the world, and arguing at other times for the opposite view, that God does not depend on the world in any way, a position that becomes foundational for the philosophy of mythology and revelation. We agree with Furhmans that the related late Schellingian doctrines of the personal nature of God, the freedom of his act of creation, and the contingency of the history of the world, are ideas that first appear in Schelling's work in 1809 and which he struggles over the next decade to make sense of in light of his prior pantheistic tendencies. See Furhmans (1940: 17–56).

36 This is not to say, *pace* Hogrebe, that "being is senseless" (*Sein ist Unsinn*) (Hogrebe, 1989: 13). Schelling remains with Kant on this point. To deny the application of categories to the real is not to equate the real with senselessness. There may be other modes of meaning beyond our comprehension.

37 See Schelling (1810a: 30): "To be sure A=A appears identical, but it might very well also have a synthetic meaning, if the one A, say, were opposed to the other. One would thus have to substitute in place of A a concept expressing a *fundamental duality within the identity* and *vice versa*. A concept of this sort, is that of an object that is at once opposed to, and the same as, itself. But the only such object is one *that is at once cause and effect of itself*, produced and product, subject and object. – The concept of an original identity in duality, and *vice*

*versa*, is thus to be found only in the concept of a *subject-object*, and only in self-consciousness does such a concept originally manifest itself."

38  See Schelling (1815: 15): "That God negates itself, restricts its being, and withdraws into itself, is the eternal force and might of God. In this manner, the negating force is that which is singularly revealing of God. But the actual being of God is that which is concealed. The whole therefore stands as A that from the outside is B and hence the whole = (A=B)."

39  For an example of this misreading, see Žižek (1996: 77).

40  See Schelling (1815: 24). The point is not unique to the third draft of *Ages*, which Žižek misleadingly suggests, but also appears in the second draft. See Schelling (1813: 134).

41  Johannes Scheffler, *Der cherubinische Wandersmann*, 1: 3, cited by Schelling (1815: 24).

42  This point is made clear in the second draft of *Ages*. See Schelling (1813: 168–169): "Now the opposition is put to work and is made perceptible to the will that wills nothing, which is not pulled into action, becoming an actual will, whereas it was previously a merely possible will. But it can only become actual as what it is. Once and for all, it is impossible for anything to be sublated. The will can therefore only become actual as the will *that wills nothing*. But since it was previously a resting will that specifically did not will anything positive, and it is now summoned to express what-is [*das Seyende*] and to express being [*das Seyn*] *as* what-is [*das Seyende*] and *as* being [*das Seyn*], it becomes from itself the will that positively wills nothing, not even itself as what-is and as being. That is, it becomes the will that opposes to itself the particularity, dispersion, and mutual freedom of the principles."

43  See Schelling (1833: 117): "This essence which is posited in the second potential is *what* the being without a beginning is, with the one difference that it (without its own assistance) is posited straightaway as essence and is correspondingly fixed . . . . A which is posited as A is no longer simply A but rather A which *is* A, not – is and is not, but emphatically is. A which is A is A which is duplicated within itself . . . thus A which is posited as A is no longer simple but duplicated A, which we can call A2."

44  See Schelling (1809: 30): "But, corresponding to the yearning, which as the still dark ground is the first stirring of divine existence, an inner, reflexive representation is generated in God himself through which, since it can have no other object but God, God sees himself in an exact image of himself. This representation is the first in which God, considered as absolute, is realized, although only in himself; this representation is with God in the beginning and is the God who was begotten *in* God himself. This representation is at the same time the understanding – the *Word* – of this yearning and the eternal spirit which, perceiving the Word within itself and at the same time the infinite yearning, and impelled by the love that it itself is, proclaims the word so that the understanding and yearning together now become a freely creating and all-powerful will and build in the initial anarchy of nature as in its own element or instrument."

45  See Schelling (1815: 8): "It is certainly impossible that the Ideal *as such* is ever the Real and vice versa, and that the Yes is ever a No and the No is ever a Yes. To assert this would mean sublimating [*aufheben*] human comprehension, the possibility of expressing oneself, even the contradiction itself. But it is certainly possible that one and the same=x is both Yes and No, Love and Wrath, Leniency and Strictness."

46  "Das Wahre ist so das Ganze bis auf Eins" (Hogrebe, 1989: 130).

47 Žižek follows Hogrebe in this respect. See Hogrebe (1989: 114–115): "That something exists means in this context: something other no longer exists, but exists as that, which no longer exists, namely as the beginning. This remains 'repressed' (*verdrungen*) in all that exists." Presumably Hogrebe puts the word "repressed" (*verdrungen*) in scare quotes because Schelling does not use the term. Indeed, it imports a whole set of un-Schellingian assumptions into the metaphysics.

48 See Welchman and Norman (2010).

49 This is a mainstay of medieval negative theology from John Scotus Eriugena to Meister Eckhart.

50 The philosophy of mythology and revelation covers 2,100 pages of lectures that remain for the most part untranslated – 25 per cent of Schelling's *Sämtliche Werke* (SSW, volumes 11–14). Two books from Schelling's *Philosophy of Mythology* (the historical-critical introduction of 1842, Schelling, SSW 11: 1–252), the philosophical introduction of 1854 (Schelling, SSW 11: 253–572), and the third book of the *Philosophy of Revelation* (Schelling, SSW 14: 1–334) have been summarized, with numerous translated citations, by Viktor Hayes (1995). Translations of *The Historical-Critical Introduction to the Philosophy of Mythology* (SSW 11: 1–252) and *The Grounding of the Positive Philosophy* (the introduction to the *Philosophy of Revelation*, SSW 13: 1–174) have recently appeared (Schelling, 1842, 1854). The English-speaking world still awaits a full translation of Schelling's last lectures, especially the *Philosophy of Revelation*, which summarizes and completes the *Philosophy of Mythology*, and, arguably, Schelling's entire career. In 1992 a manuscript was published which the editor, Walter E. Ehrhardt, claims to be the earliest version of the *Philosophy of Revelation*, a text which Schelling ostensibly dictated to one of his students in 1831 and corrected himself (Schelling, 1831). The topic of Schelling's last philosophy has been well researched in Germany. The classic German studies are Furhmans (1940), Habermas (1954), Schulz (1955), Kasper (1965), Hemmerle (1968), Frank (1975). Recent German literature includes Rosenau (1985), Buchheim (1992), Franz (1992), Wilson (1993), Hüntelmann (1995), Danz (1996), Gabriel (2006a). In French see Jankélévitch (1933), Tilliette (1970, part 2), Bruaire (1970), Marquet (1973), Maesschalk (1989), Courtine (2010). Beach's study (Beach, 1994) is to date the only book-length study in English on the late Schelling.

51 Schelling does not reject intellectual intuition in the 1821 *Erlangen Lectures* so much as re-define it as a self-diremption of reason: because there is no knowledge of distinction in the intuition, it is not the Fichtian subject's primordial self-experience but an ecstasy of the subject, a non-knowing. See Schelling (SSW 9: 229): "One calls it intuition because one grasps that in the intuition or the seen (since this word means the same) the subject loses himself, is posited outside of himself: intellectual intuition, to express that the subject here is not lost in sensible intuition, in a real object, but lost, given over to that which could not possibly be an object." By the time the positive philosophy is in full flight a decade later, the "ecstasy of reason" will become the instrument by which reason receives a truth that does not originate from itself. See Schelling (SSW 13: 162–163): "Reason can only posit the existent in which nothing of a concept, of a what, inheres as absolutely outside itself (freely, only so far as to later, a posteriori, appropriate it as its own content, and so at the same time, return to itself). In this positing, reason is therefore posited outside itself, absolutely ecstatic."

52 For Schelling's critique of the ontological argument, see Schelling (SSW 10: 15; 13: 157–158).

53 "The identity of the potencies in the absolute is not sublated [aufgehoben] when the priority of the first potency becomes real, it is rather transformed into a chain or a coherence of the same" (Schelling, 1810a: 203).

54 "At first the potencies lie in the absolute in complete indifference or indiscernibility. In the same way, the whole of time lies implicit as a unity or eternity in the absolute. Insofar as God contracts himself freely into the first potency – freely becomes one who could be all things, he makes a beginning of time (n.b. not in time). Through his self-withdrawal into the first potency, a contradiction is posited in him, which contradicts his essence, insofar as it is one nature in all potencies, so a progress from the first to the second potency develops, and thereby time. The potencies are posited as cycles of the self-revelation of God" (Schelling, 1810a: 203).

55 See Vetö (1973: 120), cited in Rosenau (1985: 86).

56 "Instead of ordering his natural life under the divine, man activates, awakens in itself, the unactivated and solely natural principle" (Schelling, 1810a: 225).

57 The ontology is rehearsed in many places in the late lectures, for example in the twentieth lecture of the *Philosophical Introduction to the Philosophy of Mythology* (SSW 11: 457–489), summarized in Hayes (1995: 152–157), and in lectures 5 to 10 of the *Urfassung* of the *Philosophy of Revelation* (Schelling, 1831: 25–63).

58 In this way Schelling solves the problem of the fourth, following Baader on this point: the fourth, which is indeed necessary, is not one of the three principles, but the whole constituted by the interactions of the three, the divine nature in Aquinas's Trinitarian theology, Eckhart's *Gottheit*, or Boehme's *Ungrund*. See Hayes (1995: 174).

59 See Frank (2004).

60 "The existent is as subject-object the spirit to whom it is given to remain in itself, or being with itself (*Ansichsein*), and in being with itself being outside itself, not losing itself and always remaining the same" (Koktanek, 1962: 64).

61 "The resemblances are not like those which exist between an original and a copy; they do not suggest a unilateral descent of the one mythology from the other, but that all mythologies have a common extraction (*Abkunft*)" (Schelling, SSW 11: 62; Hayes, 1995: 75).

62 Schelling's psycho-ontological interpretation of mythology results in a Jungian theory of archetypes *avant la lettre*, an affirmation of the existence of recurring mythic motifs which transcend cultural and temporal boundaries. For example, Schelling speaks of the myth of Prometheus, which is for him the supreme emblem of man, as "not a human invention . . . [but] one of those primordial thoughts [*Urgendanken*] which force themselves into existence and develop according to a strict logic when they find, as Prometheus found in Aeschylus, a profound spirit, a favourable soil (in which to take root)" (Schelling, SSW 11: 482; Hayes, 1995: 185). Jung is often misunderstood to have posited universal images in the human psyche; the archetypes, for Jung (when he is speaking rigorously), are not universal images but universal propensities to form certain images according to an innate logic, just as Schelling's "primordial thoughts" are the effect of the potencies on consciousness mediated through man's imagination at a particular time and place. At the same time, Schelling does not hold the common Jungian view that man is hermetically enclosed in the archetypal for the potencies that give rise to myths are teleologically ordained to the generation of a genuinely personal notion of a creator God who man meets in history.

63 "The act by which the ground of polytheism was posited did not take place within that consciousness, but occurred outside it. The first real consciousness is

already found with this occurrence, through which it is cut off [*geschieden*] from its eternal and essential being. It can no longer return to this. . . . This determination is therefore incomprehensible to consciousness. It is the unwilled and unforeseen consequence of a movement which consciousness cannot reverse or revoke. Its origin is in a region to which consciousness, once separated from it, no longer has access" (Schelling, SSW 11: 192; Hayes, 1995: 112).

64 The late Schelling's psychological interpretation of polytheism accords nicely with archetypal psychology, that of James Hillman, for example, who refuses to make gods into symbols of subjective functions while at the same time recognizing that their reality is primarily psychological. See Hillman (1975).

65 The term "tautigorical" was coined by Samuel Taylor Coleridge, one of Schelling's first English disciples. The late Schelling borrows the term from him. See Halmi (2002). "For mythology, the gods are beings who really exist. They are not something else, and they do not mean something else" (Schelling, SSW 11: 196; Hayes, 1995: 113).

66 See Beach's reliable account (Beach, 1994).

67 "But the causes and, therefore, also the objects of these representations, are the real theogonic powers as such, the very powers under whose influence consciousness is originally that-which-posits-God. It is not the mere representations of the potencies but the potencies themselves which form the content of the process. These potencies create consciousness and, since consciousness is the end of nature, they create nature. Therefore they are real powers" (Schelling, SSW 11: 207; Hayes, 1995: 115).

68 Lewis's view of the relationship of mythology to Christianity is in broad outlines identical to Schelling's. Lewis argues that primitive religions gave mythic expression to the primordial yearning in human consciousness for an intimate personal contact with the transcendent God, an encounter which would restore the fallen world's lost immediacy with the divine. Rather than one myth among others, Christianity fulfils the mythological impulse in history; it is "myth become fact" (Lewis, 1970: 63–68).

69 "Let this mind be in you, which was also in Christ Jesus: Who, being in the form of God, thought it not robbery to be equal with God: But made himself of no reputation, and took upon him the form of a servant, and was made in the likeness of men: And being found in fashion as a man, he humbled himself, and became obedient unto death, even the death of the cross. Wherefore God also hath highly exalted him, and given him a name which is above every name: That at the name of Jesus every knee should bow, of [things] in heaven, and [things] in earth, and [things] under the earth; And [that] every tongue should confess that Jesus Christ [is] Lord, to the glory of God the Father" (Philippians 2:5–11, King James Version).

70 "If the incarnation is an emptying, then the humanity or human nature of Christ must be just the pure *result* of this self-emptying, of this act in which he emptied himself not of deity – for he makes this visible again by his act – but of the *morphe theou* (the form of God). The man Christ came into being not merely because of, but in-and-through the fact that he who was in the form of God willed to empty himself of this. If the logos *merely joins* itself with the man . . . then it has *not* emptied itself but remains what it was" (Schelling, SSW 14: 158–159; Hayes, 1995: 273). " 'God became man' means: the divine became man, yet not the divine, but rather the extra-divine aspect of the divine (*das Ausser-göttliche des Göttlichen*) became man. There are here from the beginning *not* two personalities, one of which must be negated . . . but only *one* person, the divine, which reduces its extra-divine being to human being and precisely thereby

appears itself as divine. The human being is *its* being; it has willed it and given it to itself, but for that reason it itself is beyond this being . . . . As far as the divine which remained in the extra-divine is concerned the Incarnation is not a becoming other but simply a becoming-visible" (Schelling, SSW 14: 165; Hayes, 1995: 275).

# Chapter 5

# Schellingian libido theory

> Whoever wishes to grasp the concept of spirit at its most profound roots
> must therefore become fully acquainted with the nature of desire.
>
> (Schelling, 1810a: 230)

We have said that our intention in this book is not to systematize Schelling's oeuvre through the notion of the unconscious. The absence of a definitive system in Schelling is an important feature of his contribution to the philosophy of his age, an era fairly drunk on systems. It should not be understood merely negatively, as though Schelling could not achieve something which Fichte, Hegel and Schopenhauer easily did; rather the incompleteness of Schelling's philosophy is a positive feature of his thought. Instead of laying out a frame and carefully making everything accord with it, Schelling went in whatsoever direction the truth as he understood it at any given time led.[1] Nevertheless, we have discovered that Schelling's various ideas about the unconscious disclose a recurring structure in Schellingian philosophy. Far from the most inconsistent of great philosophers, Schelling suddenly appears to be one of the most consistent, following a single thought over the course of fifty-six years of active research while traversing diverse philosophical fields, genres and perspectives. The thought can be expressed purely formally but we will allow it the wealth of its natural-philosophical context and express it as a theory of desire. For Schelling, desire is never unidirectional; it is by definition divided: one desires something that is in some other respect resisted or withheld. Desire thus flourishes in negativity, as Žižek points out: "I do not actually desire what I want . . . . What I actually desire is to sustain desire itself, to postpone the dreaded moment of satisfaction" (Žižek, 1997a: 80). The question is: what is the counter-force which makes desire possible, this negative condition of the possibility of desire?

Schelling describes it in the nature-philosophy as "negative force," the power internal to an animal of resisting the outward pull of desire, the seduction of love, which calls the animal to the other. Love literally animates the world for the early Schelling, it is the "positive force" distributed throughout nature which continually destabilizes the internal equilibrium of the animal. Love is too much for the individual organism; it would tear it apart if the animal were not protected from it by a negative force stemming from within it, which allows it to consolidate its hold on its determinate matter and resist the ecstatic allure of the other. The polarization of desire is essential if nature as such, *natura naturans*, infinite productivity, is to become manifest. The argument returns in a new form in the philosophy of freedom of Schelling's middle period. The negative force is now called "ground," the positive force is "existence," and that which is revealed in the tension between these two is "personality." Ground's resistance to the ecstatic will to otherness (existence) is essential to the individuation of the self. Without this No to the outside, there would be no self at all because no boundary would be established between self and other. But if the agenda of ground, to negate the other, is not continually disrupted by the appeal of existence, the self dies, implodes, enclosing itself on a spaceless internal point which is no longer in relationship to the sources of its own life. The dark ground has a crucially positive role to play in the economy of the Schellingian self: ground without existence is a schizophrenic, lost in a world of its own; existence without ground is a hysteric, its life always abnegated, deferred, and carried by the other, to whom it can only say Yes.

The dialectic of desire returns in the philosophy of revelation. Negative force/dark ground is now first potency which resists the universal, dissociates from the divine, and materializes into the real; positive force/existence is now second potency which incarnates itself in the fallen divinity and becomes the ideal other to the material real, trebly alienated from the Godhead, first by means of materialization, second by means of incarnation into a single man, Jesus, third by means of the identification of Jesus with the unholy, i.e., the crucifixion. The later Schelling returns to his first insight into the teleology of divided desire and constructs of it an elaborate philosophy of Christianity but the essential point remains the same: the negative obstructs the positive so that something irreducible to both might be revealed. In the early Schelling, it is nature that is revealed; in the middle Schelling, it is personality; for the late Schelling, it is God himself. Let us resist the temptation to make of these three moments of revelation a Hegelian dialectic. The development of Schelling's thought might be characterized as an ever deepening understanding of what exactly is made possible, made manifest or revealed, by negative desire. We call it negative desire because it is not a positive intention of an object but a negative intention of an object, a *not wanting* rather than a wanting otherwise. Negative desire is not narcissism because it does not take the ego as its libidinal object. At the same time it is not desiring nothing. It is not the will that wills nothing, i.e., that has no will, but the will that *wills* nothing.

Schellingian libido theory cannot be mapped onto Freud for the teleology is essential to it; neither can it be mapped onto Jung for the personal *telos* is equally essential to it. It is in short a theory of libido in its own right, one, we might add, that has never developed into a practice of psychotherapy, although there is no reason why it could not. In conclusion, then, I wish to offer a few suggestions as to what a Schellingian theory of psychoanalysis would look like, by contrasting it with the main forms of analysis still widely practised today, Freudian, Jungian, and Lacanian.

While the question necessarily involves the whole of Schelling, we will restrict our view to the middle Schelling, for here is where Schelling speaks explicitly of the structure of the personality. The place he begins is Boehme's radical theory of drive (*Trieb*). In the Scholastic tradition that dominated the West until recently, drive and desire were associated with the finite and the fallen, marks of incompleteness and the relative non-existence of material being. God could not be described as either driven toward a goal, be it revelation or love, or as harbouring desires within himself: all such talk was anthropomorphic, to be negated if the being of God was to remain infinite and unsurpassable. Boehme installs both drive and desire as divine qualities: drive is at the foundation of the divine life, the impulse toward self-revelation that sets the unground into motion; desire is the means by which the unground accomplishes its goal, corresponding to conflicting "wills" generated within the divine being, the resolution of which reveals God to himself.[2] For Boehme, drive and desire are features of all that lives, whether it is infinite or finite. As Oetinger was first to point out, this amounts to a displacement of the Greek metaphysics of being (*ousia*) by the Hebrew metaphysics of life.

Drive enlivens the unground by dividing it into contesting desires: an inwardizing desire which refuses the other and an exteriorizing desire for the other. The tension between these two opposites is the key to the infinite life and self-relatedness of God. However complex the language of Boehme's doctrine of the three principles, Boehme's psychological point is simple enough to state: there is no alterity without ipseity, no self-donation without a latent self-assertion. This is not to say that love is selfish: self-assertion without self-donation is the essence of evil. But without the seed of selfishness, held in potency, not actualized, there would be no self to be overcome and given away. Personality is ipseity potentized or tinctured by alterity. The fullness of being in Boehme's view is personal: without difference, relation, and process – the play between ipseity and alterity – there is no movement, self-revelation, or relationship. The middle Schelling appropriates Boehme's notions of drive and desire with very little alteration. The will that says No to existence and contracts upon a self evacuated of actuality is confronted by the will that says Yes, which expands outward to recognize and include the other in a universe in which it accepts that it too is only a part. The two eternally struggle against one another, one momentarily taking ascendancy only to capitulate to the other the next moment. Each contains the other as a latent potency in itself. The negating potency has latent within it an affirmation of otherness; the affirming potency has latent within it an affirmation of self (Schelling, 1815: 18). Jung also insists on psychic finality – the drive that grounds Jungian libido is ultimately toward the individuation of the subject – but he does not fully understand the *telos* of libido: had he cultivated the Schellingian root of his own psychology, he could have restored the Boehmian-Schellingian answer to this question: psychic energy is teleologically oriented not simply to individuation but toward personal relationship.

We have described Schelling's model of the self as constitutively dissociative in order to distinguish it from Freud's model of the self as constitutively repressive. But we must take care not to exaggerate this distinction. In both Schelling and Freud we have a dyad of polarized vectors of desire. A self-centred chaotic "dark principle" resists an outwardly directed "light principle" or centre of consciousness. In the early Freud, the dyad is unconsciousness–consciousness; later, it becomes Id–ego. In *Beyond the Pleasure Principle*, the dyad is death-drive–life-drive, the former shutting out the exterior and abjuring all excitation, the latter actively seeking it. Schelling can and perhaps should be read through Freud, for the latter's theory of polarity is as much a product of nineteenth-century nature-philosophy as it is an application of mechanics and hydraulics to the psyche. Like death-drive, ground withdraws from externality, excitation and contact with others; it is homeostatic and conservative. Like Freud's life-drive, existence seeks excitation, progressively moving out of itself and inviting a life-generative disequilibrium into the self. The dark ground, however, does not will death; it wills itself by negating the other. It is arguable whether Schelling's speculative psychology recognizes anything like Freud's death-drive. Like Jung's, Schelling's psychology is at bottom life-affirming. The ground recoils from excitation but it does not will death or a return to the inorganic; it wills that there be nothing other than itself. If there is a death-drive in Schelling, it is the non-predicative will-lessness of the unground, the will that *wills* nothing. Schelling recognizes that traces of this pre-volitional being are found in creation. "Movement never occurs for its own sake; all movement is only for the sake of rest" (Schelling, 1813: 133). Sounding even more like Freud, Schelling writes that

> every created thing, every man in particular strives, in truth, only to return to the condition of nonwilling; not only he who strips himself away from all desirable things, but – though unknowingly – also he who abandons himself to all desires. For this man too desires only the state in which he has nothing more to wish for, nothing more to want, even if that state retreats immediately from him; and the more zealously he pursues it, the further away it is.
>
> (Schelling, 1813: 134)

The point of profoundest difference between Schelling and Freud concerns the nature of the subordination of one vector of desire to the other. In Freud's early topography (*The Interpretation of Dreams*), a third factor, "the censor," shuttles between the unconscious and the conscious, legislating what of the former is permitted into the light of the latter and under what guise. The model of repression in the early Freud is the dreamwork, in which desires that are incompatible with the ego ideal surface with the relaxation of consciousness during sleep (Freud, 1900: 174ff.). To defend itself, the psyche "censors" these desires by disguising them in the seemingly innocuous imagery of dreams that do not disturb sleep because their "manifest content" is unthreatening to the ego. For Freud, the dreamwork demonstrates the general strategy of consciousness: only by repressing its deepest impulses and impressions can sanity be maintained. Freudianism is thus most compatible with a basically gnostic view of reality: the human subject is at home neither in nature nor in its own body, and must reconfigure its environment in order to cope. Sanity is a tragic adjustment to a reality that is, from a human perspective, intolerable. Freudian repression allows Freud to explain the different directions of libido not as alternative deployments of neutral psychic energy but as repressed and free expressions of a single form of desire. Schelling has no such concept of repression, nor does he need one: there is nothing intrinsically horrible about life for Schelling. The Schellingian self does not dissociate for the sake of coping with a reality too horrible for consciousness; it dissociates for the sake of love. Freud's dark principle (the Id) is held down by consciousness. According to Schelling, the dark ground, when it acts in accordance with love, *holds itself back*; it defers to the light not because its desires are out of proportion to the modicum of pleasure reality can afford, but because only by subordinating itself to consciousness can it participate in love. This is what Wirth calls "the conspiracy of life," the clandestine coordination of opposed intentions for the sake of life and love (Wirth, 2003: 2).[3] Schelling makes it clear that the dark ground is not to be wrestled into submission by consciousness. Rather, ground and existence collaborate spontaneously. In the healthy individual, ground freely subordinates itself to existence in a spontaneous act that Schelling likens to the unreflective decision whereby a person in danger "knows" just what to do to save his or her own life (Schelling, 1813: 175). If it does not subordinate itself but instead revolts and usurps the role of the existent, the dark ground extinguishes personality, and consequently itself, like a virus that destroys itself by destroying its host.

Nothing could be further from Freud's intentions than such a teleology of psychological life, for teleology attempts to explain the lower in terms of the higher and not only implicates psychology in metaphysics but runs inexorably (so Freud thinks) into the arms of religion. Freud stops at an archaeology of the psyche: the Freudian unconscious is a residue of the past not a forerunner of the future; it does not unfold, but reacts.[4] The primal memory of the child's oceanic unity with the mother – the paradisaical time when nascent needs were satisfied before they were felt – is necessarily forgotten or repressed as the child learns to live with the daily frustration of desires inevitable in civilized life and becomes at the same time differentiated from the mother. Yet the memory of "the lost object," the body of the mother, persists in the unconscious only to reappear in dreams and neurotic symptoms. The work of classical Freudian analysis is primarily one of unearthing the frustrated desires of infancy, of bringing them into language, of naming them – so that the primitive energy they harbour ceases to obstruct civilized life and can be put instead to the service of cultural and social activities. This is the move from repression of libido to sublimation, or from neurotic suffering to ordinary unhappiness.

These basic differences between Schelling and Freud are covered over by Žižek's Lacanian reading of the *Freedom* essay and *The Ages of the World*. Žižek transforms Schelling's intelligible deed (the founding act of freedom) into a repression of psychosis, the "subjectification" of God putting an end to the mad God slipping along the chain of signifiers because he has no place in the symbolic order. Certainly there is something mad about the creativity of Schelling's God. But it is not the life-negating madness of the psychotic; it is rather the endlessly productive "divine madness" of the genius. It is only by discarding Schelling's distinction between these two types of madness that Žižek can retrofit Schelling into Lacanian psychoanalysis.

The echo between the Lacanian notion of constitutive repression and Schelling's unconscious decision goes further back than Schelling. Just as the Boehmian unground becomes self-revealed by dividing and absenting itself, and the *Ein-Sof* of the Kabbalah gives rise to a creator by becoming "nothing," so does the Lacanian subject emerge into symbolically mediated life on the grounds of a pre-subjective excision of its unbounded material reality. Fused with Freud, *zimzum* becomes the Oedipal cut by which the infant is ejected from its pre-verbal oceanic unity with the mother and takes up a position in the symbolic. But where Kabbalah, Boehme and Schelling speak of creation, production and the generation of the new, Lacan speaks of repression and the eclipse of the real. Being disappears into unconsciousness and becomes the lost object that laces the symbolic with gaps – breakdowns in meaning – rendering subjectivity a patchwork of fragments. For Lacan, we are constitutively fragmented. For a subject to achieve the wholeness it longs for is for it to cease to exist. The structure of Schelling's division of the absolute into potencies may be formally similar to Lacan's theory of repression but the context is radically different. Schellingian subjectivity does not divide itself in reaction to anything, be it trauma, the horror of non-verbal life or the prohibition of the Father; it divides for the sake of producing the new.

A different hermeneutic result is produced by reading Schelling's theory of polarity through analytical psychology. In Jung's teleology of libido, not all introversion is perverse or counter-developmental. When the conscious attitude of the personality is inadequate to new environmental conditions, the withdrawal of libido and the introversion of interests is required for the activation of latent attitudes lying dormant in the unconscious. Incest motifs in dreams and in mythology are not always symbols of counter-developmental impulses or signs of an unresolved Oedipus complex. The hero goes on a "night-sea journey" to battle the dragon because he is not yet sufficiently individuated to face the real life situation (Jung, CW 8: 60–69).[5] In the regression of libido, even in psychotic breakdowns, productive forces are at work.

> What the regression brings to the surface certainly seems at first sight to be slime from the depths; but if one does not stop short at a superficial evaluation and refrains from passing judgement on the basis of a preconceived dogma, it will be found that this "slime" contains not merely incompatible and rejected remnants of everyday life, or inconvenient and objectionable animal tendencies, but also germs of new life and vital possibilities for the future.
>
> (Jung, CW 8: 63)

Jung objects to Freud's assumption that a regression from consciousness to unconsciousness is always symptom and sickness. Drawing on pre-Freudian traditions of the unconscious, Jung makes a case for a healthy narcissism or natural introversion. Without it extroverted libido is doomed. Inevitably the psyche will find itself maladapted to conditions that arise because as a being perpetually underway, never whole, its extroverted attitudes are always to some degree inadequate to the real. In moments of conflict which appear from outside to be breakdowns, the psyche regulates itself by retreating into its own depths.

> Regression is not necessarily a retrograde step in the sense of a backward development or degeneration, but rather represents a necessary phase of development. The individual is, however, not consciously aware that he is developing; he feels himself to be in a compulsive situation that resembles an early infantile state or even an embryonic condition within the womb.
>
> (Jung, CW 8: 69)

Introversion is as essential an ingredient of mental health as ego-driven adaptation to reality. Related to this is Jung's emphasis on the present situation in the life of the neurotic as the source of psychological conflict, in contrast with Freud's search for a past trauma. The "sick" person is withdrawing into himself not primarily because of an unresolved situation from the past but because he does not have the conscious resources to face the present situation. In an act of self-regulation, the psyche is contracting so as to activate hitherto unconscious powers in the personality.

Similarly Schelling identifies a productive and positive seed of life, health and goodness in the otherwise destructive inwardizing drive of the dark ground. An unconscious desire is at work in the dark ground, a "silent . . . seeking" that "soon pulls you back to yourself" (Schelling, 1813: 136–137). The negativity of the dark ground is essential to life. "All of this – the entire fullness and future splendour of nature – is only built upon the ground of an eternal self-negating will that returns unto itself and without which nothing could be revealed anywhere" (Schelling, 1813: 140). Ground is the fastening, binding force that reins in the "expansive" "volatizing" "spiritualizing" force and prevents it from expanding to infinity (Schelling, 1813: 139). If the dark ground has its way, unchecked by existence, the individual loses touch with reality and goes mad. But if existence has its way, unchecked by ground, the individual loses touch with his life-giving depths and dies spiritually, becoming imprisoned by a "lifeless under-standing," or as Jung would describe it, fixated on an outmoded pattern of adaptation, ossified in extroversion and so unable to meet the new challenges life presents to him.

The dark ground of spirit can hold itself back in Schelling because it is not a blind-force or a mindless appetite – as the unconscious sometimes is in Freud. Ground is personal, it possesses unconscious intelligence and so acts with design but without reflective knowledge of what it is doing, why it is doing it, or where it is going. The self-centredness of ground is not something that ought not to be. Although Schelling locates the possibility of evil in the dark ground, he is careful to distinguish the possibility from the actuality of evil. The dark ground is not in itself evil; on the contrary, it is an essential ingredient of goodness, the gravitational centre of love standing in creative and productive tension with its antithesis, the other-centred and affirmative light principle. One side shuts in while the other opens out, but the opening-out is only possible because it is grounded in the closing-in. The closing-in is an opening-out, as in Heidegger's related dialectic of concealment and unconcealment (later the dyad of "earth" and "sky"). Ground is not a mindless energy that must be broken, castrated, if it is to serve the good; it is already directed to the good, only without consciousness. It does not need to be redirected, canalized or sublimated; on the contrary, consciousness must learn to trust it.[6]

At the same time, Schelling is anything but naïvely optimistic about the human condition, which Jung and Jungians on occasion are. Personality is fallen; it never achieves in this life the wholeness it longs for and in its endless pursuit of the goal it can go wrong in various ways. It can be overwhelmed by the unconscious, losing its hold on consciousness and disintegrating from within. We have called this Schellingian psychosis.

Another possibility is equally unsustainable: in its bid to defend itself from the other powers operative within it, the I can become rigidly idealized and the understanding, without living contact with the real, ossified. We have called this Schellingian neurosis. Psychosis is the result of the corruption of first potency, the life-giving dissociation from the infinite become a life-destroying separation. Neurosis is the result of the corruption of second potency, the disavowal of dissociation. Psychosis, the understanding *possessed* by ground, is a shadow of first potency, identity annulled by difference, unable to maintain itself in the face of the negative. Neurosis, ground *repressed* (here the Freudian term is not only appropriate but accurate), is a shadow of second potency, difference annulled by identity. In "living understanding," a positive dissociation of ground and existence occurs: ground grounds, identity subsists in difference, and the chaotic will of the ground is directed, transformed and fulfilled by existence. The point is neither to repress nor to identify with the negative side of personality; a difficult negotiation of these two extremes is called for. "Humanity is not served by a separation of forces (*Sonderung der Kräfte*), a repression of particular powers (*Unterdrückung einzelner Vermögen*), but only by their highest and most perfect unification."[7] The "energy" locked up in ground must be put to the service of the self, for without the conflict between ground and existence, personality is stillborn and there is no life, no movement and no growth in the self. The coordination or ruling of madness does not cancel it. Even worse than actual madness or the failure of understanding to rule the ground is an understanding in which there is no madness whatsoever, a dead and ineffective imitation of understanding, for the former has the possibility of directing itself otherwise while the latter has no energy available to it to direct (Schelling, 1810a: 233).

Such talk no doubt disturbed Hegel, for it seemed to threaten not only philosophy but Western civilization itself, which he understood to be a long pilgrimage from nature to reason. For Hegel, the true proto-Freudian of German Idealism, madness is "derangement" or reason derailed (Hegel, 1845: 123). Hegel agrees with Schelling that madness is not the opposite of reason. But whereas for Schelling madness is in touch with the living energies that are older than order, for Hegel madness is one of reason's essential stages of development gone wrong. The soul, which initially does not distinguish itself from its environment, must become rational (*Geist*), the concrete universal, through a process of particularization, distinction and return to a unity enriched by difference. In the mad, reason gets stuck in the penultimate phase of its development and fails to properly distinguish the inner from the outer world. Madness for Hegel is the psycho-physical experience of the failure of the universal to emerge from itself and become fully particular. Like the child who must break with the mother if it is to become a rational law-abiding agent, the soul must die to its natural universality and allow itself to be divided from its natural origin. They are two sides of one strategy: the subordination of nature to reason, on the one hand, supports the pathologization of the pre-rational life of the mind on the other – both profoundly un-Schellingian moves.[8]

Where Schellingian libido theory departs from all three major schools of psychotherapy, Freudian, Jungian and Lacanian, is in Schelling's insistence on a theological *telos*. In the end Schelling remains some kind of Augustinian: the Schellingian heart is restless until it rests in God. Jung flirts with such religious thoughts but always pulls away for fear of violating the scientific rigour of his work, or more likely, the fear of overstepping the Kantian limits to reason to which he seems to have committed himself as a student. In a curious way, Lacan is more Schellingian inasmuch as he insists that God must appear on the horizon of the subject's world of meaning, for the Big Other alone solidifies the fragile symbolic order upon which the sanity of the subject depends. But Lacan's Big Other is, however necessary, a big lie. For Schelling, God can neither be suspended as a question nor dismissed as a fundamental fantasy. The question of God, however unavoidable in philosophy, is not answerable by philosophy. Schelling's theology is non-foundational: at the same time that he explores the theological bankruptcy of reason, Schelling points to the reasonableness (by distinction from rational necessity) of divine revelation.

There are, then, three possibilities for the Schellingian personality, two of which lead to death and produce nothing ("madness" and "lifeless understanding"), one of which leads to life and productivity ("love"). The failure of personality, both in madness and in lifeless understanding, is the failure of freedom to achieve love. Personality is only fully realized, and understanding only fully alive, when it loves. Precisely because love effects the integration of the negative and the affirmative, ipseity and alterity, love is madness regulated, ground moderated by existence. We are only truly ourselves when we love, that is, when we love ourselves, others, and God. Schelling's lyrical words on love at the end of the *Freedom* essay are typically ignored by commentators interested in what they take to be the more radical bits – an unfortunate error, for the notion of love is Schelling at his most radical. This is not the erotic love fetishized by the romantics, nor is it the agapic love idealized to the point of evisceration by mainstream Christianity. Schellingian love is both erotic and agapic because it is as self-centred as it is other-centred. Love unites two that are really distinct – there is no room for Spinozistic monism here, no "intellectual love of God," which is merely the mode's discovery of its non-difference from everything. The dissociations in being are ultimately real for Schelling, and they must be if the transmutation of the lowest into the highest is to occur. Love is nothing less than the purpose of creation, a divine intention, which is apparently obstructed when productive dissociation disintegrates into dissociative dissociation, i.e., evil, only to be revealed in all its trans-rational glory in the incarnated, crucified and resurrected Christ.

## Notes

1 We could with Gabriel, speak of an open Schellingian system, a living system, one that does not presume to include its own foundation within it and which recognizes that every reference to the system alters it.
2 Boehme does not distinguish drive (*Triebe*) and desire (*Begierde*) in any technical sense. We are interpreting him to mean that the single will to revelation which sets the unground in motion is properly speaking drive, not desire, for it is not intentional and responsive, nor is it opposed by a counter-drive; rather, it produces its own object, the opposed wills (desires) which the unground awakens in itself, on the one hand, toward self (the dark principle), on the other, toward other (the light principle). Desire on this view is oppositional, responsive and intentional, the hunger after an object which the subject lacks.
3 See Schelling (1809: 56). In the Love and Schmidt translation, *Konspiration* is translated, accurately if somewhat prosaically, as "cooperative effort." "Conspiracy" is preferable: it connotes the spontaneous, precarious, and clandestine nature of the productive forces at work in life.
4 This point is made trenchantly clear in Ricoeur's underrated *Freud and Philosophy* (Ricoeur, 1970).
5 This alternative theory of libido is worked out in detail in Jung's *Psychology of the Unconscious*, which was first published in 1912. The book was revised significantly in 1952 and republished under the title *Symbols of Transformation* (CW 5). The first edition (Jung, 1912) heralded Jung's break with Freud. In it Jung outlines an alternative psychiatric evaluation of incest imagery. Returning to the mother is not always counter-developmental. If the extroverted attitude is inadequate to the new situation, the unconscious attitude will be compensatory. The only way to activate the compensatory attitude, to bring it to consciousness, is through a momentary *abaissement du niveau mental*, a withdrawal from the world, from social life, even from civility and normalcy, which awakens new possibilities for interacting with the world and with others.
6 "The will that produces itself through itself without the knowledge of eternity – this will is the first distant beginning toward a revelation. Without deliberation, driven by dark presentiment and longing, it posits itself as negated, as not being what-is. But it negates itself only in order to reach essence. In negating, it is thus immediately an eternal seeking and desiring of essence; and precisely in so desiring, it posits essence as in itself independent of it, as the eternal good itself, as that which alone deserves to have being in itself" (Schelling, 1813: 143).
7 Schelling, letter of 1807, cited in Gulyga (1989: 224). See Chapter 4, note 3.
8 "To such an extent as man is and acts like a creature of nature, his whole behaviour is what it ought not to be. For the spirit it is a duty to be free, and to realize itself by its own act. Nature is for man only the starting-point which he has to transform" (Hegel's *Shorter Logic*, cited in Berthold-Bond, 1995: 87). On this difference between Schelling and Hegel see McGrath (2011).

# The metaphysical foundations of Schellingian psychology

From the *Stuttgart Seminars* (Schelling, 1810a, translation mine. See SSW 7: 433–434):

> God makes himself . . . he . . . does not begin whole [*er ist nicht gleich ein von Anfang Fertiges*]. . . . What then is the primordial state, in which the pure in-itself, that primal being with nothing outside itself, finds itself?
>
> All living being [*Dasein*] begins in unconsciousness [*Bewußtlosigkeit*], from a state in which all is undifferentiated. . . . Just so does the divine life begin. . . . It is in-itself the absolute identity of the subjective and the objective . . . but it is not [yet] for-itself. . . . The entire process of the creation of the world, the always ongoing life-process in nature and history – this is nothing other than the process of becoming perfectly conscious, the perfect personalization of God. . . .
>
> In us there are two principles: an unconscious [*bewußtloses*] dark principle, and a conscious principle. The process of self-cultivation [*die Selbstbildung*] . . . consists in . . . raising that unconscious being [*das bewußtlos Vorhandene*] to consciousness, raising the innate darkness in us into the light, in a word, achieving clarity. The same is true of God. The darkness precedes him; clarity first erupts out of the night of his being [*die Nacht seines Wesens*].
>
> God has the same two principles in himself that we have in us. From the moment that we become aware of the two principles and divide ourselves within ourselves [*uns in uns Selbst scheiden*], oppose ourselves to ourselves [*uns uns selbst entgegensetzen*], raising the better part of ourselves over the lower part – from this moment consciousness begins, but not yet full consciousness. The whole of life is in truth nothing other than an ever increasing growth in consciousness [*ein immer höheres Bewußtwerden*], [but] most remain on the lower level, and although they struggle, do not achieve clarity, and perhaps none in the present life arrive at absolute clarity – a dark residue [*ein dunkler Rest*] always remains – none reach the heights of his own good or the abyss of his own evil.

This is only true of God. The beginning of consciousness in him is his division of himself from himself, his opposition of himself to himself. He has a higher and a lower in him – what we denote with the concept of potencies. God has both principles in him in an unconscious state [*im unbewußten Zustand*], but without positing the one or the other, that is, without recognizing himself in the one or the other. With the beginning of consciousness, this recognition occurs, that is, God posits himself [*setz sich selbst*] (in part) as first potency, as the unconscious [*das Bewußtloses*], however he cannot contract himself as the real [*als Reales contrahiren*] without expanding himself as the ideal [*als Ideales zu expandiren*]; he cannot posit himself as the real, as the object, without also positing himself as the subject (without thereby freeing the ideal): and both are one act, both are absolutely the same: with his actual contraction as the real [*Kontraction als Reales*], his expansion as the ideal is posited. The higher in God drives [*drängt*] the lower from himself, that from which he was previously indifferent or mixed, and vice versa, through its contraction the lower dissociates [*absondern*] itself from the higher – and this is the beginning of consciousness, as much for man as for God, his becoming personal [*Persönlichwerden*].

However, just as in the process of self-cultivation or becoming self-conscious, man shuts out from himself the dark unconscious in him, opposes it to himself, not to leave it eternally in this expulsion and darkness, but in order to raise the expelled and the dark to clarity, to make it into consciousness [*hinauszubilden zu seinem Bewußten*], so does God expel the lower part of himself from the higher and drive it away from himself, not in order to leave it in this nothingness, but in order to raise out of it, out of the expelled non-divine – out of that which he himself is not and which he separates from himself, to raise up, build up, to create, that which is similar and like him. Creation consists in the arousal of the higher, the genuinely divine, in the excluded.

# The anthropology of Schelling's *Stuttgart Seminars*

In the *Stuttgart Seminars*, which were given in the same year that Schelling is believed to have written *Clara*, Schelling offers his most detailed outline of the structure of the human self (Schelling 1810a: 229-239). Rather than speaking now in terms of a simple opposition of spirit and body mediated by soul (but while maintaining the notion of opposites and the third which unites them while transcending both), Schelling introduces a new term, *Gemüth*, which we he describes as the dark ground of the personality. Pfau translates this as "temperament." Brown identifies it with "feeling" (Brown, 1977: 175). I find neither of these translations adequate. "Temperament" sounds like a part of the self, a faculty or function, whereas *Gemüth* is not a part of the self but its ground. "Feeling" is likewise too specific for what Schelling is naming. *Gemüth* denotes the root of the whole self. Perhaps the best translation is "the heart," the turbulent, melancholic, and unsettled ground of personality. Schelling's disciple Ignaz Paul Vital Troxler describes *Gemüth* as "the true individuality of man, by means of which he is in himself most authentically, the hearth of his selfhood, the most alive centre-point of his existence" (Troxler, cited in Ellenberger, 1970: 206).

The self is composed of three powers, each of which is in turn tripartite. The distinctions are based on the logic of the grounding real, the grounded ideal, and the third which mediates the real/ideal opposition. The three powers are *Gemüth* (the real), spirit (the ideal) and soul (the third, which mediates the real and the ideal). The triadic distinctions in *Gemüth* are melancholy (*Schwermuth*), desire in its various forms (*Sucht, Begierde, Lust*) and feeling (*Gefühl*). The triadic distinctions in spirit are self-will (*Eigenwille*), universal will or understanding, and will proper, which is indifferent to both the individual and the universal. The three powers of the soul are not elaborated on. This anthropology is noteworthy for several reasons.

First, Schelling, following Renaissance hermeticists such as Cornelius Agrippa von Nettesheim, makes melancholy essential to the self. Melancholy is not merely negative, not in itself an illness or life-negating state. On the contrary, melancholy grounds the person.

The most obscure and thus the deepest aspect of human nature is that of longing [*Sehnsucht*], which is the inner gravity of the heart [*Gemüth*], so to speak; in its most profound manifestation it appears as *melancholy* [*Schwermuth*]. It is by means of the latter that man feels a sympathetic relation to nature. What is most profound in nature is also melancholy; for it too mourns a lost good, and likewise such an indestructible melancholy inheres in all forms of life because all life is *founded* upon something independent from itself.

(Schelling, 1810a: 230, translation altered)

Secondly, Schelling makes desire the origin of consciousness. This premise, more often associated with Hegel and generally connected to Freudian psychoanalysis, is in fact essentially Schellingian and in origin, Boehmian. Desire is not something which intellect directs and masters but rather the very life of consciousness, which is not to say it cannot become for it a principle of death. Desire is the quality of a being that is set over and against being as such, the state of a being for whom being is out-standing, a being "grounded in nonbeing" (Schelling, 1810a: 233). The Heideggerian overtones are impossible to miss, particularly in the German:

What we call spirit is that which exists by nature [*Geist ist das natura sua Seyende*], a flame that fuels itself. However, because as something existing, it is opposed by being [*als Seyendem das Seyn entgegensteht*], the spirit is consequently nothing but an addiction to being [*die Sucht zum Seyn*], just as the flame is addicted to matter. The deepest essence of the spirit is therefore an addiction, a desire, a lust. Whoever wishes to grasp the concept of the spirit at its most profound root must therefore become fully acquainted with the nature of desire. In desire we witness for the first time something that exists from out of itself, and desire is something entirely inextinguishable; as far as desire is con-cerned, innocence can be lost only once, for [desire] is a hunger for being, and being satiated only gives it renewed strength, i.e., a more vehement hunger. It is here that we can notice with particular clarity the inextinguishable quality of the spirit.

(Schelling, 1810a: 230, translation altered)

We can, no doubt, read this in a Lacanian register: the Schellingian self is constitutive lack, a barred subject, impossible desire, that which exists by virtue of a longing for something which is incompatible with its existence. We can also, however, read this in a Boehmian fashion: the Schellingian self is the hunger for God, the space hollowed out of being by God himself that he might have one to whom he could be revealed. The isomorph-ism between these two readings, the atheist-psychoanalytical and the personalist-theosophical, is of course no accident: the former is historically dependent on the latter.

Third, spirit is to be associated with will rather than with intellect in any Scholastic sense of a faculty independent of volition. Even in its pre-conscious phases, will is intelligent; hence Schelling regards understanding (*Verstand*) as a synonym for ideal or universal will. The opposition of self-will and understanding Schelling developed the year before in his *Freedom* essay where the two concepts were introduced as synonyms for ground and existence (Schelling, 1809: 27-33). Nothing new is added in the *Stuttgart Seminars*, although the formulations have become more succinct and trenchant. Self-will would be blind without the understanding or the ideal will; self-will is only evil if it dominates the understanding. When it subordinates itself to the universal will, self-will becomes a life-serving ground of spirit. "Virtue without an active self-will has no merit. Hence it can be argued that the good contains evil within itself. A good, unless it involves the overcoming of an evil, is not a real living good. The most active and yet subordinate self-will is the highest good [*Der aktivirteste, doch unterworfene Eigenwille ist das Höchste*]" (Schelling, 1810a: 231, translation altered).

As in *Clara*, soul is higher than heart and mind, *Gemüth* and *Geist*, for it mediates these two which oppose and exclude each other. Spirit is personal and subjective; soul is not beneath but above spirit, an "impersonal" principle that contains the key to mental health because it alone maintains the vital connection to God. "The soul constitutes the properly divine in man; hence it is something impersonal, the properly existent [*das eigentlich Seyende*], to which the personal as a non-existent [*Nichtseyendes*] shall remain subordinate" (Schelling, 1810a: 232, translation altered). The impersonal nature of soul should give us pause. Have we not argued that Schelling is above all a personalist? Have we not argued that in his middle works, of which the *Stuttgart Seminars* is a certain culmination, Schelling raises personality above being? In *Clara*, soul is what we love in a person (Schelling, 1810b: 35); how could it be impersonal? By "the impersonal" (*das Unpersönliche*), Schelling means "ontological," that which supports and sustains the being of the person. As such, soul must not be reduced to subjectivity or what was commonly understood, after Kant, as the psychological ego. The impersonal nature of soul does not mean soul is in itself unindividuated or collective, unrelated and lacking the capacity for human love: exactly the opposite is the case. Schelling is saying that relationality, individuality and the capacity to love are not *merely* personal (e.g., psychological); they are ontological. Spirit is the knower, it actively seeks and acquires knowledge, but soul is absolute knowledge. "Spirit knows but the soul does not, rather she is knowledge" (Schelling, 1810a: 232). Spirit discerns the difference between good and evil, soul is goodness itself.

There follows a somewhat schematic outline of the varieties of mental illnesses, which is most noteworthy for underscoring the psycho-medical direction of Schelling's thinking at this time. If the emotional and affective continuity of the self is disturbed, *Gemüthskrankheit* or sickness of the heart develops; if cognitive continuity is broken, idiocy (*Blödsinn*) ensues; if the communication between understanding and soul breaks down, madness proper (*Wahnsinn*) is the result. Here, Schelling adds, it is not soul that is sick but the self that has lost contact with soul. "Thus an unbroken sequence proceeds from the heart—in particular from its most profound longing [*Sehnsucht*]—and terminates in the soul. The health of the heart and the spirit hinges on the continuity of this sequence and on the continuity of a nexus between the soul and the most profound realms of the heart" (Schelling, 1810a: 232, translation altered).

# Bibliography

Abraham, Lyndy. 1998. *A Dictionary of Alchemy.* Cambridge: Cambridge University Press.

Adorno, Theodor. 1973. *Der Begriff des Unbewußten in der transzendentalen Seelenlehre.* In Theodor Adorno, *Gesammelte Schriften*, Band 1, 79–322. Frankfurt: Suhrkamp.

Atzert, Stephan. 2005. *Die Entdeckung des Unbewußten: die Bedeutung Schopenhauers für das moderne Bild des Menschen.* Schopenhauer Jahrbuch 86. Ed. Günther Baum. Würzburg: Königshausen & Neumann.

Baader, Franz Xaver von. 1963. *Sämtliche Werke.* 16 vols. Neudruck der Ausgabe Leipzig 1851–1860. Ed. Franz Hoffmann and Julius Hamberger. Darmstadt: Scientia Verlag Aalen.

Bailey, Lewis. 1914. *Milton and Jacob Boehme: A Study of German Mysticism in Seventeenth-Century England.* New York: Haskell House.

Bakan, David. 1990. *Sigmund Freud and the Jewish Mystical Tradition.* London: Free Association.

Beach, Edward Allen. 1994. *The Potencies of God(s): Schelling's Philosophy of Mythology.* Albany, NY: State University of New York Press.

Beiser, Frederick C. 2002. *German Idealism: The Struggle Against Subjectivism. 1781–1801.* Cambridge, MA: Harvard University Press.

Bell, Matthew. 2010. "Carl Gustav Carus and the Science of the Unconscious." In Angus Nicholls and Martin Liebscher, eds. *Thinking the Unconscious: Nineteenth-Century German Thought.* New York: Cambridge University Press, 156–172.

Benz, Ernst. 1955. *Schellings theologische Geistesahnen.* Wiesbaden: Akademie der Wissenschaften und der Literatur.

—— 1983. *The Mystical Sources of German Romantic Philosophy.* Allison Park, PA: Pickwick Publications.

Berdyaev, Nicolas. 1930. "Studies Concerning Jacob Boehme. Etude II. The Teaching about Sophia and the Androgyne. J. Boehme and the Russian Sophiological Current." Trans. Fr. S. Janos. Available at www.berdyaev.com/berdiaev/berd_lib/1930_349.html. Accessed 29 April 2009. Original appeared in *Journal Put'* (1930) 21: 34–62.

—— 1958. "Unground and Freedom." In Jacob Boehme, *Six Theosophical Points and Other Writings.* Trans. John Rolleston Earle. Ann Arbor, MI: University of Michigan Press, v–xxxvii. Russian original appeared in *Journal Put'* (1930) 20:

47–79. Another English translation, by Fr. S. Janos, available at www.ber-dyaev.com/berdiaev/berd_lib/1930_349.html.

Berthold-Bond, Daniel. 1995. *Hegel's Theory of Madness*. Albany, NY: State University of America Press.

Betanzos, Ramon J. 1998. *Franz von Baader's Philosophy of Love*. Ed. Martin M. Herman. Vienna: Passagen Verlag.

Betz, Otto. 1999. "Friedrich Christoph Oetinger und die Kabbala." In Friedrich Christoph Oetinger, *Biblische und Emblematisches Wörterbuch*. Ed. Gerhard Schäfer. In two parts. *Texte zur Geschichte des Pietismus*. Ed. Gerhard Schäfer. Abteil VII, Band 3. Berlin: Walter de Gruyter, Part 2, 1–41.

—— 2002. "Friedrich Christoph Oetinger als Theosoph und das hebräische Erbe im schwäbischen Pietismus." In *Glauben und Erkennen. Die Heilige Philosophie von Friedrich Christoph Oetinger. Studien zum 300 Geburtstag*. Metzingen: Franz, 94–130.

Bishop, Paul, ed. 1999. *Jung in Contexts: A Reader*. London: Routledge.

—— 2008. *Analytical Psychology and Classical German Aesthetics: Goethe, Schiller and Jung*. Vol. 1: *The Development of the Personality*. London: Routledge.

—— 2009. *Analytical Psychology and Classical German Aesthetics: Goethe, Schiller and Jung*. Vol. 2: *The Constellation of the Self*. London: Routledge.

Boehme, Jacob. 1612. *Aurora: Oder Morgenrothe im Aufgang*. BSS 1. English: *Aurora*. Trans. John Sparrow. London, 1781. *The Works of Jakob Behmen, the Teutonic Theosopher*. Vol. 1.

—— 1622. *De Signatura Rerum oder von der Geburt und Bezeichnung aller Wesen*. BSS 6. English: *De Signatura Rerum*. Trans. John Sparrow. London, 1781. *The Works of Jakob Behmen, the Teutonic Theosopher*. Vol. 4.

—— 1623a. *De Electione Gratia oder von der Gnaden-Wahl*. BSS 6. English: *De Electione Gratia*. Trans. John Sparrow. *The Works of Jakob Behmen, the Teutonic Theosopher*. London, 1781. Vol. 4.

—— 1623b. *Mysterium Magnum*. BSS 7–8.

—— 1624a. *Quaestiones theosophicae*. BSS 9.

—— 1624b. *Christosophia oder Der Weg zu Christo*. BSS 4.

—— 1781. *The Works of Jakob Behmen, the Teutonic Theosopher*. Trans. John Sparrow. London.

—— 1960. *Sämtliche Schriften* [BSS]. Faksimile-Neudruck der Ausgabe von 1730 in elf Bänden. Ed. Will-Erich Peuckert. Stuttgart: Frommanns.

—— 1997. *Jacob Böhme Werke*. Ed. Ferdinand van Ingen. Frankfurt: Deutscher Klassiker Verlag.

Bowie, Andrew. 1993. *Schelling and Modern European Philosophy*. London: Routledge.

—— 2010. "The Philosophical Significance of Schelling's Conception of the Unconscious." In Angus Nicholls and Martin Liebscher, eds. *Thinking the Unconscious: Nineteenth-Century German Thought*. New York: Cambridge University Press, 57–86.

Bricht, Martin. 1995. "Der württembergische Pietismus." In *Der Pietismus im achtzehnten Jahrhundert*. Ed. Martin Brecht and Klaus Depermann. Vol. 2: *Der Gechichte des Pietismus*. Ed. Martin Brecht. Göttingen: Vandenhoeck & Ruprecht, 225–295.

Brown, Robert. 1977. *The Later Philosophy of Schelling: The Influence of Boehme on the Works of 1809–1815.* Lewisburg, PA: Bucknell University Press.

Bruaire, Claude. 1970. *Schelling ou la quête du secret de l'être.* Paris: Seghers.

Buchheim, Thomas. 1992. *Eins von Allem. Die Selbstbescheidung des Idealismus in Schellings Spätphilosophie.* Hamburg: Felix Meiner.

Buchheim, Thomas, with Friedrich Hermanni, eds. 2004. *"Alle Persönlichkeit ruht auf einem dunkeln Grunde." Schellings Philosophie der Personalität.* Berlin: Akademie Verlag.

Buggle, Franz and Paul Wirtgen. 1969. "Gustav Theodor Fechner und die psychoanalytischen Modellvorstellungen Sigmund Freuds." *Archiv für die gesamte Psychologie* 121: 148–201.

Burdach, Karl Friedrich. 1837. *Der Mensch nach den verschiedenen Seiten seiner Natur.* Stuttgart: Becher, 1854.

Burgoyne, Bernard. 2003. "From the Letter to the Matheme: Lacan's Scientific Methods." In *The Cambridge Companion to Lacan.* Ed. Jean-Michel Rabaté. Cambridge: Cambridge University Press, 69–85.

Carus, Carl Gustav. 1831. *Vorlesungen über Psychologie.* Darmstadt: Wissenschaftliche Buchgesellschaft, 1958.

—— 1846/1851. *Psyche. Zur Entwicklungsgeschichte der Seele.* Zweite verbesserte und vermehrte Auflage. Stttgart. C.P. Scheitlin's Verlagsbuchhandlung. English: *Psyche: On the Development of the Soul. Part One, The Unconscious.* Trans. R. Welch. Zürich: Spring Publications, 1970.

—— 1944. "Über die Natur." In *Geheimnisvoll am lichten Tag. Von der Seele des Menschen und der Welt.* Ed. Hans Kern. Leipzig: Verlag Philipp Reclam, 14–23.

—— 1954. *Grundzüge allgemeiner Naturbetrachtung.* Darmstadt: Wissenschaftliche Buchgesellschaft.

Couliano, Ioan P. 1987. *Eros and Magic in the Renaissance.* Chicago: University of Chicago Press.

Courtine, Jean-François, ed. 2010. *Schelling.* Paris: Les Éditions du Cerf.

Danz, Christian. 1996. *Die philosophische Christologie F.W.J. Schellings.* Stuttgart: Frommann-Holzboog.

Davis, Douglas A. 2008. "Freud, Jung and Psychoanalysis." In *The Cambridge Companion to Jung.* Ed. Polly Young-Eisendrath and Terence Dawson. Cambridge: Cambridge University Press, 39–55.

Deghaye, Pierre. 2000. *La Naissance de Dieu, ou, La doctrine de Jacob Boehme.* Paris: Albin Michel.

Deleuze, Gilles and Felix Guattari. 1983. *Anti-Oedipus: Capitalism and Schizophrenia.* Trans. Robert Hurley, Mark Seem, and Helen R. Lane. Minneapolis: University of Minnesota Press.

—— 1987. *A Thousand Plateaus: Capitalism and Schizophrenia.* Trans. Brian Massumi. Minneapolis: University of Minnesota Press.

Dierauer, Walter. 1986. *Hölderlin und der spekulative Pietismus Württembergs. Gemeinsame Anschauugnshorizonte im Werk Oetingers und Hölderlins.* Zürich: Juris.

Dimitov, Ch.T. 1971. "A. Schopenhauer und S. Freud." *Zeitschrift für Psychosomatische Medizin und Psychoanalyse* 17: 68–83.

Dourley, John P. 2008. *Paul Tillich, Carl Jung, and the Recovery of Religion.* London: Routledge.

Drews, Arthur. 1893. *Die deutsche Spekulation seit Kant mit besonderer Rücksicht auf das Wesen des Absoluten und die Persönlichket Gottes*, 2 vols. Berlin: Paul Maeter.

Drobb, Sanford. 2000a. *Symbols of the Kabbalah: Philosophical and Theological Perspectives*. North Vale, NJ: Jason Aronson.

—— 2000b. *Kabbalistic Metaphors: Jewish Mystical Themes in Ancient and Modern Thought*. North Vale, NJ: Jason Aronson.

Dufour, Dany-Robert. 1998. *Lacan et le miroir sophianique de Boehme*. Paris: Cahiers de l'Unebévue.

Eckhart, Meister. 1955. *Deutsche Predigten und Traktate*. Ed. Josef Quint. Munich: Carl Hanser.

Ellenberger, Henry. 1956. "Fechner and Freud." *Bulletin of the Menninger Clinic* 20: 201–214.

—— 1970. *The Discovery of the Unconscious*. New York: Basic Books.

Faflak, Joel. 2008a. *Romantic Psychoanalysis: The Burden of the Mystery*. Albany: NY: State University of New York Press.

—— ed. 2008b. *Romantic Psyche and Psychoanalysis*. Romantic Circles Praxis Series. www.rec.umd.edu/praxis/

Faivre, Antoine, with Jacob Needleman, eds. 1992. *Modern Esoteric Spirituality*. New York: Crossroads.

Faivre, Antoine 1994. *Access to Western Esotericism*. Albany, NY: State University of New York Press.

—— 1996. *Philosophie de la Nature. Physique sacrée et théosophie XVIIIe–XIXe siècle*. Paris: Éditions Albin Michel.

Fechner, Gustav Theodor. 1851. *Zend-Avesta oder über die Dinge des Himmels und des Jenseits*. Leipzig: Breitkopf & Härtel.

—— 1860. *Elemente der Psychophysik*, 2 Bde. Leipzig. English: *Elements of Psychophysics*. Ed. Davis Howes and Edwin Boring. Trans. H. Adler. New York: Holt, Rinehart and Winston, 1966.

—— 1879. *Die Tagesansicht gegenüber der Nachtansicht*. Leipzig: Breitkopf & Härtel.

Ffytche, Matt. 2008. "Psychology in Search of Psyches: Friedrich Schelling, Gotthilf Schubert and the Obscurities of the Romantic Soul." In *Romantic Psyche and Psychoanalysis*. Ed. Joel Faflak. Romantic Circles Praxis Series. www.rec.umd.edu/praxis/. Accessed 4 March 2010.

—— 2012. *The Foundations of the Unconscious: Schelling, Freud and the Birth of the Modern Psyche*. Cambridge: Cambridge University Press.

Fichte, Gottlieb Johann. 1794. *The Science of Knowledge*. Ed. and trans. Peter Heath and John Lachs. Cambridge: Cambridge University Press, 1982.

—— 2002. "Some Lectures Concerning the Scholar's Vocation. Written and Delivered, Summer 1794." Trans. Daniel Breazeale. In *Philosophy of German Idealism*. Ed. Ernst Behler. New York: Continuum, 1–38.

Fink, Bruce. 1995. *The Lacanian Subject*. Princeton, NJ: Princeton University Press.

Foucault, Michel. 1962. *Mental Illness and Psychology*. Berkeley, CA: University of California Press, 1987.

—— 1966. *The Order of Things: An Archaeology of the Human Sciences*. New York: Random House, 1994.

—— 2006. *The History of Madness*. London: Routledge.

Frank, Manfred. 1975. *Der unendliche Mangel an Sein. Schellings Hegelkritik und die Anfänge der Marxschen Dialektik*. Frankfurt: Suhrkamp.

—— 2004. "Schelling and Sartre on Being and Nothingness." In *The New Schelling*. Ed. Judith Norman. New York: Continuum, 151–166.

Franz, Albert. 1992. *Philosophische Religion: Eine Auseinandersetzung mit den Grundlegungsproblemen der Spätphilosophie F.W.J. Schelling*. Amsterdam: Rodopi.

Freud, Sigmund. 1900. *The Interpretation of Dreams*. Trans. A.A. Brill. New York: Modern Library, 1994.

—— 1922. *Beyond the Pleasure Principle*. Trans. C.J.M. Hubback. Ed. Ernest Jones. London: International Psychoanalytical Press.

—— 1926. "An Outline of Psychoanalysis." Trans. James Strachey. In *An Outline of Psychoanalysis*, rev. edn. Ed. Clara Thompson. New York: Modern Library, 1955, 5–21.

—— 1953–1974. *The Standard Edition of the Complete Psychological Works of Sigmund Freud*. Trans. James Strachey. London: Hogarth Press and the Institute of Psycho-Analysis.

Freydberg, Bernard. 2008. *Schelling's Dialogical Freedom Essay: Provocative Philosophy Then and Now*. Albany, NY: State University of New York Press.

Friesen, J. Glenn. 2008. "Theosophy and Gnosticism: Jung and Franz von Baader." Unpublished lecture given at the C.G. Jung Institut, Küsnacht, 2005. www.members.shaw.ca/cgjung/Jung_Baader.html. Accessed 1 September 2010.

Fuhrmans, Horst. 1940. *Schellings letzte Philosophie. Die negative und positive Philosophie im Einsatz des Spätidealismus*. Berlin: Hans Triltsch.

—— 1954. *Schellings Philosophie der Weltalter. Schellings Philosophie in den Jarhen 1806–1821. Zum Problem des Schellingschen Theismus*. Düsseldorf: L. Schwann.

—— 1964. "Einleitung und anmerkungen zu F.W.J. Schelling." *Über das Wesen der menschlichen Freiheit*. Stuttgart: Philipp Reclam, 3–38, 139–180.

Fullenwider, Henry F. 1975. *Friedrich Christoph Oetinger. Wirkungen auf Literatur und Philosophie seiner Zeit*. Göppingen: A. Kümmerle.

Gabriel, Markus. 2006a. *Der Mensch im Mythos. Untersuchungen über Onto-theologie, Anthropologie und Selbstbewußtsein in Schellings* Philosophie der Mythologie. Berlin: Walter de Gruyter.

—— 2006b. *Das Absolute und die Welt in Schelling's Freiheitsschrift*. Bonn: University Press.

Gabriel, Markus, with Slavoj Žižek. 2009. *Mythology, Madness and Laughter: Subjectivity in German Idealism*. New York: Continuum.

Galland-Szymkoviak, Mildred. 2010. "Schelling et le problème de l'objectivité de la philosophie. De l'esthétique au politique." In *Schelling*. Ed. Jean-François Courtine. Paris: Cerf, 39–80.

Gerabek, Werner E. 1995. *Friedrich Wilhelm Joseph Schelling und die Medizin der Romantik. Studien zu Schellings Würzburger Periode*. Frankfurt: Peter Lang.

Giegerich, Wolfgang. 1994. *Animus-Psychologie*. Frankfurt: Peter Lang.

—— 2001. *The Soul's Logical Life*. Frankfurt: Peter Lang.

—— 2010. *The Soul Always Thinks*. Collected English Papers, Vol. 4. New Orleans, LA: Spring Publications.

Gödde, Günter. 1999. *Traditionslinien des "Unbewußten": Schopenhauer – Nietzsche – Freud*. Tübingen: Edition Discord.

—— 2006. "Philosophische Kontext." In *Freud-Handbuch. Leben – Werk – Wirkung*. Ed. Hans-Martin Lohmann and Joachim Pfeiffer. Stuttgart/Weimar: Verlag J.B. Metzer, 10–25.

Goethe, J.W. 1782. "Aphorism on Nature." Attributed to Goethe but likely written by Georg Christoph Tober. Trans. T.H. Huxley. Appeared in the first issue of *Nature*, 4 November 1869. www.nature.com/nature/about/first/aphorisms.html. Accessed 30 May 2009.

Goodrick-Clarke, Nicholas. 2008. *The Western Esoteric Traditions: A Historical Introduction*. Oxford: Oxford University Press.

Grant, Iain Hamilton. 2006. *Philosophies of Nature After Schelling*. New York: Continuum.

—— 2010. "Introduction to Schelling's *On the World Soul*." *Collapse* VI. Ed. Robin Mackay. Falmouth, UK: Urbanomic, 58–65.

Grassl, Hans. 1993. "Baaders Lehre vom Quaternar im Vergleich mit der Polarität Schellings und der Dialektik Hegels." In *Die Philosophie, Theologie und Gnosis Franz von Baaders. Spekulatives Denken zwischen Aufklärung, Restauration und Romantik*. Ed. Peter Koslowski. Vienna: Passagen, 31–49.

Großmann, Sigred. 1979. *Friedrich Christoph Oetingers Gottesvorstellung*. Göttingen: Vandenhoeck & Ruprecht.

Gulyga, Arsenij. 1989. *Schelling: Leben und Werk*. Stuttgart: Deutsche Verlags-Anstalt.

Habermas, Jürgen. 1954. "Das Absolute und die Geschichte: Von der Zwiespältigkeit in Schellings Denken." Dissertation. Bonn.

Hall, Stanley G. 1912. *Founders of Modern Psychology*. New York: Appleton.

Halmi, Nicholas. 2002. "When Is a Symbol Not a Symbol? Coleridge on the Eucharist." *Coleridge Bulletin*, New Series 20 (Winter): 85–92.

Hanegraaff, Wouter. 1998. *New Age Realism and Western Culture: Esotericism in the Mirror of Secular Thought*. Albany, NY: University of New York Press.

Hanegraaff, Wouter, Antoine Faivre, Roelof van den Broek, and Jean-Pierre Brach, eds. 2006. *Dictionary of Gnosis and Western Esotericism*. Leiden: Brill.

Hardenberg, Fridrich von. 1960–1988. *Novalis Schriften*. Ed. R. Samuel, H.J. Mähl, and G. Schulz. Stuttgart: Kohlhammer.

Hartmann, Eduard von. 1869. *Die Philosophie des Unbewussten*. Berlin. English: *The Philosophy of the Unconscious*. Trans. W. Coupland. London: R. Paul, Trench and Trubner, 1931.

Hartung, Walter. 1912. *Die Bedeutung der Schelling-Okenschen Lehre für die Entwicklung der Fechnerschen Metaphysik*. Leipzig: O.R. Reisland.

Hauck, Wilhelm-Albert. 1947. *Das Geheimnis des Lebens. Naturanschauung und Gottesauffassung Friedrich Christoph Oetingers*. Heidelberg: Carl Winter.

Häussermann, Friedrich. 1966–1972. "Theologia Emblematica. Kabbalistische und alchemistische Symbolik bei Fr. Chr. Oetinger und deren Analogien bei Jakob Boehme." *Blätter für Württembirgische Kirchengeschichte*. In three parts.

Hayes, Victor C. 1995. *Schelling's Philosophy of Mythology and Revelation. Three of Seven Books Translated and Reduced with General Introduction*. Armidale, Australia: Australian Association for the Study of Religions.

Hegel, G.W.F. 1801. *The Difference between Fichte's and Schelling's System of Philosophy*. Trans. H.S. Harris and Walter Cerf. Albany, NY: State University of New York Press, 1977.

—— 1807. *Hegel's Phenomenology of Spirit*. Trans. A.V. Miller. Oxford: Oxford University Press, 1977.

—— 1845. *Hegel's Philosophy of Mind. Being Part Three of the* Encyclopedia of the Philosophical Sciences *(1830). Together with the* Zusätze *in Boumann's Text*. Trans. A.V. Miller. Ed. William Wallace. Oxford: Oxford University Press, 1971.

—— 1896. *Hegel's Lectures on the History of Philosophy*, Vol. 3. Trans. E.S. Haldane and Francis H. Simson. London: Routledge & Kegan Paul.

—— 1969. *Hegel's Science of Logic*. Trans. A.V. Miller. Atlantic Highlands, NJ: Humanities Press International.

—— 1969–1971. *Werke*, 20 vols. Ed. Eva Moldenhauer and Karl Markus Michel. Frankfurt: Suhrkamp.

—— 1988. *Lectures on the Philosophy of Religion. One Volume Edition. The Lectures of 1827*. Trans. R.F. Brown, P.C. Hodgson, and J.M. Stewart, with the assistance of H.S. Harris. Berkeley, CA: University of California Press.

—— 1989–2008. *Gesammelte Werke*, 25 vols. In Verbindung mit der Deutschen Forschungsgemeinschaft. Herausgegeben von der Rheinisch-Westfälischen Akademie der Wissenschaften. Hamburg: Felix Meiner.

Heidegger, Martin. 1927. *Being and Time*. Trans. John Macquarrie and Edward Robinson. New York: State University of New York Press, 1962.

—— 1971. *Schellings Abhandlung über das Wesen der menschlichen Freiheit*. Freiburg lecture course of 1936. Tübingen: Niemeyer. English: *Schelling's Treatise on the Essence of Human Freedom*. Trans. Joan Stambaugh. Athens, OH: Ohio University Press, 1985.

—— 1991. *Die Metaphysik des deutschen Idealismus. Zur erneuten Auslegung von Schelling: Philosophische Untersuchungen über das Wesen der menschlichen Freiheit und die damit zusammenhängenden Gegenstände*. Martin Heidegger Gesamtausgabe. Vol. 49. Freiburg lecture course of 1941. Ed. Günter Seubold. Frankfurt: Klostermann.

Heidelberger, Michael. 2004. *Nature from Within: Gustav Theodor Fechner's Psychophysical Worldview*. Pittsburgh, PA: University of Pittsburgh Press.

—— 2010. "Gustav Theodor Fechner and the Unconscious." In Angus Nicholls and Martin Liebscher, eds. *Thinking the Unconscious: Nineteenth-Century German Thought*. New York: Cambridge University Press, 200–240.

Hemecker, Wilhelm W. 1991. *Vor Freud. Philosophiegeschichtliche Voraussetzungen der Psychoanalyse*. München: Philosophie Verlag.

Hemmerle, Klaus. 1968. *Gott und das Denken nach Schellings Spätphilosophie*. Freiburg: Herder.

Henry, Michel. 1993. *The Genealogy of Psychoanalysis*. Trans. Douglas Brick. Stanford, CA: Stanford University Press.

Heusser, Peter. 1984. *Der Schweizer Arzt und Philosoph Ignaz Paul Vital Troxler*. Basel: Schwabe.

Hillman, James. 1975. *Re-Visioning Psychology*. New York: Harper & Row.

Hogrebe, Wolfram. 1989. *Prädikation und Genesis. Metaphysik als Fundamentalheristik im Ausgang von Schellings "Die Weltalter."* Frankfurt: Suhrkamp.

Horn, Friedemann. 1954. *Schelling and Swedenborg: Mysticism and German Idealism*. Trans. George F. Dole. West Chester, PA: Swedenborg Foundation, 1997.

Hühn, Lore. 1998. "Die intelligible Tat. Zu einer Gemeinsamkeit Schellings und

Schopenhauers." In *Selbstbesinnung der philosophischen Moderne: Beiträge zur kritischen Hermeneutik ihrer Grundbegriffe*. Ed. Christian Iber *et al.* Cuxhaven: Junghans, 55–94.

Hüntelmann, Rafael. 1995. *Schellings Philosophie der Schöpfung: Zur Geschichte des Schöpfungsbegriffs*. Dettelbach: Röll.

Jacobs, Wilhelm G. 2001. "Diesen Vorzug haben die theosophischen System, daß in ihnen wengistens eine Natur ist. Schelling und die Theosophie." In *Die Realität des Inneren. Der Einfluß der deutschen Mystik auf die deutsche Philosophie*. Ed. Gerhard Stamer. New York: Rodopi, 140–153.

Janet, Pierre. 1889. *L'automatisme psychologique: Essai de psychologie experimentale sur les forms inférieurs de l'activité humaine*. Paris: La Société Pierre Janet, 1973.

—— 1893. *The Mental State of Hystericals: A Study of Mental Stigmata and Mental Accidents*. Trans. C.R. Corson. New York: G.P. Putnam's Sons, 1901.

Jankélévitch, Vladmir. 1933. *L'Odyssée de la conscience dans la dernière philosophie de Schelling*. Paris: L'Harmattan, 2005.

Jarrett, James L. 1999. "Schopenhauer and Jung." In *Jung in Contexts: A Reader*. Ed. Paul Bishop. London: Routledge, 193–204.

Jaspers, Karl. 1933. *Man in the Modern Age*. Trans. Eden and Cedar Paul. London: Routledge, 1951.

—— 1955. Schelling. *Größe und Verhängnis*. Munich: Piper.

Johnston, Adrian. 2008. *Žižek's Ontology: A Transcendental Materialist Theory of Subjectivity*. Evanston, IL: Northwestern University Press.

Jonas, Hans. 1963. *The Gnostic Religion: The Message of the Alien God and the Beginnings of Christianity*, 2nd rev. edn. Boston: Beacon Press.

Juliusburger, Otto. 1912. "Die Beduetung Schopenhauers für die Psychiatrie." *Allgemeine Zeitschrift für Psychiatrie und psychisch-gerichtliche Medizin* 69: 618–638.

Jung, C.G. 1912. *Psychology of the Unconscious: A Study of the Transformations and Symbolisms of the Libido, a Contribution to the History of the Evolution of Thought*. Trans. Beatrice M. Hinkle. London: Kegan Paul Trench Trubner, 1916.

—— 1934. *Modern Psychology. Notes and Lectures given at the Eidgenössische Technische Hochschule, Zürich, by Prof. Dr. C.G. Jung, October 1933–February 1940*. Compiled and trans. Elizabeth Welsh and Barbara Hannah. Zürich, 1959. Privately published, 2nd edn.

—— 1953–1977. *The Collected Works of C.G. Jung* [CW], 20 vols. Ed. H. Read, Michael Fordham, and Gerhard Adler. Trans. R.F.C. Hull. London: Routledge.

—— 1963. *Memories, Dreams, Reflections*. Ed. Aniela Jaffé. Trans. Richard and Clara Winston. New York: Vintage Books, 1989.

Kant, Immanuel. 1798. *Anthropology from a Pragmatic Point of View*. Ed. Hans Rudnick. Trans. V.L. Dowdell. Carbondale and Edwardsville, IL: Southern Illinois Press, 1978.

—— 1799. *Religion within the Limits of Reason Alone*. Trans. Theodore M. Greene and Hoyt H. Hudson. New York: Harper & Row, 1960.

—— 1922. *Metaphysische Anfangsgründe der Naturwissenschaft*. Ed. Artur Buchenau and Ernst Cassirer. *Immanuel Kants Werke*. Band IV. Berlin: Bruno Cassirer, 367–478.

Kasper, Walter. 1965. *Das Absolute in der Geschichte. Philosophie und Theologie der Geschichte in der Spätphilosophie Schellings*. Mainz: Grünewald.

Kern, Hans. 1937. *Die Seelenkunde der Romantik* [On G.H. Schubert]. Berlin: Widukind.

Kerner, Justinus. 1829. *The Seeress of Prevorst*. Trans. Catherine Crowe. New York: Partridge & Brittan, 1855.

Kerslake, Christian. 2007. *Deleuze and the Unconscious*. New York: Continuum.

Koktanek, Anton Mirko. 1962. *Schellings Seinslehre und Kierkegaard*. Munich: Oldenbourg.

Korff, Herman A. 1954–1956. *Geist der Goethezeit. Vesuch einer Ideelen Entwicklung der klassische-Romantischen Literaturgeschichte*, 4 vols. Leibzig: Koehler Amelang. 1954. Vol. 2: *Klassik*; 1956a. Vol. 3: *Frühromantik*; 1956b. Vol. 4: *Hochromantik*.

Kosloswki, Peter. 2001. *Philosophien der Offenbahrung. Antiker Gnostizismus, Franz von Baader, Schelling*. Paderborn: Ferdinand Schöningh.

Koyré, Alexandre. 1929. *La Philosophie de Jacob Böhme*. Paris: Vrin, 1971.

Lacan, Jacques. 1966. *Écrits*. Paris: Seuil.

—— 1978. *The Four Fundamental Concepts of Psycho-Analysis*. Ed. Jacques-Alain Miller. Trans. Alan Sheridan. New York: W.W. Norton & Company.

—— 2002. *Écrits: A Selection*. Trans. Bruce Fink. New York: W.W. Norton & Company.

Lauer, Christopher. 2010. *The Suspension of Reason in Hegel and Schelling*. New York: Continuum.

Laughland, John. 2007. *Schelling versus Hegel: From German Idealism to Christian Metaphysics*. Aldershot, UK: Ashgate.

Leibniz, Gottfried W. 1705. *New Essays on Human Understanding*. Trans. P. Remnant and J. Bennett. Cambridge: Cambridge University Press, 1981.

Lewis, C.S. 1970. *God in the Dock: Essays on Theology and Ethics*. Grand Rapids, MI: Eerdmans.

Maesschalk, Marc. 1989. *Philosophie et révélation dans l'itinéraire de Schelling*. Paris: Bibliothèque Philosophique de Louvain.

Magee, Glenn A. 2001. *Hegel and the Hermetic Tradition*. Ithaca, NY: Cornell University Press.

Marquard, Odo. 1987. *Transzendentaler Idealismus, Romantische Naturphilosophie, Psychoanalyse*. Köln: Verlag für Philosophie.

—— 2004. "Several Connections Between Aesthetics and Therapeutics in Nineteenth-Century German Philosphy." In *The New Schelling*. Ed. Judith Norman. New York: Continuum, 13–29.

Marquet, Jean-François. 1973. *Liberté et existence dans la philosophie de Schelling*. Paris: Cerf.

Matthews, Bruce. 2011. *Schelling's Organic Form of Philosophy: Life as the Schema of Freedom*. Albany, NY: State University of New York Press.

Mayer, Paola. 1999. *Jena Romanticism and Its Appropriation of Jakob Böhme*. Montreal and Kingston: McGill-Queen's University Press.

McGrath, S.J. 2006. "Boehme, Schelling, Hegel, and the Hermetic Theology of Evil." *Philosophy and Theology* 18(2): 257–285.

—— 2008. "Jakob Böhmes Begriff des Bösen." In *Unheilvolles Erbe? Zum Verständnis der Erbsündenlehre*. Ed. Helmut Hoping and Michael Schultz. *Quaestiones Disputatae*. Ed. Peter Hünermann and Thomas Södung, Vol. 231. Freiburg: Herder, 50–76.

—— 2009. "Hermeneutics and the Unconscious: The Mercurial Play of Interpretation in Phenomenology, Psychoanalysis, and Alchemy." In *The Task of Interpretation: Hermeneutics, Psychoanalysis, and Literary Studies*. Ed. Dariusz Skórczewski, Andrzej Wiercinski, and Edward Fiawa. Lublin, Poland: Catholic University of Lublin, 45–72.

—— 2010a. "Sexuation in Jung and Lacan." *International Journal of Jung Studies* 2(1): 1–19.

—— 2010b. "Schelling on the Unconscious." *Research in Phenomenology* 40: 72–91.

—— 2011. "Madness as a Philosophical Problem in Hegel." In *Madness*. Ed. Daniela Fargions and Johnathan Sunley. Inter-Disciplinary Press.

Meynert, Theodor. 1892. *Sammlung von populärwissenschaftlichen Vorträgen über den Bau und die Leistungen des Gehirns*. Wien/Leipzig: Braunmüller.

Midelfort, H.C. Erik. 2005. *Exorcism and Enlightenment: Johann Joseph Gassner and the Demons of Eighteenth-Century Germany*. New Haven, CT: Yale University Press.

Mills, John. 2002. *The Unconscious Abyss: Hegel's Anticipation of Psychoanalysis*. Albany, NY: State University of New York Press.

Milton, John. 2003. *Paradise Lost*. London: Penguin.

Müller, Max, ed. 1879. *The Upanishads*. Oxford: Clarendon Press. www.sacred-texts.com/hin/sbe01/index.htm#section_001

Neugebauer, Jörg. 2007. "Das Unbewußte bei Schelling." *Beiträge zur geistigen Situation der Gegenwart* Jg. 8, Heft 3. www.philosophia-online.de/mafo/heft2007-3/Neu_Sch.htm. Accessed 6 August 2010.

Nicholls, Angus and Martin Liebscher, eds. 2010. *Thinking the Unconscious: Nineteenth-Century German Thought*. New York: Cambridge University Press.

Nicolaus, Georg. 2011. *C.G. Jung and Nikolas Berdyaev: A Critical Comparison*. London: Routledge.

Nietzsche, Friedrich. 1978. *Thus Spoke Zarathustra*. Trans. Walter Kauffman. New York: Penguin.

Noll, Veit. 2009 "Goethes' Naturfragment." In Veit Noll, *Zwei Teilnehmende des Weimarer Kulturkreises um Anna Amalia und Goethe in der Zeit von 1775–1785. Aufsätze mit Bezug auf Johann August von Einsiedel (1754–1837) und Emilie von Werthern (1757–1844) zu Goethe und Anna Amalia*. Salzwedel: Verlag Egon Wogel, 5–23, 129–131.

Norman, Judith, ed. 2004. *The New Schelling*. New York: Continuum.

Novalis. 1969. *Werke*. Ed. Gerhard Schulz. Munich: C.H. Beck.

Oetinger, Friedrich Christoph. 1765. *Theologia ex idea vitae deducta*. Ed. Konrad Ohly. In two parts. Texte zur Geschichte des Pietismus. Abteil VII. Band 2. Berlin: Walter de Gruyter, 1979.

—— 1776. *Biblisches und Emblematisches Wörterbuch*. Ed. Gerhard Schäfer. In two parts. Texte zur Geschichte des Pietismus. Abteil VII, Band 3. Berlin: Walter de Gruyter, 1999.

—— 1920. "Kurzer Auszug der hauptlehren Jakob Böhms." In *Schriften Jakob Böhmes*. Ed. Hans Kayser. Leipzig: Insel, 54–94.

—— 1977a. *Sämtlichen Schriften*. Ed. Karl Chr. Eberhard Ehmann. *Zweiter Abteilung. Theosophische Schriften*, 3 vols. Stuttgart: J.F. Steinkopf. Facsimile of the 1776 edition.

—— 1977b. *Die Lehrtafel der Prinzessin Antonia*. Ed. Reinhard Breymayer and

Friedrich Häussermann. In two parts. Texte zur Geschichte des Pietismus. Abteil VII. Band 1. Berlin: Walter de Gruyter.

O'Regan, Cyril. 1994. *The Heterodox Hegel*. Albany, NY: State University of New York Press.

—— 2001. *The Gnostic Return of Modernity*. Albany, NY: State University of New York Press.

—— 2002. *Gnostic Apocalypse: Jacob's Böhme's Haunted Narrative*. Albany, NY: State University of New York Press.

Orth, Johannes. 1914. *Der psychologische Begriff des Unbewussten in der Schelling'schen Schule (Novalis, G.H. Schubert, K.F. Burdach, C.G. Carus)*. Ludwigshafen am Rhein.

Paracelsus. 1979. *Selected Writings*. Ed. Jolande Jacobi. Princeton, NJ: Princeton University Press.

Pfau, Thomas, ed. 1994. *Idealism and the Endgame of Theory: Three Essays by F.W.J. Schelling*. Trans. Thomas Pfau. Albany, NY: State University of New York Press.

Pietsch, Roland. 1999. "Friedrich Christoph Oetinger und Jakob Boehme." In Friedrich Christoph Oetinger. 1776. *Biblisches und Emblematisches Wörterbuch*. Ed. Gerhard Schäfer. In two parts. Texte zur Geschichte des Pietismus. Abteil VII, Band 3. Berlin: Walter de Gruyter, 1999, Part 2, 71–85.

Platner, Ernst. 1776. *Philosophische Aphorismen nebst einigen Anleitungen zur philosophischen Geschichte*. Leibzig: Schwickertscher Verlag.

Pound, Marcus. 2008. *Žižek: A (Very) Critical Introduction*. Grand Rapids, MI: Eerdmans.

Rank, Otto. 1910. "Schopenhauer und der Wahnsinn." *Zentralblatt für Psychoanalyse* 1: 69–74.

Ricoeur, Paul. 1970. *Freud and Philosophy: An Essay on Interpretation*. Trans. Denis Savage. New Haven, CT: Yale University Press.

Rosenau, Hartmut. 1985. *Die Differenz im Christologischen Denken Schellings*. Frankfurt: Peter Lang.

Samuels, Andrew. 1986. *Jung and the Post-Jungians*. London: Routledge.

Schelling, Friedrich Wilhelm Joseph von. 1797. "Ideas on a Philosophy of Nature as an Introduction to this Science." SSW 2: 1–73. Trans. Priscilla Hayden-Roy. In *Philosophy of German Idealism*. Ed. Ernst Behler. The German Library, Vol. 23. New York: Continuum, 1987, 167–202.

—— 1798. *Von der Weltseele, eine Hypothese der höheren Physik*. Friedrich Wilhelm Joseph Schelling Historisch-Kritische Ausgabe Werke 6. Ed. Kai Torsten Kanz and Walter Schieche. Stuttgart: Frommann-Holzboog, 2000.

—— 1799a. *First Outline of a System of the Philosophy of Nature*. SSW 3: 1–268. Trans. Keith R. Peterson. Albany, NY: State University of New York Press, 2004.

—— 1799b. *Einleitung zu dem Entwurf eines Systems der Naturphilosophie oder über den Begriff des Spekulativen Physik*. SSW 3: 269–326.

—— 1800. *System of Transcendental Idealism*. SSW 3: 327–624. Trans. Peter Heath. Charlottesville, VA: University Press of Virginia, 1978.

—— 1804a. "System of Philosophy in General and of the Philosophy of Nature in Particular." SSW 6: 131–156. Trans. Thomas Pfau. In *Idealism and the Endgame of Theory: Three Essays by F.W.J. Schelling.* Ed. Thomas Pfau. Albany, NY: State University of New York Press, 1994, 139–194.

—— 1804b. *Philosophy and Religion.* SSW 6: 11–70. Trans. Klaus Ottmann. Putnam, CT: Spring Publications, 2010.

—— 1809. *Philosophical Inquiries into the Essence of Human Freedom.* SSW 7: 331–416. Trans. Jeff Love and Johannes Schmidt. Albany, NY: State University of New York Press, 2006.

—— 1810a. "Stuttgart Seminars." SSW 7: 417–486. Trans. Thomas Pfau. In *Idealism and the Endgame of Theory: Three Essays by F.W.J. Schelling.* Ed. Thomas Pfau. Albany, NY: State University of New York Press, 1994, 195–268.

—— 1810b. *Clara or, On Nature's Connection to the Spirit World.* SSW 9: 1–110. Trans. Fiona Steinkamp. Albany, NY: State University of New York Press, 2002.

—— 1811. *Die Weltalter: Fragmente. In den Urfassungen von 1811 und 1813.* Ed. Manfred Schröter. Munich: Beck, 1946

—— 1813. *The Ages of the World.* 2nd draft. Trans. Judith Norman. Ann Arbor, MI: University of Michigan Press, 1997.

—— 1815. *The Ages of the World.* 3rd draft. SSW 8: 195–344. Trans. Jason M. Wirth. Albany, NY: State University of New York Press, 2000.

—— 1831. *Urfassung der Philosphie der Offenbarung.* Ed. Walter E. Ehrhardt. Hamburg: Felix Meiner, 1992.

—— 1833. *On the History of Modern Philosophy.* SSW 10: 1–20. Trans. Andrew Bowie. Cambridge: Cambridge University Press, 1994.

—— 1842. *Historical-Critical Introduction to the Philosophy of Mythology.* SSW 11: 1–252. Trans. Mason Richey and Markus Zisselsberger. Albany, NY: State University of New York Press, 2007.

—— 1854. *The Grounding of the Positive Philosophy. The Berlin Lectures.* SSW 13: 1–174. Trans. Bruce Matthews. Albany, NY: State University of New York Press, 2008.

—— 1856–1861. *Sämtliche Werke* [SSW], 14 vols. Ed. Karl Friedrich Anton Schelling. Stuttgart and Augsburg: J.G. Cotta.

—— 1927–1946/1954. *Schellings Werke, Nach der Oringal in neuer Anordnung,* 12 vols, plus one *Nachlass* vol. Ed. Manfred Schröter. Munich: C.H. Beck.

—— 1976–. *F.W.J. Schelling Historisch–kritische Ausgabe.* Im Auftrag der Schelling-Kommission der Bayerischen Akademie der Wissenschaften. Ed. H.M. Baumgartner, W.G. Jacobs, H. Krings, and H. Zeltner. Stuttgart/Bad Cannstatt: Frommann-Holzboog.

Schneider, Robert. 1938. *Schelling und Hegels schwäbischen Geistesahnen.* Würzurg: K. Triltsch.

Scholem, Gerschom. 1960. *Zur Kabbala und ihrer Symbolik.* Zürich: Rhein-Verlag.

—— 1962. *Von der mystischen Gestalt der Gottheit. Studien zu Grundbegriffen der Kabbala.* Zürich: Rhein-Verlag.

—— 1974. *Kabbalah.* New York: Meridian.

Schopenhauer, Arthur. 1819/1844. *The World as Will and Representation,* 2 vols. New York: Dover.

—— 1836. *On the Will in Nature.* Trans. E.F.J. Payne. New York: Berg, 1992.

—— 1851. *Parerga and Paralipomena: Short Philosophical Essays,* 2 vols. Trans. E.F.J. Payne. Oxford: Clarendon Press, 1974.

—— 1986. *Sämtliche Werke*, 5 vols. Ed. Wolfgang von Löhneysen. Frankfurt: Suhrkamp.

Schubert, Gotthilf. 1806–1821. *Ahndungen einer allgemeinen Geschichte des Lebens.* Leibzig.

—— 1808. *Ansichten von der Nachseite der Naturwissenschaften.* Darmstadt: Wissenschaftliche Buchgesellschaft, 1967.

—— 1814. *Die Symbolik des Traumes.* Stuttgart: Besler Presse, 1968.

—— 1817–1844. *Altes und Neues aus dem Gebiete der inneren Seelenkunde.* Leibzig.

—— 1830. *Die Geschichte der Seele.* Hildesheim: Olms, 1961.

—— 1845. *Die Krankheiten und Störungen der menschlichen Seele.* Tübingen: Cotta.

Schulz, Walter. 1955. *Die Vollendung des deutschen Idealismus in der Spätphilosophie Schellings.* Stuttgart: Koohlhammer.

Schulze, Wilhelm August. 1955. "Jacob Boehme und die Kabbala." *Judaica. Beiträge zum Verständnis des Jüdischen Schicksals* 11: 12–29, 209–216.

—— 1957a. "Schelling und die Kabbala." *Judaica. Beiträge zum Verständnis des Jüdischen Schicksals* 13: 65–98, 143–170, 210–232.

—— 1957b. "Oetinger's Beitrag zur Schellingschen Freiheitslehre." *Zeitschrift für Theologie und Kirche* 54: 213–225.

Shamdasani, Sonu. 2003. *Jung and the Making of Modern Psychology: The Dream of a Science.* Cambridge: Cambridge University Press.

Shaw, Devin Zane. 2011. *Freedom and Nature in Schelling's Philosophy of Art.* New York: Continuum.

Silberer, Herbert. 1914. *Hidden Symbolism of Alchemy and the Occult Arts.* Trans. Smith Ely Jelliffe. New York: Dover, 1971.

Snow, Dale E. 1996. *Schelling and the End of Idealism.* Albany, NY: State University of New York Press.

Sokowlowski, Robert. 2008. *Phenomenology of the Human Person.* Cambridge: Cambridge University Press.

Spinoza, Benedict de. 1955. *The Chief Works of Benedict de Spinoza*, Vol. II. Trans. R.H.M. Elwes. New York: Dover.

Steinkamp, Fiona. 2002. "General Introduction." In F.W.J. Schelling, *Clara* Trans. Fiona Steinkamp. Albany, NY: State University of New York Press, vii–xl.

Swedenborg, Emanuel. 1758. *Heaven and Hell.* Trans. George F. Doyle. West Chester, PA: Swedenborg Foundation, 2000.

Tillich, Paul. 1910. *The Construction of the History of Religion in Schelling's Positive Philosophy: Its Presuppositions and Principles.* Trans. Victor Nuovo. Lewisburg, PA: Bucknell University Press, 1974.

—— 1912. *Mysticism and Guilt-Consciousness in Schelling's Philosophical Development.* Trans. Victor Nuovo. Lewisburg, PA: Bucknell University Press, 1974.

Tilliette, Xavier. 1970. *Une philosophie en devenir.* Paris: J. Vrin.

Troxler, Ignaz. 1812. *Blicke in das Wesen des Menschen.* Aaran: Sauerländer.

Uslar, Detlev von. 1987. *Sein und Deutung. Grundfragen der Psychologie.* Stuttgart: Hirzel.

Van Ingen, Ferdinand. 1997. "Jacob Böhme: Leben und Werke." In *Jacob Böhme Werke.* Ed. Ferdinand van Ingen. Frankfurt: Deutscher Klassiker Verlag, 795–831.

Vater, Michael. 1978. "Introduction." In F.W.J. Schelling, *System of Transcendental*

*Idealism (1800)*. Trans. Peter Heath. Charlottesville, VA: University Press of Virginia, xi–xxxvi.

—— 2000. "Intellectual Intuition in Schelling's Philosophy of Identity 1801–1804." In *Schelling Zwischen Fichte und Hegel*. Ed. Christoph Asmuth, Alfred Denker, and Michael Vater. Amsterdam: B.R. Grüner, 213–234.

Vetö, Miklos, ed. 1973. *F.W.J. Schelling. Stuttgarter Privatvorlesungen*. Version inédite, accompagnée du texte des Oeuvres. Torino: Bottega d'Erasmo.

Völmicke, Elke. 2005. *Das Unbewusste im deutschen Idealismus*. Würzburg: Königshausen & Neumann.

Waterfield, Robin. 2001. *Jacob Boehme*. Western Esoteric Masters Series. Berkeley, CA: North Atlantic Books.

Weeks, Andrew. 1991. *Böhme: An Intellectual Biography of the Seventeenth-Century Philosopher and Mystic*. Albany, NY: State University of New York Press.

Welchman, Alistair and Judith Norman. 2010. "Creating the Past: Schelling's *Ages of the World*." *Journal of the Philosophy of History* 4: 23–43.

Whyte, Lancelot Law. 1960. *The Unconscious Before Freud*. New York: Basic Books.

Wieland, Wilhelm. 1956. *Schellings Lehre von der Zeit*. Heidelberg: Carl Winter Universitäts Verlag.

Wilson, John Elbert. 1993. *Schellings Mythologie. Zur Auslegung der Philosophie der Mythologie und der Offenbarung*. Stuttgart: Frommann-Holzboog.

Wirth, Jason. 2003. *The Conspiracy of Life: Meditations on Schelling and His Time*. Albany, NY: State University of New York Press.

—— ed. 2004. *Schelling Now: Contemporary Readings*. Bloomington, IN: Indiana University Press.

Yates, Francis. 1964. *Giordano Bruno and the Hermetic Tradition*. Chicago: University of Chicago Press, 1991.

—— 1979. *The Occult Philosophy in the Elizabethan Age*. New York: Routledge.

Zentner, Marcel. 1995. *Die Flucht ins Vergessen: Die Anfänge der Psychoanalyse Freuds bei Schopenhauer*. Darmstadt: Wissenschaftlichen Buchgesellschaft.

Žižek, Slavoj. 1996. *The Indivisible Remainder: On Schelling and Other Matters*. London: Verso.

—— 1997a. *The Abyss of Freedom*. An essay by Slavoj Žižek with the text of Schelling's *Die Weltalter* (2nd draft, 1813) in English translation by Judith Norman. Ann Arbor, MI: University of Michigan Press.

—— 1997b. "Desire:Drive=Truth:Knowledge." www.lacan.com/zizek-desire.htm. Accessed 2 May 2011.

—— 2001. *The Fragile Absolute: Or, Why is the Christian Legacy Worth Fighting For?* London: Verso.

—— 2003. *The Puppet and the Dwarf: The Perverse Core of Christianity*. Cambridge, MA: MIT Press.

—— 2006. *The Parallax View*. Cambridge, MA: MIT Press.

Zovko, Marie-Elise. 1996. *Natur und Gott: Das wirkungsgeschichtliches Verhältnis Schellings und Baaders*. Würzburg: Konigshausen and Neumann.

# Index